Configurational
Comparative
Methods

APPLIED SOCIAL RESEARCH
METHODS SERIES

Series Editors

LEONARD BICKMAN, Peabody College, Vanderbilt University, Nashville

DEBRA J. ROG, Westat

Configurational Comparative Methods

Qualitative Comparative Analysis (QCA)
and Related Techniques

EDITED BY
BENOÎT RIHOUX
Université catholique de Louvain

CHARLES C. RAGIN
University of Arizona

APPLIED SOCIAL RESEARCH METHODS SERIES

Volume 51

Los Angeles • London • New Delhi • Singapore

For information:

SAGE Publications, Inc.
2455 Teller Road
Thousand Oaks, California 91320
E-mail: order@sagepub.com

SAGE Publications India Pvt. Ltd.
B 1/I 1 Mohan Cooperative
   Industrial Area
Mathura Road, New Delhi 110 044
India

SAGE Publications Ltd.
1 Oliver's Yard
55 City Road
London EC1Y 1SP
United Kingdom

SAGE Publications Asia-Pacific Pte. Ltd.
33 Pekin Street #02-01
Far East Square
Singapore 048763

Printed in the United States of America

Library of Congress Cataloging-in-Publication Data

Configurational comparative methods: Qualitative Comparative Analysis (QCA) and related techniques/[edited by] Benoît Rihoux, Charles C. Ragin.
      p. cm. —(Applied social research methods series; 51)
Includes bibliographical references and index.
ISBN 978-1-4129-4235-5 (pbk.)
   1. Social sciences—Comparative method. 2. Social sciences—Research—Methodology. I. Rihoux, Benoît, 1965- II. Ragin, Charles C.

H61.C59125 2009
300.72—dc22   2008017858

Printed on acid-free paper

08   09   10   11   12   10   9   8   7   6   5   4   3   2   1

Acquiring Editor:	Vicki Knight
Associate Editor:	Sean Connelly
Editorial Assistant:	Lauren Habib
Production Editor:	Sarah K. Quesenberry
Copy Editor:	Tony Moore
Typesetter:	C&M Digitals (P) Ltd.
Proofreader:	Dorothy Hoffman
Indexer:	Claude Rubinson
Marketing Manager:	Stephanie Adams

Brief Contents

Detailed Contents

List of Boxes, Figures, and Tables

Boxes

Figures

Tables

Acknowledgments

This textbook is the result of a collective endeavor, not only because it involves seven contributors but also because it has been made possible by the support of numerous colleagues, collaborators, and students around the globe.

We are indebted to the late Kriss Drass for software development. Kriss was responsible for implementation of all versions of QCA-DOS through 3.0 and for all versions of FSQCA through 0.9. Sean Davey has taken on responsibility for subsequent versions of FSQCA (1.0 through 3.0), including implementation of the fuzzy-set truth table procedure and the various procedures for counterfactual analysis.

We thank Nancy Martin for translation work during the early stages. We also wish to mention some colleagues who have played active roles in setting up activities and further developing the COMPASSS network, which has provided opportunities to develop new ideas and collaborative projects: Peter Bursens, Heike Grimm, David Levi-Faur, Axel Marx, Daishiro Nomiya, Wendy Olsen, Fritz Sager, and Geert Van Hootegem. We also thank close colleagues and friends with whom we have debated at length over comparative methods, among them Frank Aarebrot, David Collier, André-Paul Frognier, Gary Goertz, Airo Hino, Bruce Kogut, Lars Mjøset, and Marc Swyngedouw.

We also wish to thank Academia-Bruylant for its support in the publication of a first, French-language, textbook on csQCA (De Meur & Rihoux, 2002), which paved the way for this first comprehensive English-language textbook, *Configurational Comparative Methods*. The completion of this volume was also made possible by the support of the Fonds de la Recherche Fondamentale Collective (FRFC), through the Fonds National de la Recherche Scientifique (FNRS, Belgium), with the research grant on *"Analyse de l'émergence des nouvelles institutions à parties prenantes multiples (multi-stakeholder) pour la régulation politique et sociale des conditions de travail et de la protection de l'environnement dans des marchés globaux"* (ref. 2.4.563.05.F). Work was also facilitated by a grant from the European Science Foundation (ESF), to organize an exploratory workshop on "Innovative comparative methods for policy analysis: An interdisciplinary European endeavour for methodological advances and improved policy analysis/evaluation," held in Erfurt from September 25–28, 2004 (ref. EW03–217). The fine working atmosphere and bibliographical resources at the *Centre de Politique Comparée* (*Université catholique de Louvain*) also helped us a great deal in finalizing the manuscript.

We are thankful to numerous colleagues who have given us feedback in the course of the development of the FSQCA and TOSMANA software, including

Helen Giesel, Gary Goertz, Bruce Kogut, Jon Kvist, Carsten Schneider, Steve Vaisey, and Claudius Wagemann. More specifically, we received most useful feedback on previous versions of this textbook from Simone Ledermann, Raphaela Schlicht, Carsten Schneider, Svend-Erik Skaaning, and Claudius Wagemann, as well as from two anonymous reviewers. We also received specific comments from Olaf Van Vliet and Maarten Vink. Finally, we owe special thanks to Svend-Erik Skaaning, who has replicated the QCA analyses with some of his students at the University of Aarhus while we were finalizing this textbook—this has been most helpful in the technical consolidation of Chapters 3 through 5.

The list of colleagues, researchers and students who have given us feedback on "bits and pieces" of this textbook in conferences, seminars, and courses is naturally too long to mention, but their comments have also been valuable. In particular, we thank participants to courses we taught at the ECPR Summer School in Methods and Techniques (Ljubljana), the Essex Summer School in Social Science Data Analysis and Collection (Colchester), the Oslo Summer School in Comparative Social Science Studies, the Institute for Qualitative and Multi-Method Research (Phoenix), and the Ecole d'été en méthodes quantitatives en sciences sociales (Lille). Naturally, the organizers of these venues are also to be thanked—nothing replaces such training venues when it comes to testing teaching material and new ideas.

Last but not least, we thank the Sage team for their diligent support and efficiency, in particular Lisa Cuevas for enabling the ship to set its sails, Vicki Knight for ensuring safe arrival at the harbor after a long voyage, Sean Connelly for overall satellite guidance, Sarah Quesenberry for skillfully operating the dry dock facilities, Tony Moore and Dorothy Hoffman for polishing every square inch and checking every bolt from bow to stern, and finally Lauren Habib and Stephanie Adams for spreading the word around the globe, so that crowds will come visit this first vessel of its kind as it embarks on the conquest of the seven seas. On the practical side, in the team of contributors to this book, Sakura Yamasaki and Damien Bol have played a crucial role in the maintenance of the COMPASSS bibliographical database out of which the list of references has been extracted. All this being said, we fiercely claim intellectual property on any remaining error, approximation, or omission.

Introduction

Benoît Rihoux

Charles C. Ragin

WHY COMPARE? WHY CONFIGURATIONAL COMPARATIVE METHODS?

Comparison lies at the heart of human reasoning and is always there in the observation of the world—"thinking without comparison is unthinkable" (Swanson, 1971, p. 45). Indeed, even the observation of singular phenomena is empty if we do not engage in a comparison: A phenomenon or object can be identified as such only if it is recognized as different from other phenomena or objects (Aarebrot & Bakka, 2003). For instance, we know that apples are not pears because we have compared the two.

More specifically, comparison is a key operation in any empirical *scientific* effort. There is a long line of scholars who have reflected upon this—and applied this empirically—all the way from Aristotle (probably the founder of a rigorous comparative approach) to de Tocqueville, Weber and Durkheim, and on to more contemporary works by Sartori (e.g., 1970, 1991), Lijphart (e.g., 1971) and Marradi (1985). For one thing, any descriptive effort, any typology or classification involves comparison (Bailey, 1994). To consider both apples and pears as belonging to the category of "fruits," we must compare "fruits" and "non-fruits" in the broader category of "plants," and so on. Once we have defined the category of "fruits," we can come to the conclusion that an orange is also a fruit, by comparing some key properties of an orange with those of an apple and of a pear. While also being a fruit, an orange shares some specific characteristics with lemons and grapefruits. Thus oranges and lemons, on the one hand, and apples and pears, on the other hand, belong to two different subtypes of fruits.

Of course, such everyday comparisons may seem trivial, and indeed many of those mental operations remain implicit in our reasoning. The purpose of this textbook is to demonstrate that comparison, as a basic and powerful mental operation, can be translated into a set of systematic comparative *methods and techniques*. Although this volume is not about fruits, we shall demonstrate that such methods and techniques can indeed be fruitfully applied in many disciplines, in the social sciences broadly defined, and also beyond.

Systematic comparison is a key operation in all experimental and natural sciences. For instance, we know that water is boiling when it is heated to 100°C because we have compared the state of water below 100°C, at 100°C, and above 100°C, while controlling for contextual parameters such as atmospheric pressure and altitude above sea level. Incidentally, because we are able to control all these contextual parameters, and because we are able to manipulate one specific condition—temperature—we are able to demonstrate that a change in temperature actually *causes* the water to boil. This is why the experimental sciences are able to make such strong and simple causal statements.

Yet, in most social and behavioral sciences, perhaps with the exception of some branches of psychology, real-life laboratory-like experimentation is neither empirically possible nor ethically desirable. To pursue our example further: In antiquity, slaves were used to scientifically demonstrate that water that is brought to a boiling temperature also happens to burn human skin, by comparing the effect of plunging the hand of a slave into lukewarm, as compared to boiling, water. And Cleopatra used slaves to examine the more or less lethal effects of various poisons in her apples and oranges. Obviously, contemporary social scientists cannot do this, nor would they want to.

This is where the comparative *method* comes into play. It can be considered a crude substitute for experimentation (Lijphart, 1971): We observe empirical phenomena—analytical units, "cases" (Ragin & Becker, 1992)—while also controlling for contextual conditions (see Chapter 1). In social science, those cases, as we know, are intrinsically complex, multifaceted, often with blurred boundaries. This is why "thick," single-case studies have always played an important role in many disciplines: They allow a deep understanding of that single case. The main limitation of single-case studies, however, is that it is very difficult to engage in any form of generalization, as the key findings and conclusions are mostly limited to that single case.

How can one compare these complex cases? During recent decades, an increasing number of social scientists have been opting for *multiple case studies* as a research strategy. This strategy aims at meeting the need to gather in-depth insight into different cases and to capture their complexity, while still attempting to produce some form of generalization (Ragin, 1987). It also coincides, during the last few years, with renewed interest in case-oriented research (e.g., George & Bennett, 2005; Gerring, 2006; Mahoney & Rueschemeyer, 2003). Such a strategy is also adopted because many relevant and interesting objects are "naturally" limited in number: nation states or regions, political crises, wars, firms of a certain type, and so on. These are naturally limited, or "small-N" (or "intermediate-N"—see Chapter 2), populations of cases.

In many instances the (ex post) comparison of case study material is rather "loose" or not formalized. The major ambition of the methods and techniques presented in this textbook is *to allow systematic cross-case comparisons, while at the same time giving justice to within-case complexity, particularly in small- and intermediate-N research designs.*

The cover heading for all these methods and techniques is Configurational Comparative Methods (CCM). In a nutshell, this heading indicates that in order to enable the systematic comparative analysis of complex cases, those cases must be transformed into *configurations*. Simply said, a configuration is a specific combination of factors (or stimuli, causal variables, ingredients, determinants, etc.—we call these *conditions* in CCM terminology) that produces a given *outcome* of interest. As shall be explained at length in the next chapters, the conditions will be envisaged in a combinatorial way—hence enabling one to model quite a high level of complexity even with only a few conditions.

One key question we shall address is the following: Which conditions (or combinations thereof) are "necessary" or "sufficient" (or possibly both necessary *and* sufficient) to produce the outcome? In a non-formal way (for more on this, see p. 10, Box 1.3; see also Caramani, 2008), let us say at this stage that:

- A condition is *necessary* for an outcome if it is always present when the outcome occurs. In other words, the outcome cannot occur in the absence of the condition.

- A condition is *sufficient* for an outcome if the outcome always occurs when the condition is present. However, the outcome could also result from other conditions.

For instance, holding competitive elections is a *necessary* condition for a state to be considered democratic. However, it is not a *sufficient* condition because comprehensive civil liberties must also be present for a state to be considered democratic. Nonetheless, the *absence* of competitive elections is a *sufficient* condition to qualify a state as *non*-democratic, as a democracy cannot exist without competitive elections.[1]

Under the heading of CCM, we place four specific techniques: Qualitative Comparative Analysis using conventional, crisp sets (csQCA, often simply labeled QCA in the literature), multi-value QCA (mvQCA), fuzzy-set QCA (fsQCA), and MSDO/MDSO (most similar, different outcome/most different, same outcome).

Box 0.1
About Terminology and Labels:
QCA, csQCA, mvQCA, fsQCA, and Software

QCA using conventional Boolean[2] (or "crisp") sets was developed first, which is why the label "QCA" is so often used to name this technique. In this volume, however:

- We use the label *QCA* as an umbrella term that captures the three main types (Boolean, multi-value, and fuzzy set) as a group. After all, they share many commonalities (see Chapter p. 1).

(Continued)

(Continued)

- When referring explicitly to the original Boolean version of QCA, we use *csQCA*[3] (where "cs" stands for "crisp set"; see Chapter 3, p. 33).

- When referring explicitly to the version that allows multiple-category conditions, we use *mvQCA* (where "mv" stands for "multi-value"; see Chapter 4, p. 69).

- When referring explicitly to the fuzzy-set version, which also links fuzzy sets to truth table analysis, we use *fsQCA* (where "fs" stands for "fuzzy set"; see Chapter 5, p. 87).

- Finally, we use *fuzzy sets* to designate the original fuzzy set analysis as developed by Ragin (2000).

When referring to software, we use:

- *QCA-DOS* to refer to the original program for crisp-set analysis developed by Charles Ragin and Kriss Drass.

- *TOSMANA* to refer to the mvQCA program developed by Lasse Cronqvist.

- *FSQCA* to refer to the fuzzy-set version developed by Charles Ragin, Kriss Drass, and Sean Davey.

Note that all existing versions of QCA software (QCA-DOS, TOSMANA, and FSQCA) are capable of performing conventional crisp-set analysis of the type described in Ragin (1987) and De Meur and Rihoux (2002).

These four techniques form the core of this book. Although these are quite specific techniques, we will also tackle broader issues that any social scientist inevitably confronts, no matter what methodology he or she uses—e.g., causality, operationalization, generalization, temporality, mechanisms, and process.

Box 0.2
Goals of This Textbook

1. Provide a broad introduction to the comparative template: the purpose of systematic comparison and the key operations thereof (especially case and variable selection)

2. Present the main assumptions and underpinnings of the configurational comparative approach

3. Using one concrete example throughout, introduce the key operations and workings of four specific techniques: csQCA, mvQCA, fsQCA, and MSDO/MDSO

4. Examine the strengths and limitations of these techniques, and provide a critical overview of real-life applications produced so far

5. Provide useful resources and tips, and identify "good practices" for practitioners, so they can better exploit the potential of these techniques

STRUCTURE OF THIS BOOK

After this introductory chapter, whose aim is to lay out the basic purpose and aims of this book, Chapter 1 presents the whole approach behind QCA and related techniques. First, this approach is discussed more at the epistemological level, with a key focus on "small- and intermediate-N" research situations. Some key features of QCA are also laid out: the interplay between theoretical and case-oriented knowledge, a specific understanding of causality and complexity, and particular goals when it comes to generalizing findings. We also present different ways to exploit QCA—it is indeed suited for several different purposes.

In Chapter 2, we tackle issues of comparative research design and all the practical steps that need to be performed before QCA techniques (csQCA, mvQCA, or fsQCA) are actually implemented. The key practical questions deal with strategies of case selection, as well as model specification—especially the selection of the explanatory variables (called *conditions*). In this context, MSDO/MDSO is presented as a specific technique that can be used as a help in this challenging process of selecting cases and conditions. An empirical study is introduced as an example: a comparative analysis of the survival or breakdown of democracies in Europe during the inter-war period.

Chapters 3 to 5 then present the three core QCA techniques: first crisp-set QCA (csQCA), followed by multi-value QCA (mvQCA), and finally fuzzy-set QCA (fsQCA)—this sequence follows the way the data are coded: from completely dichotomous (only [0] or [1] scores on all variables) to much more fine-grained ones. All three techniques are discussed from A to Z, along with their key practical steps. The specificity of each technique is also underlined, along with the more basic or more advanced uses. Throughout these three chapters, the same "inter-war project" data are used, so as to show which added value is brought by each of the techniques. Many good practices tips are given along the way.

In Chapter 6, we provide a broad review of applications of these techniques, in many different fields, on different topics, and with different uses of the techniques. The real-life applications presented here have been selected because they exemplify some good practices, as well as the potential and limitations of the techniques. All the main steps of a QCA procedure are revisited in this way, from the prior steps of case selection and model specification to more advanced features such as the treatment of the so-called contradictory simplifying assumptions. Because of their specificities, csQCA, mvQCA, and fsQCA applications are discussed separately.

Next, Chapter 7 addresses all the main critiques that have been issued vis-à-vis QCA and its different techniques. There are many of such critiques, from dichotomization to temporality, through case sensitivity and the use of non-observed "logical remainder" cases. For each one of these critiques, we discuss to what extent the critique is valid and, if it is, to what extent the difficulty or limitation can be technically addressed.

Finally, in Chapter 8, we provide an open and prospective conclusion, as indeed QCA is an expanding and moving field. Some particularly promising paths are further discussed, such as using the different QCA techniques in a sequence or engaging in a fruitful dialogue (or confrontation) with other techniques, qualitative or quantitative. The last sections are devoted to specific topics on which some innovations can be expected or are already underway, particularly in terms of software development and more advanced uses of the techniques.

At the end of the book, we have also gathered a set of key resources, such as a glossary, an extensive bibliography, author and subject indexes, and links to various resources on the Web.

HOW TO READ THIS BOOK

This volume has been designed to follow a logical sequence, from general considerations to the presentation of specific techniques, then from these techniques to comments on applications, strengths, and limitations, with practical tips throughout. Readers who intend to engage in rigorous hands-on use of these techniques are thus best advised to read the whole textbook from beginning to end. Readers who wish to have a quick overview of the possibilities and key features of the techniques are advised to start from Chapter 6 (review of applications) and then to consult, in a selective way, sections from Chapters 3 to 5, depending on which pertain most directly to their specific research purposes. Six types of pedagogical resources have been inserted for all readers.

Box 0.3
Pedagogical Resources in This Textbook

- Chapter-opening summaries, listing the main goals of each chapter
- Chapter-concluding summaries, listing key points as well as key complementary readings for each chapter
- Illustrations and examples, to make technical aspects more accessible
- Basic technical definitions, explicating specific terminology
- "Good practices" boxes, listing key hands-on advice for using the techniques in appropriate ways
- A glossary, an index, and a list of key resources, toward the end of the volume—and more on a specific "resources" Web page at www.compasss.org/Textbook.htm.

COMPANION READINGS

Naturally, as this textbook covers a lot of ground in a relatively restricted volume, some key companion readings are recommended to get a more fine-grained picture of QCA and its techniques. Although many volumes have touched upon QCA to some extent,[4] there are three core companion volumes to this one. On the one hand, the two agenda-setting volumes by Charles Ragin, *The Comparative Method* (1987) and *Fuzzy-Set Social Science* (2000), lay out all the fundamentals and the overall ambition of QCA in its different variations. They have been recently complemented by a volume updating and extending the whole discussion around fuzzy sets (Ragin, 2008).

On the other hand, the focus of the textbook by Schneider and Wagemann (2007 in German; forthcoming in English) is, altogether, more technical; it provides, in particular, detailed discussions on necessity and sufficiency, consistency and coverage, Boolean algebra and set theoretic operations, measurement, concept formation, advanced features of fuzzy sets, and more information on the use of software. As a contrast, our textbook is more broad and encompassing, at a more introductory-to-intermediate level. What's specific about this volume is that it provides a state-of-the-art, basic treatment of all three main QCA techniques as well as what is "upstream" (comparative research design in particular), an extensive discussion of the strengths and limitations as well as published applications in many fields and disciplines—all of this in a relatively compact format. Thus the more focused and technically elaborate Schneider and Wagemann textbook is to be considered as a complementary resource to our textbook—along with resources on the Web (see p. 179). A specific piece on good practices in QCA, by Wagemann and Schneider (2007; Schneider & Wagemann, 2008) as well, is also complementary to the advice offered in this book.

For those who read French, the De Meur and Rihoux textbook (2002) can still be useful, in particular in its discussion of the Boolean foundations of QCA and in its visual representations of the data and key operations. The concise textbook by Caramani (2008) is useful for an in-depth look into the "black box" of QCA (technical aspects, fine-grained discussion of causation and control) and to reflect more thoroughly on epistemological and practical issues of comparative research design. Finally, two recent volumes are particularly helpful "upstream": that of Goertz (2006b), for the practical stages of comparative research design, case selection, concept formation and measurement; and that of Gerring (2006), also for case selection and for a reflective view on how case-oriented knowledge and "case intimacy" can be gained before engaging in comparative analysis.

Key Points

- Comparison is a key operation in any empirical scientific effort.

- This book is about specific comparative *methods and techniques* that enable systematic cross-case comparisons, while at the same time attending to within-case complexity, particularly in small- and intermediate-N research designs.

- The "QCA" label designates the whole approach, and more specific labels (csQCA, mvQCA, fsQCA) designate particular techniques.

- In QCA, complex cases are transformed into *configurations*: specific combinations of *conditions* linked to a given *outcome*.

Key Complementary Readings

Caramani (2008), Lijphart (1971), Ragin (1987, 2000, 2008), Schneider & Wagemann (2007, forthcoming).

NOTES

1. Example suggested by Lasse Cronqvist.

2. "Boolean" simply means that variables can be coded only [0] or [1]—that is, they have to be dichotomized. See the subsection on dichotomization, p. 39.

3. Note that, in most publications so far, csQCA has simply been referred to as "QCA"—hopefully, the more precise and unambiguous label "csQCA" will be used from now on.

4. Quite a few other textbooks with a broader methodological purpose cover QCA to some extent. We particularly recommend the following three, because they put QCA (and its logical foundations) within a broader setting in a thoughtful way: Becker (1998), Pennings, Keman, & Kleinnijenhuis (1999), and Peters (1998).

1

Qualitative Comparative Analysis (QCA) as an Approach

Dirk Berg-Schlosser
Gisèle De Meur
Benoît Rihoux
Charles C. Ragin

Goals of This Chapter

After reading this chapter, you should be able to:

- Locate QCA as an approach and grasp its key epistemological foundations

- Understand how and why QCA is "case oriented" and how one should use QCA to engage in a dialogue between cases and theories

- Understand the specific conception of causality conveyed in QCA—*multiple conjunctural causation*—and its practical consequences

- Reflect on the usefulness of QCA to reach a certain level of generalization beyond the observed cases

- Grasp key common features of QCA techniques in terms of formalization, replication, transparency, and different types of uses

- Become accustomed to some key technical terms and use the appropriate, QCA-specific terminology

LOCATING QCA

Epistemological Foundations

To better understand QCA and its various techniques and applications, it is important to locate it both in its historical epistemological context and in its relationship vis-à-vis other methods of social scientific inquiry.[1] In its more recent developments it dates back to systematic comparative procedures as they originated in the natural sciences in the 18th and 19th centuries, as, for example, in Linnaeus' (1753) work in botany or Cuvier's (1812) studies in anatomy.

The logical foundations for this method were laid by Hume (1758) and, in particular, J. S. Mill's (1967 [1843]) "canons." Among these, the "method of agreement" and the "method of difference" are the most important. The first refers to eliminating all similarities but one: "If two or more instances of the phenomenon under investigation have only one circumstance in common, the circumstance in which alone all the instances agree is the cause (or effect) of the given phenomenon" (p. 390). By contrast, the Method of Difference establishes the absence of a common cause or effect, even if all other circumstances are identical:

> If an instance in which the phenomenon under investigation occurs, and an instance in which it does not occur, have every circumstance in common save one, that one occurring only in the former; the circumstance in which alone the two instances differ, is the effect, or the cause, or an indispensable part of the cause, of the phenomenon. (p. 391)

Both methods thus are concerned with the systematic matching and contrasting of cases in order to establish common causal relationships by eliminating all other possibilities. Both procedures are, however, somewhat extreme in the sense that they attempt to establish a single common cause, or its absence, by controlling all other possibilities and the entire environment.

Mill also devised a combination of the two which he called the "Joint Method of Agreement and Difference" or the "Indirect Method of Difference," which consists of a double application of the Method of Agreement:

> If two or more instances in which the phenomenon occurs have only one circumstance in common, while two or more instances in which it does not occur have nothing in common save the absence of that circumstance, the circumstance in which alone the two sets of instances differ, is the effect, or the cause, or an indispensable part of the cause, of the phenomenon. (p. 396)

This "quasi-experimental" design is, however, as Mill himself stated, less convincing than the pure Method of Difference.

Mill's "canons" imply rather rigid "positivist" assumptions about relationships of cause and effect and the state of valid theory in any given area of research. On the whole, such relatively mechanical and deterministic relationships can be established only rarely even in the "hard" sciences. By themselves, therefore, these methods do not produce any new discoveries unless some truly relevant factors have been included. Similarly, they may not *prove* any causal relationship, because it is most often impossible (in social science at least) to test a clear and complete (preconceived) model of such links and to sufficiently "control" for other factors.[2] They constitute, however, a valuable step toward eliminating irrelevant factors and approximating causal conditions in the "real" world. In this sense they correspond to Popper's (1959) famous principle of "falsification." Or as it was expressed in another classic of this period, Mill's methods are nevertheless

> of undoubted value in the process of attaining truth. For in eliminating false hypotheses they narrow the field in which true ones may be found. And even where these methods may fail to eliminate all irrelevant circumstances, they enable us with some degree of approximation to so establish the *conditions for the occurrence* of a phenomenon, that we can say one hypothesis is logically preferable to its rivals. (Cohen & Nagel, 1934, p. 267; emphasis added).

The various techniques of QCA precisely identify and narrow down such "conditions of occurrence." As will be demonstrated and exemplified in the chapters that follow, these techniques are important tools for reducing the enormous complexity that we routinely confront in the social sciences. As Mill (1967 [1843]) himself put it,

> in politics and history . . . Plurality of Causes exists in almost boundless excess, and effects are, for the most part, inextricably interwoven with one another. To add to the embarrassment, most of the inquiries in political science relate to the production of effects of a most comprehensive description, such as the public wealth, public security, public morality, and the like: results liable to be affected directly or indirectly either in *plus* or in *minus* by nearly every fact which exists, or event which occurs, in human society. (p. 452; emphases in the original)

"Small-N" Research and "Macro-Comparative" Analysis . . . and Beyond

Initially, in the late 1980s and early 1990s, QCA was mostly developed for applications in political science (comparative politics) and historical sociology (e.g., welfare state studies). Thus, quite naturally, QCA has been initially conceived, in those social scientific disciplines, as a "macro-comparative" approach—because the specific subject matter in those disciplines necessitates empirical research at the "macro" level of entire societies, economies, states, or other complex social and cultural formations (Berg-Schlosser & Quenter, 1996).

In the present world, but also if we include relevant historical cases, the maximum number of such cases is of necessity quite limited, as for example the current 200 or so independent countries worldwide, 50 states in the United States, or 27 EU member countries. In fact, for many meaningful macro-level comparisons, the number of cases with useful and comparable data is even more limited—for example, the set of OECD countries, sub-Saharan countries, or a given set of European regions that have received, say, some structural funds for economic development. This is why QCA is still widely seen as a "small-N" approach. Out of this fact arises the characteristic "small-N–many variables" dilemma for this type of research (see, e.g., Lijphart, 1971, 1975; see also Chapter 2 on how to address this problem).

In a more general way, QCA techniques can be located in a two-dimensional matrix listing numbers of variables and numbers of cases in relation to other supplementary or neighboring approaches (Figure 1.1).

The realm of QCA techniques—that is, the "comparative method" in the more narrow sense of the term—thus has to be distinguished, in particular, from the "statistical method," which proceeds on the basis of a large number of cases, drawn on a random basis if possible, and a relatively small number of variables. Both methods have their respective strengths and weaknesses (for extensive discussions, see Brady & Collier, 2004; King, Keohane, & Verba, 1994; see also p. 170), but rather than merely adopting insights from large-scale quantitative inquiries or simply increasing the number of cases as much as possible, QCA follows a different path with several distinct emphases, as will be demonstrated in the next sections.

As QCA techniques and their applications have been developing, this positioning of QCA as a "small-N" and "macro-comparative" approach needs to be nuanced somewhat, in at least two respects. On the one hand, technically speaking, the "small-N" zone is now usually associated with a really low number of cases—say, between 2 cases (this is a "very small-N," but it does enable some form of binary comparison) and around 10 to 15 cases. Beyond this—say, between 10 and 15 and 50 and 100 cases—one finds oneself rather in an "intermediate-N" situation, which is still quite a small number of cases relative to the requirements of most quantitative (read: statistical) techniques. Besides, as shall be discussed later (see p. 174), QCA techniques have been fruitfully applied in "large-N" research designs as well. On the other hand, an increasing number of scholars, in fields such as organizational sociology, management studies, and education studies, among others, have begun to apply QCA techniques at other levels, notably at the "meso" level (the level of organizations, social networks, collective actors, etc.) or even, more recently, at the "micro" level (small groups or individuals) (see p. 173).

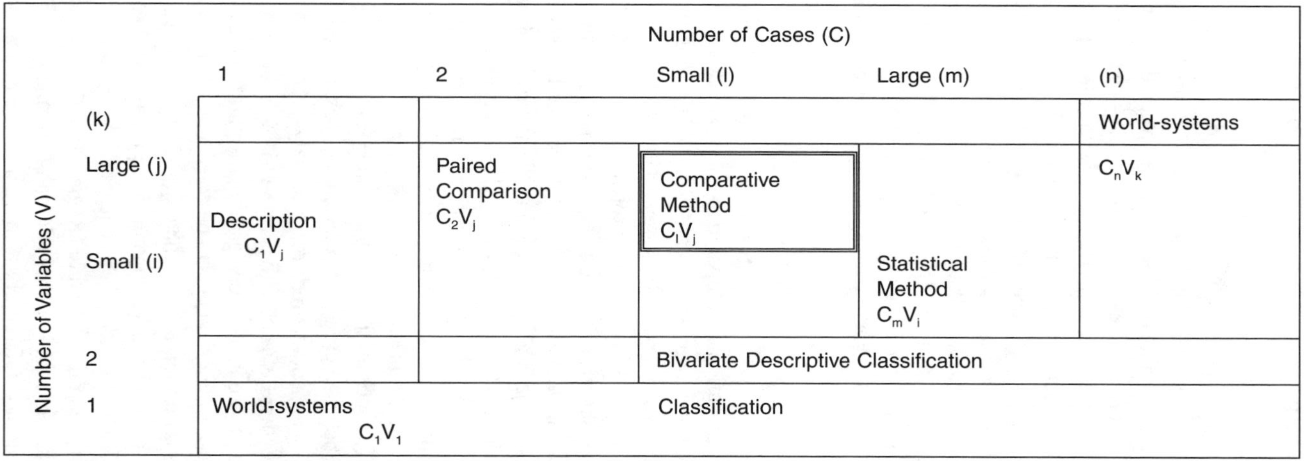

Number of Cases (C)

Number of Variables (V)	1	2	Small (l)	Large (m)	(n) World-systems
(k)					$C_n V_k$
Large (i)	Description $C_1 V_j$	Paired Comparison $C_2 V_j$	Comparative Method $C_l V_j$	Statistical Method $C_m V_i$	
Small (i)			Bivariate Descriptive Classification		
2					
1 World-systems	$C_1 V_1$		Classification		

Figure 1.1 Comparative Analysis: A Typology

Source: Adapted from "Die Vergleichende Methode in der Politikwissenschaft," by F. H. Aarebrot and P. H. Bakka, in *Vergleichende Politikwissenschaft: Ein Einführendes Studienhandbuch* (4th ed.), p. 65, by D. Berg-Schlosser and F. Müller-Rommel (Eds.), 2003, Wiesbaden, Germany: VS-Verlag.

KEY FEATURES AND ASSUMPTIONS OF QCA

In some respects, it can be said that QCA techniques strive to meet advantages of both the "qualitative" (case-oriented) and "quantitative" (variable-oriented) techniques. This was indeed the main ambition expressed when the first technique—initially known as QCA and now referred to as csQCA—was developed in the late 1980s and presented as a "synthetic strategy" to "integrate the best features of the case-oriented approach with the best features of the variable-oriented approach" (Ragin, 1987, p. 84). Indeed, as we explain below, csQCA and the other QCA techniques do combine distinctive strengths of both approaches (Rihoux, 2003, 2006, 2008a, 2008b), but altogether they are more clearly located on the side of "case-oriented" methods (Rihoux & Lobe, 2009). QCA techniques allow the systematic comparison of cases, with the help of formal tools and with a specific conception of cases. This is where configurations come in.

Cases and Theory

Techniques of configurational comparative analysis (CCA) are "case oriented" in the sense that they deal with a limited number of complex cases in a "configurational" way (see p. xix). This means that each individual case is considered as a complex combination of properties, a specific "whole" that should not be lost or obscured in the course of the analysis—this is a *holistic* perspective. The cases dealt with are (or should be) well known rather than anonymous, as, for example, individuals are at the micro level in large-scale survey research. Rather than being a drawback, this can become a considerable advantage that enables the researcher to go back to these cases or consult historians, country experts, and others to clarify further aspects of cases or to check and improve the relevant data.

In the process of configurational comparative analysis, the researcher engages in a dialogue between cases and relevant theories. Indeed, the choice of the variables (conditions and outcome) for the analysis must be theoretically informed. In this sense, there is a deductive aspect to QCA; however, QCA techniques can also be used more inductively, gaining insights from case knowledge in order to identify the key "ingredients" to be considered (Rihoux, 2003, 2006; Rihoux & Lobe, 2009). Further, a key richness of QCA techniques is that they use a formal language (Boolean or set-theoretic; see Chapters 3 to 5) that can be very easily translated into a theoretical discourse (and vice versa); indeed, theoretical discourse is set-theoretic by nature (Ragin, 2000, 2008) and QCA techniques enable a rich dialogue with theory (Befani, Ledermann, & Sager, 2006).

With regards to theories, QCA is best located in the more general area of "medium range" theorizing in social research (Merton, 1968; Mjøset, 2001) and thus has to be distinguished from contemporary "grand" and potentially universal social theories such as those of Habermas, Bourdieu, Luhmann or Giddens, which remain highly speculative and are actually not designed to be empirically testable.[3] In this sense, QCA is, again, more modest and context sensitive in the tradition of "grounded" approaches that are historical, qualitative, and empirically differentiated (Glaser & Strauss, 1967; discussed by Mjøset, 2003).

Seen in this perspective, QCA can lay the groundwork and be extended to even more demanding types of analyses—for example, taking into account the temporal dimension and the various "paths," "critical junctures," and overall dynamics that can be found in systematic comparative historical studies (see, e.g., Pierson, 2004; see also pp. 161–163, 173). Similarly, it can be applied conjointly at several levels of analysis—for example, linking the meso and macro levels when social cleavages and party systems are linked in empirical democratic theory. Furthermore, the specific "conditions of occurrence" identified by QCA can be integrated in the general model of social explanation as explicated in Coleman's "bathtub" (1990) and further elaborated by Esser (1993). In substance, Coleman formalizes the articulation between macro-level and micro-level changes in a given society, where societal change at the macro level or group-level change at the meso level are actually grounded in changes at the level of the constituent individuals (i.e., the micro level). In this way, structure- and actor-related aspects can be combined and brought into a more general historical or "medium-range theorizing" perspective.

In practical terms, theory plays an important role at crucial stages in the application of QCA techniques. First, "upstream," when the model has to be elaborated, theory points at useful conditions to be included in the model and helps to operationalize them (how to measure their intensity, which thresholds to use, etc.). Theories also guide the selection of cases, in the attempt to include both the important or typical cases and the more paradoxical or contrary ones (see also p. 20). QCA indeed tends to give explanations without dismissing "exceptions" or "outliers." These nonconforming cases, on the contrary, often shed a special light on the understanding of specific processes.

Second, during the analysis, theoretical knowledge, as well as a deep knowledge of the empirical field, will help researchers make decisions regarding several practical QCA operations such as the operationalization of variables and the treatment of the so-called contradictory configurations—in short, cases that display the same values on the *condition* variables but lead to different *outcomes* (much more on this p. 44). Theoretical knowledge is also important in a key step of the analysis in QCA: the inclusion of non-observed cases, the so-called logical remainders (see p. 59). Third and not least, "downstream," after the analysis, theory will help the researcher sort the different (otherwise logically equivalent—i.e., equally parsimonious) solutions and justify any reasoned preferences among them.

Causality, Complexity, and Parsimony

QCA techniques allow for "conjunctural causation" across observed cases. This means that different constellations of factors may lead to the same result, as, for example, different "paths" in democratization research (e.g., Berg-Schlosser, 1998; Collier, 1999) or different social forces leading to the emergence of welfare states in Western Europe (e.g., Alber, 1982; Esping-Andersen, 1990). More precisely, QCA develops a conception of causality that leaves room for complexity, referred to as "multiple conjunctural causation."

Box 1.1
"Multiple Conjunctural Causation" in a Nutshell

It is a conception of causality according to which:

1. Most often, it is a combination of causally relevant conditions that generates the outcome (AB → Y).

2. Several different combinations of conditions may produce the same outcome (AB + CD → Y, + indicates a Boolean or[4]).

3. Depending on the context, a given outcome may result from a condition when it is present and also when it is absent (AB → Y but also aC → Y). In this example, [A] combined with [B] produces the occurrence[5] of the outcome, but its absence [a] combined with [C] also produces the outcome.

In other words: Different causal "paths"—each path being relevant, in a distinct way—may lead to the same outcome (De Meur & Rihoux, 2002). The term "multiple" refers to the number of paths, while the term "conjunctural" conveys the notion that each path consists of a combination of conditions. Thus multiple conjunctural causation contains the notion of *equifinality,* which simply means that different paths can lead to the same outcome. It should be noted that this runs completely against key assumptions on which mainstream statistical techniques rest—for example, additivity, meaning that a given factor is assumed to have the same incremental effect on the outcome across all cases, regardless of the values of other causally relevant conditions (Schneider & Wagemann, 2007, forthcoming).

Since it views causality as context and conjuncture specific, QCA rejects any form of permanent causality (Ragin, 1987). This is in line with the earlier works of J. S. Mill (see p. 2). Bottom line: By using QCA, the researcher is urged not to specify a single causal model that best fits the data, as one usually does with statistical techniques, but instead to determine the number and character of the different causal models that exist among comparable cases (Ragin, 1987).

It thus goes beyond the (often superficial or misleading) means, correlations, and regressions—computed across all cases at the same time—which average out the respective constellations and ignore specific, distinct patterns and "outliers" (see, e.g., also Berg-Schlosser & Cronqvist, 2005; Berg-Schlosser & Quenter, 1996; Ragin, 2006a).[6] Actually, with QCA, if a given combination of conditions "explains" only one single case, it is not a priori considered as less relevant or less important than another combination of conditions that would account for, say, 10 or 15 cases—because each case matters in most applications of QCA (see pp. 23, 155). In this sense, QCA moves away, quite radically, from simplistic, probabilistic causal reasoning (De Meur & Rihoux, 2002); in its case-orientedness, it is more geared toward diversity (Ragin, 2006a).

Thus QCA broadens the usual frame in the analysis of causality, by relaxing several common assumptions. First, "additivity" is no longer assumed: This means that the idea that each single cause has its own separate, independent impact on the outcome is abandoned and replaced by the assumption that "conjunctural causation" is at work, meaning that several causes can be simultaneously present (or be combined, somehow), constituting a "causal combination," for the outcome to occur. Second, a given causal combination may not be the only route to a specific result; other combinations also may be able to produce it. Third, the uniformity of causal effects is not assumed; on the contrary, a given condition may, combined with different others, sometimes act in favor of the outcome, and sometimes, differently combined, act against it. Fourth, causality is not assumed to be symmetrical—rather, causal asymmetry is assumed, meaning that the presence and the absence of the outcome, respectively, may require different explanations.

Box 1.2
Causal Relations in QCA:
Assumptions That Are *Not* Taken Onboard

It is crucial to bear in mind that QCA does *not* take onboard some basic assumptions that lie at the heart of the mainstream statistical approach (and thus underlie most statistical techniques). In QCA:

- Permanent causality is *not* assumed.
- Uniformity of causal effects is *not* assumed.
- Unit homogeneity is *not* assumed.
- Additivity is *not* assumed.
- Causal symmetry is *not* assumed.

Note that other core mainstream statistical assumptions, such as linearity, and so on, are not taken onboard either.

Of course, QCA techniques do not guarantee the final grasp of the "true" causal grounds of a given phenomenon because the issue of causality is a much more complex matter (see, e.g., Abell, 2004; Gerring, 2005; Mahoney, 2004). Besides, the conclusions of any empirical analysis (QCA or any other) are totally dependent on the choice of "ingredients" put under the microscope, including the condition variables as they have been operationalized as well as the selection of cases. Yet, if several competing theories try to explain the same result, QCA techniques will quickly disqualify the theories that are unable to discriminate correctly between cases with and without the outcome under study. This will be indicated by the presence of so-called contradictory configurations (see p. 44).

Among the remaining theories, those that best satisfy the "parsimony principle" (Occam's "razor") will emerge. The parsimony principle, successively reinvented and reinforced through the centuries, can be translated into the commonsense adage: "Why make complicated when one can make simple?" Or, as Einstein put it in his famous dictum: One should express things "as simply as possible, but no simpler." To sum up: QCA techniques strive to achieve some form of "short" (parsimonious) explanation of a certain phenomenon of interest, while still providing appropriate allowance for causal complexity.

Naturally, the search for causal regularities implies the acceptance of the postulate that there are indeed underlying causal regularities in human and social phenomena, even if sketchy (Ragin, 1987, p. 19; Skocpol, 1984, pp. 374–375; Zelditch, 1971). In QCA, as discussed in Box 1.3, two key regularities are framed in terms of necessity ("necessary [combinations of] conditions") and sufficiency ("sufficient [combinations of] conditions"). In fact, any empirical scientific process—even those within the "hard" sciences—is based on this postulate. The opposing postulate, that of an "unstructured chaos" of phenomena, would preclude the search for explanations as well as for meaning.

Box 1.3
Necessity and Sufficiency Back in the Picture[7]

Note that the key concepts of *necessity* and *sufficiency* (as defined on p. xix) are very much in line with the multiple conjunctural view on causation. Indeed, a given path toward an outcome usually consists in a combination of conditions that is *sufficient* (a sufficient *combination* or "intersection" of conditions) to produce that outcome. However, this path is not always *necessary*, as some other alternative paths (with different conditions, at least partly) could very well produce the same outcome. Let us pursue the example used on p. xix and consider three possible conditions leading to the outcome "building a democratic state":

- Condition A: Hold regular competitive elections.
- Condition B: Ensure comprehensive civil liberties.
- Condition C: Ensure independence of political decision-makers vis-à-vis the military leadership.

In this example, there could be two paths leading to the outcome of interest:

- Path 1: the combination of A and B
- Path 2: the combination of A and C

This can be translated as follows:

- Path 1 is the first *sufficient combination of conditions* leading to the outcome.
- Path 2 is the second *sufficient combination of conditions* leading to the outcome.

Neither of these two paths, considered separately, is both sufficient *and* necessary (as there is always an alternate path leading to the outcome). Note, finally, that one condition (A: Hold regular competitive elections) is present in both paths. Hence, we can say that:

- A is a *necessary condition* for the outcome to occur (because it is always present when the outcome occurs).
- However, it is *not* a sufficient condition, because condition A alone does not produce the outcome—it needs to be combined with either condition B or C.

Modest Generalization

Generalization is an important part of any empirical scientific endeavor. The goal of research is not limited to description, as exhaustive as possible, of some corpus of observations. The search for "explicit connections" (Ragin & Rihoux, 2004a) or "specific connections" (see Rihoux, 2008b) takes an important part in the process of understanding. Explicit connections give a formal shape to observed regularities that occur in the data set, and this allows for further investigations, as they are dissected to elaborate an "explanation"— an attempt to describe the mechanism at work. They also give a predictive tool, providing assertions on the behavior of new, not yet observed cases and therefore offering an opportunity to test the model and go a step further.

Without the ambition to generalize, in the search for explanations, research would produce only tautologies and descriptions. This is not to say that more interpretive or "thick" descriptive work is devoid of value—indeed such work can yield very useful insights to grasp phenomena, to understand their deeper mechanisms, to gain an understanding of complex cases (Gerring, 2006; Ragin & Becker, 1992). But it is crucial to recognize the importance of producing new conjectures and to take the risk of confronting them with new data.

The degree of maturity and robustness of a generalization will strongly depend on the quality of the empirical data set constructed by the researcher, and it will generally be a long and hard job to produce it, with many trials and errors, new questionings, and assessments. Contrary to popular myth, those readjustments should not be considered opportunistic manipulations of data; they are necessary steps in their elaboration as researchers increase their substantive and theoretical knowledge—this is why QCA techniques, as shall be demonstrated in further chapters, are iterative by nature.

A good index of the quality of research results could be precisely their ability to withstand refutation when confronted with new cases. In this respect, we should remember that a theory maximizes its robustness when it avoids individualizing explanations—that is, when it avoids providing a specific "explanation" for each specific case (it is then only an accumulation of "descriptions," and not an "explanation"). Only generalization makes it possible to achieve more succinct explanations—such as in the example in the previous section, where condition A is identified as a key regularity (a necessary condition). This again speaks strongly in favor of parsimony.

Yet, the efforts toward generalization that have a reasonable chance of success must stay inside the initial "homogeneity space," within which the empirical data set is contained (see p. 20.). Nothing supports the idea that conditions not included in the analysis would *not* affect the results of the analysis. Hence a well-executed QCA should go beyond plain description and consider "modest generalizations": QCA results may be used in support of "limited historical generalization" (Ragin, 1987, p. 31). More specifically, from a systematic comparison of comparable cases, it is possible to formulate propositions that we can then apply, with appropriate caution, to other similar cases—that is, cases that share a reasonable number of characteristics with those that were the subject of the QCA. Note that this view on generalization is much more modest than statistical inference, which allows very broad generalizations (from a sample of, say, 1,000 respondents to a population of millions of individuals).

Data, Replicability, and Transparency

As mentioned above, QCA techniques require that each case be broken down into a series of features: a certain number of condition variables and an outcome variable. For instance, if we consider athletes as cases, if the outcome is the ability to throw a discus beyond 60 meters, then some conditions could be being tall (versus not tall), being fast (versus slow), being muscular (versus thin), and so on. Then we could measure these attributes for each "case" (athlete): Case 1 could be tall, fast, and muscular; Case 2 not tall, fast, and thin; and so on.

This means that, as with statistical analyses, QCA techniques allow one to develop an *analytical* strategy. However, this segmentation into variables does not affect the perception of each case as a whole. The aim here is to allow for major concerns of both quantitative (defining variables) and qualitative (keeping in touch with the *holistic* perspective) approaches. Having done so, one will be able to compare cases as "whole units," each one of these being defined as a combination of features (i.e., as a *configuration,* as defined p. xix).

In this analytical process, QCA techniques enable us to take into account both "qualitative" and "quantitative" phenomena. When the first QCA technique (csQCA) was developed, Ragin, and several other scholars, used the "qualitative" label to refer to phenomena that vary by kind rather than by degree and also to stress the importance of considering cases as specific and complex configurations, or combinations, of features (Ragin, Berg-Schlosser, & De Meur, 1996, p. 749). Incidentally, we should mention here that it is perfectly possible to work with "subjective" or "qualitative" data using QCA. The only practical requirement is to be able to transform these data into categories or numbers. For instance, if our cases are political parties after a given election and a condition is defined as "perception of electoral defeat by the party activists," the nature of the data could be very subjective (i.e., based on discussions with party activists, assessment of the "tone" in the party press, a feeling about the atmosphere in the post-election party congress, using participant observation methodology, etc.). For any given party, one could still allocate a numerical score of "1" ("yes, or mostly yes") or "0" ("no, or mostly no") on this condition.

However, csQCA, as well as the other QCA techniques, is also able to consider phenomena that are "more" or "less" similar—that is, to express a degree of (dis)similarity (the differences therefore being of a quantitative nature)—as well as phenomena that differ by their nature (the differences being in this case qualitative). For instance, a "wealth versus poverty" variable could be based on some fine-grained data on yearly income of individuals—this would then be a typically "quantitative" measurement of wealth versus poverty. Alternatively, one could consider—for instance, following some official UN or OECD criteria—that the crucial analytical difference is to consider whether a given individual is "poor" or "not poor." Usually, this is done by specifying an income threshold (say, below 1,000 EUR/month, in a country such as Germany) below which one is considered "poor." This is exactly what will be done in the basic, dichotomous csQCA: switching, in the course of the analysis, from quantitative (numerical) to dichotomous (still numerical, but tapping a more qualitative distinction) variables, using substantive knowledge to guide the dichotomization. By dichotomizing the originally fine-grained (quantitative) data, our aim is to identify what can be considered a more fundamental, more basic distinction, of a more qualitative nature.

In this process, similarly to the quantitative (mainly statistical) approach, QCA offers tools that are both formalized and replicable. QCA techniques are formalized in the sense that they are based on a particular language (Boolean algebra and set theory) whose rules and well-defined solutions formalize and translate the rules of logic (formal operations and algorithms; see Chapters 3 to 5). Because these formal rules are fixed and stable, they allow replicability. Simply stated, this means that another researcher using the same data set and selecting the same options will obtain the same results (King et al., 1994, p. 26). This is a major asset of QCA techniques compared to many ad hoc or less formalized qualitative techniques. From a certain perspective, one could say that replicability provides the "scientific" character of the approach, in the sense that it eliminates vagueness and interpretation in the application of techniques (mathematics, for example, is universal as far as technique is concerned).

Another advantage of QCA techniques is their transparency. They demand that the researcher, at several points in the analysis, acts with transparency in his or her choices—selecting variables, processing them, choosing tools for the analysis, intervening during the analysis, and so on. During this process, the researcher regularly refers back to the cases with all their richness and specificity. This back-and-forth "dialogue with the cases," combined with the transparency of choices, is unquestionably a virtue of QCA techniques. What also makes this transparency possible for QCA techniques is that the formal language used by the software takes its inspiration from principles used in everyday life and, for this reason, can be more easily understood by non-specialists.

With most statistical tools, the researcher enters the data and the software finds the "solution." In contrast, QCA opens the "black box" of formalized analysis, by demanding from researchers not only that they make choices but also that they account for them. Using QCA, researchers must be engaged in the analytic process, for it is not mechanical or "push-button." For sure, such requirements should also apply to statistical work. The difference, with QCA, is that the user is more active, gets a better grip on the "mechanics" of the formal operations,[8] makes more decisions in the course of the analysis, and follows an iterative logic, with frequent "returns to the cases." Researchers may feel uncomfortable with this, but this lack of comfort is beneficial, because it compels them to use critical thought during the analysis and opens up the research to others for confirmation or falsification (Popper, 1963).

FIVE TYPES OF USES OF QCA TECHNIQUES

QCA techniques may be exploited in at least five different ways. According to their specific needs, researchers can use different features of QCA. Here, we consider only the three versions of QCA (csQCA, mvQCA, fsQCA). MSDO/MDSO is a technique geared toward one specific type of usage.

Box 1.4
Five Types of Uses of QCA Techniques

1. Summarizing data

2. Checking coherence of data

3. Checking hypotheses or existing theories

4. Quick test of conjectures

5. Developing new theoretical arguments

First, QCA techniques may be used in a straightforward manner, simply to *summarize data*, to display them in a more compact way, and to describe more synthetically the relevant empirical universe. This is thus a purely descriptive use of QCA. More specifically, this is done by means of using the software to generate a synthetic table that shows, in a straightforward way, how some cases cluster together—the so-called truth table (see Chapters 3 to 5). In this way, the researcher will be able to bring to light similarities between cases that may, at first sight, seem quite different. QCA is therefore an excellent tool for data exploration.

Second, the researcher may take advantage of QCA to *check the coherence* of the data. During the analysis, one often detects contradictory configurations—that is, cases that are identical with respects to causal conditions, but different in outcome (see p. 44). Contradictions are plainly displayed in the truth table produced by the software. Detecting contradictions, however, does not necessarily mean that researchers have failed. On the contrary, contradictions will tell them something about the cases they are studying. By seeking a solution to these contradictions, the researcher will both get a more thorough knowledge of relevant cases (through his or her "dialogue with the cases") and develop a more coherent body of evidence (see p. 48).

Third, QCA may be used to *test hypotheses* or *existing theories*. More precisely, it enables us to corroborate or falsify these hypotheses or theories. When using QCA in this way, the researcher aims at operationalizing some theory or hypothesis, as explicitly as possible, by defining a series of conditions that should yield a particular outcome. QCA is a powerful tool for this kind of application because it allows theory testing or hypothesis testing that is both systematic and empirical. When the researcher discovers, through QCA, a large number of contradictory configurations, it may enable him or her to falsify the theory or hypothesis (a very important achievement from a Popperian perspective; see above and p. 50). Furthermore, QCA allows us to refine the hypothesis testing process, by taking into account the actual number of cases related to falsification or corroboration.

A fourth use, close to the former one, is the *quick test of any conjecture* formulated by the researcher him- or herself—that is, without testing a preexisting theory or model as a whole. This is another way of using QCA for data exploration. The researcher specifies an expression (a formula) reflecting a specific conjecture, for example, to test an ad hoc theory or part of a theory. This yields a truth table, which allows the researcher to check whether his or her conjecture was accurate—whether it is confirmed or falsified by the set of cases under analysis.

Last but not least, QCA also may be used in the process of *developing new theoretical arguments* in the form of hypotheses. By obtaining a truth table free of contradictions and then conducting QCA, the researcher obtains a reduced expression (called a "minimal formula"). This may then be interpreted through a "dialogue with the cases" to yield new theoretical arguments. In this way, QCA can be used in a more grounded manner.

One specific technique is especially relevant for this fifth use of QCA. It consists of revising by hand the reduced expression (results of truth table analysis) generated by the software. More specifically, the researcher treats these results as a conventional algebraic expression (Boolean sums of products) and factors it to highlight shared conditions, or to rearrange it in other algebraically acceptable ways so that it speaks as directly as possible to theoretical and substantive interests (see, for example, p. 58). As such, however, QCA does not yield new theories. What it may do, once performed, is to help the researcher generate some new insights, which may then be taken as a basis for a further theoretical development or for reexamination of existing theories. Only by returning to empirical cases will it be possible to evaluate whether it makes sense to highlight a particular condition.

Key Points

- The logical foundations of QCA date back to previous work by J. S. Mill, and in particular to Mill's "canons."

- QCA was initially geared toward "small-N" designs (few cases) and macro-level cases; however, the niche for QCA applications has broadened to "intermediate-N" and "larger-N" designs and also to more meso-level or micro-level cases.

- QCA techniques feature strengths of both qualitative and quantitative techniques but are still located closer to "case-oriented" techniques.

- QCA conveys a particular conception of causality: "multiple conjunctural causation." It is a nonlinear, non-additive, non-probabilistic conception that rejects any form of permanent causality and that stresses equifinality (different paths can lead to the same outcome), complex combinations of conditions, and diversity.

- It is possible to produce generalizations with QCA; however, these are only "modest" generalizations.

- QCA techniques are analytical, transparent, and replicable and can process various sorts of data, from more quantitative (numerical) to more qualitative or subjective; they require an ongoing dialogue between case-oriented knowledge and theoretical knowledge.

- QCA techniques can be exploited in several different ways.

Key Complementary Readings

Goertz (2006b), Mill (1843), Popper (1963), Ragin (1987, 2000, 2003, 2006a).

NOTES

1. For a complementary view, see Caramani (2008).
2. And also because of the "limited diversity" problem (see p. 27).
3. A note of nuance: One may attempt to empirically and systematically test some fragments of such grand theories—see for instance how Andersen (2005) succeeds in testing Luhmann's systems theory. Part of Bourdieu's own work has also consisted in deriving concrete and testable empirical propositions from his grand theoretical framework—but alas only very few of his contemporary "believers" have followed that path.
4. See p. 34 and Box 3.1: Main Conventions and Operations of Boolean Algebra.
5. Ibid.
6. It is fair to say that the broad majority of mainstream statistical work does little to deal with causal complexity. However, some suggestions have been made in the

statistical literature as to how to deal with issues such as asymmetrical causation, necessity, sufficiency, and so on. See Schneider and Wagemann, 2007, forthcoming.

7. Example suggested by Lasse Cronqvist, further elaborated by Benoît Rihoux. For more extensive discussions, see Goertz, 2006b, Schneider and Wagemann, 2007, forthcoming; Wagemann & Schneider, 2007.

8. These logical operations, as well as all their underlying assumptions, are much simpler than statistical operations. Very few users are really able to understand the deep mechanisms and assumptions at work behind the statistical operations.

2

Comparative Research Design

Case and Variable Selection

Dirk Berg-Schlosser
Gisèle De Meur

Goals of This Chapter

After reading this chapter, you should be able to:

- Clearly delimit the universe of investigation within which you select your cases, with a key preoccupation in the definition of the *outcome* of interest

- Choose the type of research design that is most suited to your needs: "most similar" systems design, "most different" systems design, or a combination of both

- Make well-informed choices on the exact number of cases that will be included in the analysis, on methodological and practical grounds

- Proceed to model building—namely, identify potential conditions to be included in the model(s), relying on case-based knowledge and theoretical considerations

- Grasp the key goals and steps of MSDO/MDSO, a formalized procedure that, among other things, makes it possible to decrease the number of conditions when "candidate" conditions are too numerous to proceed with QCA

Each empirical field of study can be described by the cases ("units"[1]) analyzed, the characteristics of cases ("variables") being considered, and the number of times each case is observed ("observations") (King, Keohane, & Verba, 1994, pp. 51 ff.). We focus especially on the first two aspects, cases and variables. For many analyses it is indispensable to examine variation over time, and such longitudinal study can be conducted using both quantitative (e.g., Petersen, 1993) and qualitative (e.g., Griffin, 1993; Heise, 1989) methods. However, studies of this type pose their own special problems (see p. 161), which are not dealt with at this point and are not the key focus of the research designs and techniques discussed in this chapter.

In case-oriented, small- and intermediate-N situations, which is the domain we are mostly concerned with here (see pp. 3–5), both case selection and variable selection are essential for the further steps of inquiry. Both should be guided by explicit theoretical concerns, but, at least initially, they also may be exploratory in nature, starting at a relatively low level of theory building ("analytic induction," Blalock, 1984). Only in later stages can the range of explanations be determined and systematically tested. In any event, it is of crucial importance before engaging in QCA proper (through csQCA, mvQCA, fsQCA) to develop a specific *comparative research design.* Naturally, developing a research design covers many other aspects than simply case and variable selection—but we choose to concentrate on these two operations because they are particularly crucial in *comparative* research designs.

CASE SELECTION

Outcome and Area of Homogeneity

At the outset of any investigation an area of *homogeneity*, a "domain of investigation" must be defined that establishes boundaries within which cases are selected. Cases must parallel each other sufficiently and be comparable along certain specified dimensions. This is the meaning of the common adage that "apples and oranges" should not be compared. In this regard, the subject matter and the problem we are interested in (the *outcome*, in QCA terminology) must first be specified to make any sense. Thus, these fruits may well be compared concerning their sugar or water contents, their nutritional value, and so on, provided that some other dimensions on which they share some common properties (e.g., they both grow on trees, they are both suitable for human consumption) have been made explicit. The specification of relevant cases at the start of an investigation thus amounts to an explicit or implicit hypothesis that the cases selected are in fact alike enough to permit comparisons. In other words, the cases must share enough background characteristics, which in turn can be considered as "constants" in the analysis. Thus, the primary consideration in delimiting cases for a small- or intermediate-N comparative study is the outcome.

Box 2.1
An Empirical Example Used
Throughout This Textbook: The "Inter-war Project"

From here onwards, and all the way through this chapter and the three following (Chapters 3 to 5), we shall use, as a "real-life" example, a large-scale international research project on the survival or breakdown of democracies in Europe in the inter-war period (the "inter-war project," Berg-Schlosser & Mitchell, 2000, 2003).

In the inter-war project, the breakdown or survival of democratic regimes in inter-war Europe—the outcome the research team was striving to explain—presupposes the prior existence of some form of democracy in the selected cases. In addition, some limitations in time and space can also enhance the homogeneity and thus the comparability of the cases examined. For example, certain kinds of colonial or other forms of external domination or religious-cultural influences may be useful criteria for selecting a specific group of cases. A key point to remember is that a clear definition of the *outcome* of interest must be explicated at a very early stage of the QCA, because it is indispensable for the selection of cases.

A second consideration concerns the extent of diversity within the selected universe. In this regard, a maximum of *heterogeneity* over a minimum number of cases should be achieved. In the inter-war project, for instance, both survivors and breakdowns of democracy should be considered, and among the latter perhaps some more specific variants such as fascist versus more generally authoritarian outcomes. Generally, it is advantageous to include cases with a "positive" and cases with a "negative" outcome.

The "Most Similar" Versus "Most Different" Systems Designs

Once the universe of investigation and the outcome of interest have been clearly identified, two opposite strategies now become possible. One is the *most similar*, the other the *most different* systems design.

These have been explicitly formulated and discussed by Przeworski and Teune (1970)—these authors use the term *system* to designate a complex case. The most similar systems design is "based on a belief that a number of theoretically significant differences will be found among similar systems and that these differences can be used in explanation" (p. 39). By matching these similar cases as much as possible, most of the variables can be "controlled." Mill's (1967 [1843]) "indirect method of difference" (see p. 2), where different outcomes may be attributed to the remaining factors that differentiate these cases, now becomes applicable. Even though only rarely just a single factor will remain to which the effect can be attributed, at least many others can be excluded, and the remaining ones can be examined more closely in a theoretically guided qualitative manner. The "internal validity" of the observed relationships thus can be greatly enhanced (see also Cook & Campbell, 1979).

The opposite strategy, the "most different" systems design, "seeks maximal heterogeneity in the sample of systems, [and] is based on a belief that in spite of intersystemic differentiation, the populations will differ with regard to only a limited number of variables or relationships" (Przeworski & Teune, p. 39). This "contrasting" of cases thus eliminates all factors across the observed range that are not linked to an identical outcome. In this way, more "universal" explanations are sought as far as the selected area of homogeneity is concerned. To some extent, thus, the "external validity" of some hypothesized causal relationship (which have to be identified at the disaggregated level, not at the system level) can be extended and the range of its applicability including certain limitations in time and space can be established.

These designs can be visualized in a simple manner showing the respective intersections for a systematic matching and contrasting of cases. Consider Figure 2.1, which visually represents the contrasting emphases of MSDO (*m*ost *s*imilar [systems with a], *d*ifferent *o*utcome) and MDSO (*m*ost *d*ifferent [systems with a], *s*imilar *o*utcome). In this figure, each circle represents a case, and the intersections represent their commonalities. In an example of three cases that are, in one instance, "most similar" but have a different outcome (MSDO) the commonalities of the cases are indicated by the white area, whereas the shaded areas indicate their remaining idiosyncrasies in which the reasons for the different outcome may lie. Conversely, for most different systems with the same outcome (MDSO) the white areas indicate their specific conditions, whereas the shaded areas for two or three cases respectively indicate their remaining commonalities in which the reasons for the same outcome may be sought.

Until recently, however, such designs had not been fully operationalized and, indeed, Przeworski and Teune themselves did not specify any concrete case selection procedures. It also must be noted that it is only by linking the specific outcomes to these designs that they can approximate Mill's "quasi-experimental" methods. The MSDO design (most similar, different outcome) in this respect is mostly applicable for "very small-N" situations, where paired comparisons or the systematic matching of very few cases (often just three or four) may lead to a narrowing down of the "conditions of occurrence" for exploratory purposes, in order to identify some factors that may possibly be

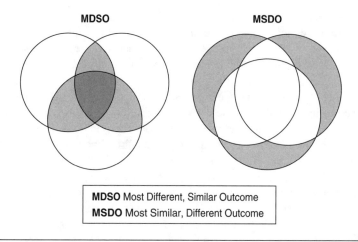

Figure 2.1   Most Different and Most Similar Systems Designs

responsible for the respective outcome. Conversely, the MDSO technique (most different, similar outcome) can cover an already somewhat larger but still limited number of cases in an order of magnitude of, say, 15 to 25, such as the EU member states or similar still sufficiently comparable groups of cases. This design allows for the testing of hypotheses in this somewhat larger universe showing their "external validity" and the specific realm of already somewhat more developed "medium-range" theories.[2]

Further Guidance for Case Selection

An important difference between the case-oriented and relatively small- or intermediate-N approach presented here and the usual large-N statistical "variable-oriented" analyses lies in the fact that case selection by itself is a process guided by the underlying research question and the preliminary hypotheses one may have in this respect. This process of case selection, therefore, can be as tentative and iterative as the variable selection and model specification in statistically oriented research. Thus, in small- or intermediate-N situations the relevant population of cases cannot simply be constituted by purely mechanical procedures like, for example, random sampling. Even if the two more general criteria mentioned above (sufficient homogeneity of the universe of cases considered and maximum heterogeneity within this universe) are taken into account, the inclusion of each case should be justified on theoretical grounds (Mahoney & Goertz, 2004; Ragin, 1994). This also means that the number of cases analyzed often cannot be fixed a priori, but new cases may be added, or others dropped, in the ongoing process of research when new hypotheses arise that can be confirmed with more similar or falsified with other contrary cases. In the inter-war project, for example, the case of Estonia was added at a later stage when the specific conditions for the survival of democracy in Finland could be contrasted with the breakdown of democracy in this otherwise very similar case (De Meur & Berg-Schlosser, 1996).

The procedure of case selection often meets discipline-specific constraints. For instance, in some disciplines, as in political science, the possible units at the macro level (e.g., states and their political systems, cities, policies) are mostly institutionally "given." They then may or may not be selected for inclusion in the study. In other disciplines, such as social anthropology, for example, certain ethnic groups or smaller units like clans may be considered relevant, but their social boundaries may be more fluid, and a precise delineation of the population of cases to be included in the study may be more difficult. Similarly, in sociology, again depending on the research question, varying units like families, school classes, interest groups, and so on may be considered where the relevant population of cases may pose some problems, and the particular choices made must be made explicit (see also Ragin, 2004).

Furthermore, there are, of course, a number of pragmatic considerations concerning the kind and overall number of cases selected. One's own familiarity with the cases, language skills, accessibility of sources and data, the possibility of cooperating with other case experts, and, last but not least, the availability of funding and other resources always play a role. This should enable the researcher to develop a certain degree of "intimacy" (Ragin, 1994) with each one of the cases under consideration. In other words, there must be sufficient "case-based knowledge" before engaging in the further technical operations of QCA. However, as important as case knowledge should be, the primary concern should still be the original research question and the subsequent use of theory to guide case selection.[3]

Box 2.2
"Good Practices" (1): Case Selection in
Small- and Intermediate-N Research

- Make sure that all cases share enough background characteristics.
- Make sure that you have a very clear definition of the *outcome* you are trying to "explain" across the cases.
- Generally, it is best to include both cases with a "positive" outcome and cases with a "negative" outcome.

- Don't take your population (or sample) of cases as a "given"; leave open the possibility to include additional cases or to remove cases at a later stage of the research.

- If you engage in a small- or intermediate-N design: When pondering on how many cases you can manage, ask yourself whether you can gain sufficient familiarity (empirical "intimacy") with each case.

- If you engage in a large-N design, make sure you gain sufficient familiarity with the *types* (kinds or categories) of cases.

THE SELECTION OF CONDITIONS

In a similar manner, the selection of conditions must be guided by theoretical criteria. Here, however, we are confronted with the opposite embarrassment—namely, a potential abundance of conditions to be considered. Given the state of theory for most empirical questions in the social and behavioral sciences, and in particular the existence of numerous competing theories, a large number of conditions often cannot be excluded a priori. This predicament is exacerbated if we seek to go beyond "universalizing" explanations and explore diversity (i.e., "variation finding"; see Tilly, 1984) or address patterns of "multiple conjunctural causation" (see p. 8). Ideally, the researcher should try to narrow his or her perspective to only a few "core" theories, but even then, the sheer number of competing "explanations" of the outcome of interest often remains too great. How should a researcher choose a smaller set of conditions if too many theories seem relevant? We discuss four concrete strategies.

The first conventional strategy for limiting the number of conditions is to test any relevant hypothesis for the outcome concerned in a strictly "Popperian" falsificatory manner (see p. 3). Thus, for example, the well-known thesis that "the more well-to-do a nation, the greater the chances that it will sustain democracy" (Lipset, 1960, p. 31) can be tested in this way. In the contemporary world, this hypothesis is verified for about 70% of the cases that are relatively well established and consolidated democracies. However, the hypothesis does not account for poor countries with relatively stable democracies like Botswana, India, and Papua New Guinea or for the failure of democracy in relatively well-developed ones like Weimar Germany. Indeed, in the inter-war project, a specific test of this hypothesis across Europe produced a score of only 10 out of 18 "correct" results (Berg-Schlosser & De Meur, 1994).

Following a second, complementary strategy, such a hypothesis must thus be modified and specified more closely if it is to satisfy any epistemological criteria more demanding than vague "probability." One way to do this is to test "conjunctural hypotheses," in which the selection of conditions is guided by explanations that are combinatorial in nature (see, e.g., Amenta & Poulsen, 1994; see also p. 125). In this way, certain constellations of conditions—for example, concerning conditions favorable to democracy in a number of poor countries or unfavorable in some richer countries—can be identified and tested.

Third, widening the horizon still further, investigators may adopt a "perspectives" approach—that is, supplying a mixed bag of conditions derived from the main theoretical perspectives in the empirical literature. This approach is probably the most common way of dealing with complex problems in empirical social scientific research. The investigator takes a thorough look at the state of the art in any given area and then develops a specific research design that takes the wider range of these conditions into account. At the same time, he or she develops a way to adjudicate between competing explanations and to allow for "interaction effects" among certain conditions. To stay within our previous example of empirical democratic theory, the works of Dahl (1971; 1989) and the overview by Lipset (1994) discuss a wide range of factors that are conducive to more stable forms of democracy in the modern world. These reviews do not, however, consider the relative "weight" these factors or their possible interaction effects.

But even such broad overviews may not address all possibly relevant conditions or all relevant interactions. Often, therefore, researchers must adopt a fourth, "comprehensive" strategy, relying on all existing theories, hypotheses, and explanations. Even though the "all" in this formulation can never be fully satisfied, it points to the potential for complexity on the variables side of the "many variables, few cases" dilemma (see the limited diversity problem, next page). Pursuing our example of the inter-war project, as this project mostly mobilizes a political science and sociology literature, such a comprehensive approach can be structured with broad "systems" models of the Parsonsian or Eastonian kind, which potentially comprise all relevant aspects and interactions to be considered. The different subsystems or categories of such a model can be "filled" using a theoretically and historically informed listing of conditions (as in the "perspectives" approach). Still, even the comprehensive approach offers no assurance that all relevant factors and interactions have been taken into account.

In the inter-war project, for example, the authors departed from a relatively comprehensive "system" model in Easton's (1965) sense, by distinguishing seven major categories of conditions: (1) general historical and geopolitical background conditions; (2) socioeconomic development; (3) social cleavage structure; (4) political-cultural traditions; (5) intermediary structures, major interest groups, and party systems; (6) institutional setup of the central political system and the administrative apparatus; and (7) external (international) factors. Within each category, several conditions were then identified, depending on the state of empirical democratic theory within each category (for further details, see Berg-Schlosser & Mitchell 2000; 2003). Over and above these "system-derived" conditions, two further sets of conditions were included: some conditions to tap the crisis effects concerning the social and political turbulences in many countries (formation of new states, establishment of new democratic regimes, and the effects of the Great Depression after 1929) and some specific actor-related conditions (major interventions by leading personalities or collective actors such as the military). Obviously, it was not possible to process this very long list of conditions (61 "system-derived" conditions plus 4 crisis- and 8 actor-related conditions) in one single model for further empirical analysis, especially in a small- or intermediate-N setting.

In this process of condition selection, it is very important to keep the number of conditions quite low, especially in small- or intermediate-N research designs.[4] The key issue here is not so much the absolute number of conditions but rather the *ratio* between their number and the number of cases. Consider some binary conditions (dichotomized: only "0" or "1" values). As their number increases, the number of possible combinations of these variables increases exponentially (De Meur & Rihoux, 2002; Ragin, 1987). If there are only two conditions, there are only four combinations. But then the figures rise very quickly: for instance, 8 combinations (i.e., 2^3) for 3 conditions, 64 combinations (i.e., 2^6) for 6 conditions, 512 combinations (i.e., 2^9) for 9 conditions, and so on.

Thus the number of possible logical combinations of conditions can quickly exceed the number of cases, and the empirically observed cases will occupy only a tiny proportion of the potential "logical space" (as shall also be demonstrated further with Venn diagrams; see Chapter 3, Figures 3.2 and 3.3). This is the *limited diversity* problem: The observed data are far less rich than the potential property space delineated by the conditions. The danger, if we proceed and use these data to perform QCA treatment, is that we shall obtain an individual explanation for each individual case. In the extreme, only a *description* of the cases—of each separate case—will be obtained, rather than a genuine explanation. For this reason, it is better to select a limited number of potential conditions. This further reinforces the more general argument in favor of parsimony (see p. 10): The fewer the number of "causes" we need to explain a phenomenon of interest, the closer we come to the "core" elements of causal mechanisms. Moreover, the better we are able to identify fundamental causes, the easier it will be to produce results that may be tested on other cases, and eventually corroborated or falsified. It is exactly this "falsifiability" of results that gives a method its scientific quality (Popper, 1963; see also p. 3).

The initial complexity of possible factors influencing the outcome can also be reduced by a number of stepwise multi-methodological procedures. In the inter-war project, for example, the seven major categories of conditions were tested separately with csQCA but also with other outcome-oriented techniques such as Discriminant Analysis (a statistical technique) to identify strong bivariate relationships. In a second step, only conditions displaying strong relationships were retained across all categories and tested again, also showing some specific combinations of factors. Other procedures, like confirmatory factor analysis, may also be employed to process together conditions that load on the same dimension—for example, values of urbanization, industrialization, and literacy being combined to a single measure of "modernization." Some other factors could also be combined by logical procedures, such as taking together the existence of large landlords and a rural proletariat as a common factor of feudal or quasi-feudal patterns of landholding. In this way, the 61 original conditions were reduced to 8 "super conditions," also corresponding to major tenets in empirical democratic theory, and the relationship between the number of conditions and the number of cases considered thus became much more favorable (De Meur & Berg-Schlosser, 1996).

Box 2.3
"Good Practices" (2): Condition Selection in Small- and Intermediate-N Research Designs

- Do not include a condition that does not vary across the cases. In other words, "a variable must vary," otherwise it is a constant.

- Keep the number of conditions relatively low. A large number of conditions tends to "individualize" each case, making it difficult to find any regularity or any synthetic explanation of the outcome across the cases.

- Altogether, a good balance must be reached between the number of cases and the number of conditions. The ideal balance is not a purely numerical one and will most of the time be found by trial and error. A common practice, in an intermediate-N analysis (say, 10 to 40 cases) would be to select from 4 to 6–7 conditions.

- For each condition, formulate a clear hypothesis regarding its connection to the outcome; if possible, formulate this hypothesis in the form of a statement about necessity and/or sufficiency.

MSDO/MDSO: A SYSTEMATIC PROCEDURE
FOR MATCHING CASES AND CONDITIONS

To establish which cases are "most similar" or "most different" in any given research situation, rather than proceeding from merely intuitive "hunches" or purely pragmatic reasons like knowing the history and language of a particular country, several specific problems must be addressed. These follow from the necessity of measuring the proximity or remoteness of pairs of cases in the heterogeneous, multidimensional space defined by the conditions. These distance measures provide the basis for determining the "most different" and "most similar" pairs or groups of cases with regard to the outcome. The two main issues are (a) choosing from among a variety of different ways of measuring the distance between pairs of cases in a multidimensional space and (b) assigning relative weights to the conditions that define this space. In this way the complexity of the data can be retained as much as possible in the complexity of the proximity measure.

The purpose of this section is to present, in a nutshell, a systematic procedure to achieve these goals—it is called MSDO/MDSO. Ultimately, it also allows, through the systematic matching and pairing of cases, to identify some key conditions that can either be used for further, more qualitative, interpretation of some clusters of cases or be considered as a way to identify "core" conditions that can be used in a subsequent application of QCA. The MSDO/MDSO procedure is designed for research situations in which the conditions ("explanatory factors") are—or can be—grouped into categories or clusters. It is also particularly helpful when conditions are numerous.

Box 2.4
Main Steps of the MSDO/MDSO Procedure

Full details, with the "inter-war project" example (with seven clusters of conditions), can be found via the resources Web page (see the Appendix). See also De Meur and Berg-Schlosser (1994) and De Meur (1996) on this same example, as well as De Meur, Bursens, and Gottcheiner (2006) for another empirical application.

1. Preparing the data: Each variable (conditions and outcome) is dichotomized, for each case.

2. Computing "distance matrices" between pairs of countries, for each cluster of conditions. As a measure of distance, a "Boolean distance" is used: the number of Boolean (i.e., dichotomized, with 0 or 1 values) conditions by which two cases differ from one another. This makes it possible to identify, for each of the seven distance matrices, the minimum distance obtained for countries with different outcomes (MSDO) and the maximum distance for countries with the same outcome (MDSO)—some key pairs of MSDO cases and MDSO cases are thus singled out.

(Continued)

(Continued)

3. Aggregating the data matrixes: The results of the previous step are aggregated, considering all seven clusters of conditions—this produces a comprehensive distance matrix.

4. Defining levels of (dis)similarity: The comprehensive distance matrix is marked at different levels. First, for each pair of countries, the clusters of conditions in which the distance is equal to either the minimum (for countries with a different outcome) or to the maximum (for countries with the same outcome) are identified. These are the "level 0" (i.e., strongest, "purest") similarities or dissimilarities. Lower levels of similarity (or dissimilarity) can also be taken into account ("level 1," "level 2," etc.). Thus, different levels of (dis)similarity can be obtained for all clusters of conditions. Enabling the computation of lower levels of (dis)similarity allows one to maintain a broader "reservoir" of conditions to be kept for the next steps.

5. Synthesizing (dis)similarity: The information across all seven clusters of cases is synthesized so as to obtain a complete picture of the (dis)similarities of all the cases, within the MDSO zone for cases with the same outcome, and within the MSDO zone for cases with a different outcome.

6. Producing overall similarity and dissimilarity graphs: For each level of (dis)similarity (see Step 4), only those pairs of cases that are most (dis)similar (i.e., that display the largest number of clusters of conditions with highest levels of (dis)similarity) are retained. This information is then translated into a "similarity graph" or a "dissimilarity graph," which visualizes the constellations of cases with the greatest (dis)similarities. Those graphs are eventually merged into aggregated graphs, in which the different levels of (dis)similarity are superimposed.

7. Systematic matching and contrasting of cases: On the basis of the established (dis)similarities and dissimilarities, in a final step, the most different cases with the same outcome (MDSO) and the most similar cases with a different outcome (MSDO) can be selected. It is then possible to list the individual conditions (in each cluster of conditions) that characterize the remaining (dis)similarities. It is among these selected conditions that the reasons for the common (or contrasted) outcome may be determined.

A practical note: At this stage of development, the technical steps and terminology of this procedure are not so easy to grasp for users not specifically trained in formal language. They are also quite labor-intensive if they have to be done manually. This is why software for automating these procedures has been developed (see resources Web page listed in the Appendix).

Once this stepwise procedure has been completed, it is then possible to reexamine specific groups of cases (MDSO or MSDO cases), pairwise, three by three, and so on, and to use qualitative judgment and "thick" case knowledge to examine the remaining (dis)similarities in greater detail. Thus, the final step after the MSDO/MDSO procedure can be, on the one hand, a re-interrogation of some key groups of cases (of the MDSO or MSDO type, depending on the goals of the researcher) in a more qualitative way *and* also in a more focused way, because what needs to be interpreted is specifically the interplay of some more crucial conditions that have been singled out through the MSDO/MDSO procedure. Such more qualitative, historically informed interpretation can yield some "causal" insights as to how and why those core conditions have led (or have not led) to the outcome of interest in the contrasted or similar cases.

On the other hand, the MSDO/MDSO procedure can also be used as a prior step, in the process of model specification, before one engages in QCA proper. Indeed, MSDO/MDSO identifies some particularly crucial conditions that seem to be at the heart of what brings together (or differentiates) cases with a similar (or different) outcome. For instance, using the inter-war project data, selections of such conditions could be used for various QCA tests.

To sum up, the MSDO/MDSO procedure provides a further extension, operationalization, and application of Mill's methods, including the possibility of "conjunctural" patterns of causation and the implications for the necessary "dialogue between theory and data" in a "case-oriented" manner. It can be used to produce substantial tests and further refinements of theory when many competing theories abound (see also Berg-Schlosser, 2004). It leaves some room for flexibility—for example, allowing for more or less stringent criteria of (dis)similarity, depending on how restrictive the researcher wants to be with regard to the number of conditions to be kept for further analyses.

Key Points

- From the outset, a sufficiently homogeneous domain of investigation must be delineated, from which cases will be selected.

- A clear definition of the outcome of interest must be laid out at a very early stage of the analysis, because it is indispensable for case selection.

- In most small- or intermediate-N research designs, it is useful to have meaningful variation in the outcome—that is, to select cases with both "negative" and "positive" outcomes.

- It is important to keep the number of conditions reasonably low; the greater the number of conditions, the more one runs the risk of "individualizing" the explanation of each case.

- There are different, complementary strategies for reducing the number of conditions when there are many "candidate" theories.

- The MSDO/MDSO procedure (systematic matching and contrasting of cases) can be used either for further, more qualitative, interpretation of clusters of cases or as a prior step to further QCA analyses—by identifying crucial conditions.

- MSDO/MDSO is best suited for research situations in which the conditions can be grouped into clusters.

- MSDO/MDSO leaves room for flexibility, in particular with regard to the stringency of criteria of (dis)similarity across cases.

Key Complementary Readings

Berg-Schlosser & De Meur (1997), De Meur & Berg-Schlosser (1994), De Meur et al. (2006), Ebbinghaus (2005), Mahoney & Goertz (2004), Przeworski & Teune (1970).

NOTES

1. Note that "units" do not always equate with "cases." For instance, a case (unit of *analysis*) could be a country, whereas a unit of *observation* within that case could be a given region or a given political institution, or that country at a given point in time.

2. A somewhat different aspect of "most different systems designs" when they are applied to "multi-level analyses"—linking, for example, the "meso" level of party systems to the "macro" overall country level—is discussed by Tiemann (2003).

3. For further elaborations with regard to case selection in small- and intermediate-N settings, see Ebbinghaus (2005), Gerring (2006), Mahoney and Goertz (2004).

4. Note that this advice to keep models sufficiently "short" is also valid in statistical research. For example, Achen (2005) argues that regression analysts should work with five or six independent variables

3

Crisp-Set Qualitative Comparative Analysis (csQCA)

Benoît Rihoux
Gisèle De Meur

Goals of This Chapter

After reading this chapter, you should be able to:

- Understand the key operations of Boolean algebra and use the correct conventions of that language

- Transform tabular data into Venn diagrams and vice versa; interpret Venn diagrams

- Replicate a standard csQCA procedure, step by step, using the software

- In the course of this procedure, dichotomize your variables (conditions and outcome) in an informed way, and at a later stage, use an appropriate strategy for solving "contradictory configurations"

- Weigh the pros and cons of using *logical remainders* (non-observed cases)

- Read and interpret the *minimal formulas* obtained at the end of the csQCA

csQCA was the first QCA technique developed, in the late 1980s, by Charles Ragin and programmer Kriss Drass. Ragin's research in the field of historical sociology led him to search for tools for the treatment of complex sets of binary data that did not exist in the mainstream statistics literature. He adapted for his own research, with the help of Drass, Boolean algorithms that had been developed in the 1950s by electrical engineers to simplify switching circuits, most notably Quine (1952) and McCluskey (1966). In these so-called minimization algorithms (see Box 3.2), he had found an instrument for identifying patterns of multiple conjunctural causation and a tool to "simplify complex data structures in a logical and holistic manner" (Ragin, 1987, p. viii).

csQCA is the most widely used QCA technique so far. In this chapter, a few basic operations of Boolean algebra will first be explicated, so the reader can grasp the nuts and bolts of csQCA. Then, using a few variables from the interwar project (see Chapter 2), the successive steps, arbitrations, and "good practices" of a standard application of csQCA will be presented.

THE FOUNDATION OF CRISP-SET QCA: BOOLEAN ALGEBRA IN A NUTSHELL

George Boole, a 19th-century British mathematician and logician, was the first to develop an algebra suitable for variables with only two possible values, such as propositions that are either true or false (Boole, 1847; 1958 [1854]). Following intuitions by Leibniz one century before him, Boole is the originator of mathematical logic that allows us to "substitute for verbal reasoning a genuine symbolic calculation" (Diagne, 1989, p. 8). This algebra has been studied further by many mathematicians and logicians over the last few decades. It has been central to the development of electronic circuits, computer science, and computer engineering, which are based on a binary language, and has led to many applications, mostly in experimental and applied scientific disciplines. Only a few basic principles and operations will be presented here (for more details, see, e.g., Caramani, 2008; De Meur & Rihoux, 2002; Ragin, 1987, pp. 89–123; Schneider & Wagemann, 2007, forthcoming). Boolean algebra, as any language, uses some conventions that need to be understood before engaging in csQCA.

Box 3.1
Main Conventions and Operations of Boolean Algebra

1. The main *conventions* of Boolean algebra are as follows:

   - An *uppercase* letter represents the [1] value for a given binary variable. Thus [A] is read as: "variable A is large, present, high, . . ."

   - A *lowercase* letter represents the [0] value for a given binary variable. Thus [a] is read as: "variable A is small, absent, low, . . ."

   - A *dash* symbol [-] represents the "don't care" value for a given binary variable, meaning it can be either present (1) or absent (0). This also could be a value we don't know about (e.g., because it is irrelevant or the data is missing). It is *not* an intermediate value between [1] and [0].

> 2. Boolean algebra uses a few basic *operators*, the two chief ones being the following:
>   - Logical "AND," represented by the [*] (multiplication) symbol. NB: It can also be represented with the absence of a space: [A*B] can also be written as: [AB].
>   - Logical "OR," represented by the [+] (addition) symbol.
> 3. The connection between conditions and the outcome: The arrow symbol [→][1] is used to express the (usually causal) link between a set of conditions on the one hand and the outcome we are trying to "explain" on the other.

With this very basic language, it is possible to construct very long and elaborate expressions and also to conduct a complex set of operations. One key operation, which lies at the heart of csQCA, is called *Boolean minimization.*

Box 3.2
What Is Boolean Minimization?

It is the "reduction" of a long, complex expression into a shorter, more parsimonious expression. It can be summarized verbally as follows: "if two Boolean expressions differ in only one causal condition yet produce the same outcome, then the causal condition that distinguishes the two expressions can be considered irrelevant and can be removed to create a simpler, combined expression" (Ragin, 1987, p. 93). Let us use a very simple example. Consider the following Boolean expression, with three condition variables (R, B, and I) and one outcome variable (O) (*Formula 1*):

$$R * B * I + R * B * i \rightarrow O$$

This expression can be read as follows: "[The presence of R, combined with the presence of B and with the *presence* of I] OR [The presence of R, combined with the presence of B and with the *absence* of I] lead to the presence of outcome O."

Notice that, *no matter which value the [I] condition takes* (0 or 1), the [I] outcome value is the same. This means, in verbal reasoning, that the [I] condition is superfluous; it can thus be removed from the initial expression. Indeed, if we remove the [I] condition, we are left with a much shorter, *reduced expression* (which is called a *prime implicant*) (*Formula 2*):

$$R * B \rightarrow O$$

(Continued)

(Continued)

> It is read as follows: "The presence of R, combined with the presence of B, leads to the presence of outcome O." This reduced expression meets the parsimony principle (see p. 10). We have been able to explain the O phenomenon in a more parsimonious way, but still leaving room for complexity, because for O to be present, a *combination* of the presence of R and the presence of B must occur.
>
> In other words, to relate this again to necessity and sufficiency (see p. 10): the presence of R is necessary (but not sufficient) for the outcome; likewise, the presence of B is necessary (but not sufficient) for the outcome. Because neither of the two conditions is sufficient for the outcome, they must be combined (or "intersected," through Boolean multiplication, see Box 3.1) and, together, they could possibly[2] form a necessary *and* sufficient *combination* of conditions leading to the outcome.

Boolean minimization can also be grasped in a more visual way. Let us consider again the same example and provide more explicit labels for the three conditions: respectively, R stands for "RIGHT," B stands for "BELOW," and I stands for "INSIDE." As these are binary conditions, each divides the universe of cases into two parts: those that meet the condition (value 1) and those that do not (value 0). So we have three conditions:

- RIGHT (1 value) versus not-right (0 value)
- BELOW (1 value) versus not-below (0 value)
- INSIDE (1 value) versus not-inside (0 value)

Because each condition divides the universe into two parts, the set of three conditions divides it in 2 * 2 * 2 = 8 zones, called "elementary zones." Within each zone, the values for conditions of each case are the same. Let us also suppose that we know the value of the outcome variable for each one of these 8 zones. The data can first be presented in tabular format (see Table 3.1).

The first column of Table 3.1 contains the case labels ("caseid"), from "case1" to "case8." The following three columns contain all logically possible combinations (there are 8 of them—i.e., 2^3; see p. 27) of the binary RIGHT, BELOW, and INSIDE conditions. Finally, the fifth column contains the value of the OUTCOME for each one of the 8 combinations. The first six cases display a [0] outcome (Boolean notation: [outcome]), while the last two display a [1] outcome (Boolean notation: [OUTCOME]). The Boolean expression that was minimized above (see Formulas 1 and 2 in Box 3.2.) corresponds simply to a translation of the two bottom rows of this table.

Table 3.1   Raw Data Table (3-Condition Example)

caseid	Right	Below	Inside	Outcome
case1	0	0	0	0
case2	1	0	0	0
case3	0	0	1	0
case4	1	0	1	0
case5	0	1	0	0
case6	0	1	1	0
case7	1	1	1	1
case8	1	1	0	1

This same data can be represented in a visual way, in a *Venn diagram* (see also p. 23), showing visually that each condition cuts the universe of cases in two (Figure 3.1) and making the 8 basic zones visible.
In this Venn diagram:

- Condition [RIGHT] cuts the space vertically: All cases on the right-hand side of the vertical line have a (1) value for this condition, whereas all cases on the left-hand side of this line ("not right") have a (0) value for this condition.

- Condition [BELOW] cuts the space horizontally: All cases below the horizontal line have a (1) value for this condition, whereas all cases above this line ("not below") have a (0) value for this condition.

- Finally, condition [INSIDE] cuts the space between what's inside or outside the square in the middle: All cases inside the square have a (1) value for this condition, whereas all cases outside the square ("not inside") have a (0) value for this condition.

This Venn diagram also contains information about where each case is located. In this simple example, each basic zone is occupied by a single case. In addition, the diagram contains information about the value of the outcome variable. Let us consider only the [1] outcome. It corresponds to the dark-shaded area, at the bottom right of the diagram, and corresponds indeed to

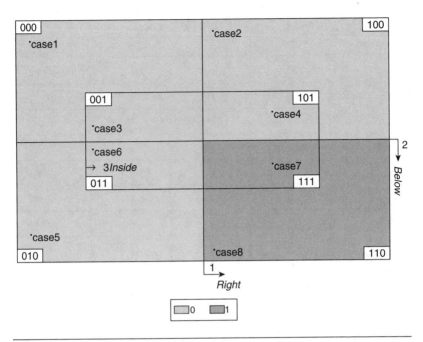

Figure 3.1   Venn Diagram Corresponding to Table 3.1 (3 Condition Variables)*

* Venn diagram produced by the "visualizer" tool, TOSMANA 1.3.0.0 software

case7 and case8 (as in the last two lines of Table 3.1). This light shaded area can be expressed, in Boolean notation, as follows (*Formula 3*):

RIGHT * BELOW * INSIDE + RIGHT * BELOW * inside → OUTCOME

Note that this formula is exactly the same as Formula 1. It is read as follows: "The outcome is present for case7 [a case that is on the right AND below AND *inside*] OR for case8 [a case that is on the right AND below AND *not inside*]."

This is a long formulation, which requires the description of each basic zone: It describes first the basic zone where case7 stands, then the one where case8 stands. Technically speaking, this formula contains two *terms* (each term is a combination of conditions linked by the "AND" operator), and each term contains all three conditions. This is precisely where the Boolean minimization intervenes: It makes possible describing these two zones with one simpler and shorter expression, consisting of only one *term*. Indeed, we notice, visually, that the two basic zones where cases 7 and 8 stand, when combined, form a larger square: All the cases that are located below the horizontal line, AND all the cases that are located on the right-hand side of the vertical line. This larger zone can be expressed as (*Formula 4*):

RIGHT * BELOW → OUTCOME

Note that this formula is exactly the same as Formula 2. It means that we simply need to know about two conditions—[RIGHT] and [BELOW]—to account for the outcome, which corresponds to cases 7 and 8. We need not know whether or not those cases are inside or "not inside" the middle square, because this information is superfluous: What is shared by these two cases with a [1] outcome is that they are "on the right AND below." So we can simply remove the [INSIDE/not inside] condition.

As we shall see later, this is exactly the operation that is performed by the software on more complex data sets, with more conditions, and also with "empty" basic zones (i.e., with no cases observed). Of course, this makes the operations somewhat more complex, so it is best to let the computer perform the algorithms (in csQCA, the software uses the Quine minimization algorithm).

Now that we have introduced the basics of Boolean language and operations, we can present key practical steps of csQCA. We shall pursue the same example as in Chapter 2, from the inter-war project, where the cases are 18 European countries.

STEP 1: BUILDING A DICHOTOMOUS DATA TABLE

Of course, building a relevant data table requires previous work: A well-thought-out comparative research design, and in particular rigorous case and variable selection (see Chapter 2). Remember, also, that at this stage the researcher is supposed to have gained adequate substantive knowledge about each case and theoretical knowledge about the most relevant variables (conditions, in particular) included in the analysis.

Among the large variety of approaches dealing with the more general conditions favoring the emergence and consolidation of democratic political systems in different parts of the world (see p. 26: list of main categories of conditions in the inter-war project), we have selected one that addresses overall socioeconomic and "structural" factors. Of course, for a more comprehensive account other factors such as specific historical and cultural conditions, inter-mediate organizations, institutional arrangements, actor-related aspects, and so on must also be considered (for an application of such a more comprehensive design, see also Berg-Schlosser, 1998). For purposes of illustration, however, using the selected approach will suffice—in short, for the sake of clarity, we need a relatively simplified theory, which does not entail too many conditions.

As a reminder, the specific outcome we are trying to "explain" here is the survival or breakdown of democratic systems in Europe during the inter-war period. Why is it that some democratic systems survived, while others collapsed? In QCA terminology, this variable we seek to explain is called the *outcome.*

The most influential study dealing with the more general socioeconomic preconditions of democracy was S. M. Lipset's *Political Man* (1960), in particular his chapter "Economic Development and Democracy." There, he (re)stated the general hypothesis that "the more well-to-do a nation, the greater the chances that it will sustain democracy" (p. 31). Indeed, among the "stable European democracies" analyzed by Lipset were cases like Belgium, the Netherlands, Sweden, and Great Britain, which all showed high levels of wealth, industrialization, education, and urbanization. Under his (very broad) category of "unstable democracies and dictatorships" figured countries like Greece, Hungary, Italy, Poland, Portugal, and Spain, with lower levels in this regard. However, he also noted that

> Germany is an example of a nation where growing industrialization, urbanization, wealth and education favoured the establishment of a democratic system, but in which a series of adverse historical events prevented democracy from securing legitimacy and thus weakened its ability to withstand crisis. (p. 20)

This statement certainly applies to Austria as well, but the kind of "adverse historical events" and their specific roots were not investigated by Lipset. Similarly, the fact that countries like Czechoslovakia, Finland, and France (which also had higher levels of development and democratic institutions, and which, as far as internal factors were concerned, survived the economic crisis of the 1930s) were grouped by Lipset in the same "unstable" category, was not very helpful from an analytical viewpoint. In later years, Lipset's work was followed by a number of conceptually and statistically more refined studies and drew considerable criticism as well. However, when he later reviewed his original study, he still found its basic tenets confirmed (Lipset, 1994; see also Diamond, 1992).

For each of the four main dimensions discussed by Lipset (wealth, industrialization, education, and urbanization), we have selected one major indicator as listed in Table 3.2. and have provided the data for each one of the 18 cases (countries) considered.

In this example, we have 18 cases (each case being a row in Table 3.2). The outcome variable (SURVIVAL) is already of a dichotomous nature:

Table 3.2   Lipset's Indicators, Raw Data (4 Conditions)

CASEID	GNPCAP	URBANIZA	LITERACY	INDLAB	SURVIVAL
AUS	720	33.4	98	33.4	0
BEL	1098	60.5	94.4	48.9	1
CZE	586	69	95.9	37.4	1
EST	468	28.5	95	14	0
FIN	590	22	99.1	22	1
FRA	983	21.2	96.2	34.8	1
GER	795	56.5	98	40.4	0
GRE	390	31.1	59.2	28.1	0
HUN	424	36.3	85	21.6	0
IRE	662	25	95	14.5	1
ITA	517	31.4	72.1	29.6	0
NET	1008	78.8	99.9	39.3	1
POL	350	37	76.9	11.2	0
POR	320	15.3	38	23.1	0
ROM	331	21.9	61.8	12.2	0
SPA	367	43	55.6	25.5	0
SWE	897	34	99.9	32.3	1
UK	1038	74	99.9	49.9	1

Labels for conditions:

CASEID: Case identification (country name) abbreviations: AUS Austria; BEL Belgium; CZE Czechoslovakia; EST Estonia; FIN Finland; FRA France; GER Germany; GRE Greece; HUN Hungary; IRE Ireland; ITA Italy; NET Netherlands; POL Poland; POR Portugal; ROM Romania; SPA Spain; SWE Sweden; UK United Kingdom

GNPCAP: Gross National Product/Capita (ca. 1930)

URBANIZA: Urbanization (population in towns with 20,000 and more inhabitants)

LITERACY: Literacy

INDLAB: Industrial Labor Force (including mining)

(Details of sources in Berg-Schlosser & Mitchell, 2000, 2003.)

The [0] outcome value stands for "breakdown of democracy" (for 10 cases), and the [1] outcome value stands for "survival of democracy" (for the other 8 cases).

However, the four variables that are supposed to "explain" the outcome, which are called *conditions*[3] in QCA terminology, are continuous (interval-level) variables. To be used in csQCA, those original conditions must be dichotomized according to relevant thresholds.

To dichotomize conditions, it is best to use empirical (case-based) and theoretical knowledge (see "good practices" box, below). In this example, we have chosen to set the dichotomization thresholds as follows[4]:

- [GNPCAP]: Gross National Product/Capita (ca. 1930): 0 if below 600 USD; 1 if above.

- [URBANIZA]: Urbanization (population in towns with 20,000 and more inhabitants): 0 if below 50%; 1 if above.

- [LITERACY]: 0 if below 75%; 1 if above.

- [INDLAB]: Industrial Labor Force (incl. mining): 0 if below 30% of active population; 1 if above.

Box 3.3
"Good Practices" (3): How to Dichotomize
Conditions in a Meaningful Way

- Always be transparent when justifying thresholds.

- It is best to justify the threshold on substantive and/or theoretical grounds.

- If this is not possible, use technical criteria (e.g., considering the distribution of cases along a continuum; see also p. 79). As a last resort, some more mechanical cutoff points such as the mean or median can be used, but one should check whether this makes sense considering the distribution of the cases.[5]

- Avoid artificial cuts dividing cases with very similar values.

- More elaborate technical ways can also be used, such as clustering techniques (see p. 130), but then you should evaluate to what extent the clusters make theoretical or empirical sense.

- No matter which technique or reasoning you use to dichotomize the conditions, make sure to code the conditions in the correct "direction," so that their presence ([1] value) is theoretically expected to be associated with a positive outcome ([1] outcome value).

We thus obtain a dichotomized data table (Table 3.3). Already before engaging in csQCA proper, exploring this table visually, in a non-formal way, we can easily see that some cases corroborate very neatly the Lipset theory, by looking at the most extreme cases.

Table 3.3   Lipset's Indicators, Dichotomized Data (4 Conditions)

CASEID	GNPCAP	URBANIZA	LITERACY	INDLAB	SURVIVAL
AUS	1	0	1	1	0
BEL	1	1	1	1	1
CZE	0	1	1	1	1
EST	0	0	1	0	0
FIN	0	0	1	0	1
FRA	1	0	1	1	1
GER	1	1	1	1	0
GRE	0	0	0	0	0
HUN	0	0	1	0	0
IRE	1	0	1	0	1
ITA	0	0	0	0	0
NET	1	1	1	1	1
POL	0	0	1	0	0
POR	0	0	0	0	0
ROM	0	0	0	0	0
SPA	0	0	0	0	0
SWE	1	0	1	1	1
UK	1	1	1	1	1

For instance, Belgium (row 2) is a "perfect survivor case," corroborating Lipset's theory: A [1] value on all four conditions leads to the [1] outcome value [SURVIVAL]. Conversely, Portugal (row 14) is a "perfect breakdown case," corroborating Lipset's theory: A [0] value on all four conditions leads to the [0] outcome value [survival]. However, for many other cases, the picture looks more complex.

STEP 2: CONSTRUCTING A "TRUTH TABLE"

The first step for which we need csQCA proper (in terms of specific software treatment[6]) corresponds to a first "synthesis" of the raw data table. The result thereof is called a *truth table*. It is a *table of configurations*—remember that a configuration is, simply, a given combination of conditions associated with a given outcome. There are five types of configurations, each of which may correspond to none, one, or more than one case.

Box 3.4
Five Types of Configurations

- Configurations with a [1] outcome (among the *observed* cases); also called "1 configurations."

- Configurations with a [0] outcome (among the *observed* cases); also called "0 configurations."

- Configurations with a "–" ("don't care") outcome (among the *observed* cases); also called "don't care configurations." It means that the outcome is indeterminate. This is to be avoided, since the researcher is supposed to be interested in explaining a specific outcome across well-selected cases.[7]

- Configurations with a « C » (« contradiction ») outcome, called *contradictory configurations*. Such a configuration leads to a « 0 » outcome for some observed cases, but to a « 1 » outcome for other observed cases. This is a logical contradiction, which must be resolved (see p. 48) before engaging further in the csQCA.

- Finally, configurations with an "L" or "R" ("logical remainder") outcome. These are logically possible combinations of conditions that have *not* been observed among the empirical cases.

Table 3.4 displays the truth table corresponding to the dichotomized data in Table 3.3.

Table 3.4   Truth Table of the Boolean Configurations

CASEID	GNPCAP	URBANIZA	LITERACY	INDLAB	SURVIVAL
SWE, FRA, AUS	1	0	1	1	C
FIN, HUN, POL, EST	0	0	1	0	C
BEL, NET, UK, GER	1	1	1	1	C
CZE	0	1	1	1	1
ITA, ROM, POR, SPA, GRE	0	0	0	0	0
IRE	1	0	1	0	1

Box 3.5
"Good Practices" (4): Things to Check to Assess the Quality of a Truth Table

- Check again that there is a mix of cases with a "positive" outcome and cases with a "negative" outcome (see Box 2.2, good practices for the case selection).

- Check that there are no counterintuitive configurations. In this example, these would be configurations in which all [0] condition values lead to a [1] outcome, or all [1] condition values lead to a [0] outcome.

- Check for cross-condition diversity; in particular, make sure that some conditions do not display exactly the same values across all cases; if they do, ask yourself whether those conditions are too "proximate" to one another (if they are, they can be merged).

- Check that there is enough variation for each condition (a general rule: at least 1/3 of each value) (see also Box 2.3, good practices for condition selection: "a variable must vary"...).

If one of these criteria is not met, reconsider your selection of cases and/or conditions or possibly the way you have defined and operationalized the outcome.

It is also useful, at this stage, to check for the necessity and sufficiency of each condition with regard to the outcome.

This truth table (Table 3.4) shows only the configurations corresponding to the 18 *observed* cases. It already allows us to "synthesize" the evidence substantially, by transforming the 18 cases into 6 configurations. We find out the following:

• There are two distinct configurations with a [1] outcome, corresponding respectively to Czechoslovakia and Ireland.

• There is one configuration with a [0] outcome, corresponding to five cases (Italy, Romania, Portugal, Spain, and Greece). It fits quite neatly with the Lipset theory, because a [0] value for all four conditions leads to a [0] outcome (breakdown of democracy).

We also notice that there are 3 *contradictory configurations* (the first 3 rows in the truth table), corresponding to no less than 11 cases out of the 18. In other words: Lipset's theory—in the way we have operationalized it, at least—does not enable us to account for 11 out of 18 cases. The third contradictory configuration is particularly troubling: It contains [1] values on all of the conditions and yet produces the [0] outcome for one case (namely, Germany), whereas it produces the expected [1] outcome for the other 3 cases (Belgium, Great Britain, and the Netherlands).

The data in this truth table can once again be visualized through a Venn diagram, a bit more complex than Figure 3.1 because it contains 4 conditions instead of 3 (Figure 3.2).

This Venn diagram has 16 basic zones (configurations)—that is, 2^4 zones. It is constructed using the same logic as Figure 3.1. In this empirically grounded example, we can observe four types of configurations:

• Two configurations with a [1] outcome, covering respectively the cases of Czechoslovakia and Ireland.

• One configuration with a [0] outcome, covering the five cases of Italy, Romania, Portugal, Spain, and Greece.

• Three contradictory configurations, covering in all 11 cases (the shaded zones corresponding to the "C" label).

• Finally, many non-observed, "logical remainder" ("R") configurations—10 altogether. Thus, there is limited diversity (see p. 27) in the data: As the 18 observed cases correspond to only 6 configurations, the remaining Boolean property space is devoid of cases. As will be shown at a later stage, these "logical remainder" configurations will constitute a useful resource for further analyses.

One way to look at this evidence, from a purely numerical perspective, would be to state that the model "fits" 7 out of 18 cases. This is, however, not a correct

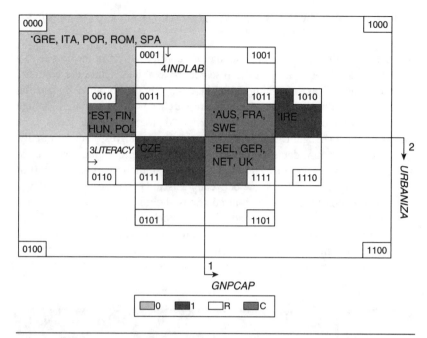

Figure 3.2   Venn Diagram Corresponding to Table 3.4 (4 Conditions)*

* Venn diagram produced by the "visualizer" tool, TOSMANA 1.3.0.0 software.

way to proceed; remember that QCA is a case-oriented method (see p. 6), and that each case matters. From this perspective, it is a problem that so many contradictions occur. Hence these contradictions first have to be resolved before proceeding to the core of csQCA—namely, Boolean minimization.

At this stage of the analysis, it is also useful to check for the necessity and sufficiency of each condition with regard to the outcome. Let us assume a model that contains three conditions, A, B and C. For condition A, for instance, assessing its *consistency* as a necessary condition means answering the following question: "To what extent is the statement 'condition A is necessary for the outcome' consistent?" Technically, this can be computed as follows: [the number of cases with a [1] value on the condition AND a [1] outcome value, divided by the total number of cases with a [1] outcome value]. For more details, see Goertz (2006a), Ragin (2006b), and Schneider and Wagemann (2007, forthcoming).

STEP 3: RESOLVING CONTRADICTORY CONFIGURATIONS

It is perfectly normal to detect contradictory configurations in the course of a csQCA. It does not mean that the researcher has failed. Quite the contrary, contradictions tell us something about the cases we are studying. By seeking a resolution of these contradictions, the researcher will get a more thorough knowledge of the cases (through his or her "dialogue with the cases"), be forced to consider again his or her theoretical perspectives, and, eventually, obtain more coherent data. Remember that QCA techniques are best used in an iterative way (see p. 14). Thus addressing contradictions is simply part of this iterative process of "dialogue between ideas and evidence" (Ragin, 1987).

Insofar as possible, all such contradictions should be resolved or, at least, one should strive to reduce contradictions as much as possible (Ragin, Berg-Schlosser, & De Meur, 1996, p. 758)—because, eventually, the cases involved in those contradictory configurations will be excluded[8] from the analysis. Once again, this is problematic given the case-oriented nature of QCA.

Box 3.6
"Good Practices" (5): How to Resolve
Contradictory Configurations[9]

There are basically eight strategies. In real-life research, it is advisable to at least consider all those strategies, and most often it will turn out that some combination is useful.

1. Probably the easiest one: Simply add some condition(s) to the model. Indeed, the more complex the model—the more numerous the conditions—the less likely contradictions will occur, because each condition added constitutes a potential additional source of differentiation between the cases. Of course, such a strategy should not be pursued in a "hope-and-poke" way; it should be cautious and theoretically justified. It is advisable to add conditions one by one, not to obtain too complex a model. Otherwise, you run the risk of creating a greater problem of "limited diversity" (see p. 27) and thus of "individualizing" explanations of each particular case; this means that csQCA will have missed its purpose of reaching some degree of parsimony (see p. 10).

2. Remove one or more condition(s) from the model and replace it/them by (an)other condition(s).

3. Reexamine the way in which the various conditions included in the model are operationalized. For instance, it may be that the threshold of dichotomization for a given condition is the source of the contradiction between two cases. By adjusting the threshold, it may be possible to resolve the contradiction. Alternatively, the contradiction could be due to data quality problems—in that case, one could collect complementary or revised data. This is the most labor-intensive option but very much to be advocated from a case-oriented perspective.

4. Reconsider the outcome variable itself. This strategy is often overlooked. If the outcome has been defined too broadly, it is quite logical that contradictions may occur. For instance, Rihoux (2001) noticed, during some exploratory csQCA analyses, that his initial outcome variable—major organizational change in a given political party—could in fact be decomposed into two opposed subtypes: organizational adaptation and organizational radicalization. By focusing the outcome solely on organizational adaptation, he was able to resolve many contradictory configurations.

5. Reexamine, in a more qualitative and "thick" way, the cases involved in each specific contradictory configuration. What has been missed? What could differentiate those cases, that hasn't been considered, either in the model or in the way the conditions or the outcome have been operationalized?

6. Reconsider whether all cases are indeed part of the same population (cf. case selection, p. 20). For instance, if it is a "borderline" case that is creating the contradiction, perhaps this case should be excluded from the analysis.

7. Recode all contradictory configurations as [0] on the outcome value. This solution, suggested by Ragin (1987), treats contradictory configurations as "unclear" and thus decides to accept fewer minimizable configurations in exchange for more consistency in the cases/outcome relationship.

8. Use frequency criteria to "orientate" the outcome. Let us consider a contradictory configuration that involves nine cases. If, say, it leads to a [1] outcome for eight cases and to a [0] outcome for only one case, one could consider that the "most frequently traveled path" wins—thus the outcome would be considered as having a [1] value for all nine cases. Note, however, that this more probabilistic strategy is disputable from a "case-oriented" perspective.

Of course, the strategy(ies) chosen must be justified on empirical grounds (case-based knowledge) and/or on theoretical grounds and not be the result of some opportunistic "manipulation."

If none of these strategies, or a combination thereof, resolves the contradictory configurations, some cases will have to be removed from the key minimization procedure. In such an event, there are basically four options:

- Choose to move on and proceed with csQCA, even though there are still one or more contradictory configuration(s) left. There are then two sub-options: Either delete the cases involved in the contradictions from the data table or keep them in the data table.[10] Those cases still involved in the contradictory configuration(s) could then be interpreted separately (apart from the csQCA procedures proper), using a more qualitative-historical, case-specific approach.

- Consider using mvQCA or fsQCA (see Chapters 4 and 5), which are able to process more fine-grained data. Indeed, the reason csQCA easily produces contradictions is simply because dichotomization strongly reduces the richness of the data and hence also masks potential differences across the cases (see p. 148: "costs" and "benefits" of dichotomization).

- Consider turning to other techniques, quantitative or qualitative. We recommend that you at least try out mvQCA and/or fsQCA first (or in parallel, so you can weigh the strengths and limitations of the QCA techniques vis-à-vis the other techniques), because these two other QCA techniques will allow you to keep some key strengths of the QCA approach (both analytic and case-oriented, etc.—see Chapter 1).

- ... or, if you are using csQCA for theory-testing, stop there and happily conclude that csQCA has allowed you to falsify the theory (see pp. 3, 16).

Technically speaking, if the decision is to proceed with csQCA, it is necessary to produce a revised dichotomized data table, which enables the software to produce a revised truth table. In real-life research, experience shows that several iterations may be necessary to obtain a contradiction-free truth table.

For this textbook example, we opt for the pragmatic way: Add a fifth condition to the model. In substance, we choose to add a "political–institutional" condition to the four more socioeconomic conditions derived from Lipset's theory. This fifth condition is governmental stability (GOVSTAB). The threshold is placed as follows: A score of [0] (low stability) if 10 cabinets or more have governed during the period under investigation and a score of [1] (high stability) if fewer than 10 cabinets have governed during that same period.

The addition of this fifth condition can be justified on theoretical grounds: For the cases of "breakdown of democracy": In the context of already less favorable socioeconomic circumstances, governmental instability further weakens the political system, the institutional capacity to address problems, and the credit of democratic institutions. Conversely, for the "survivors," more stable governments are able to consolidate democratic institutions and enhance their capacity to confront political challenges.

We thus obtain a new raw data table (Table 3.5, with one additional column as compared to Table 3.2), which is dichotomized (Table 3.6). The software then produces a new truth table (Table 3.7).

Table 3.5   Lipset's Indicators, Raw Data, Plus a Fifth Condition

CASEID	GNPCAP	URBANIZA	LITERACY	INDLAB	GOVSTAB	SURVIVAL
AUS	720	33.4	98	33.4	10	0
BEL	1098	60.5	94.4	48.9	4	1
CZE	586	69	95.9	37.4	6	1
EST	468	28.5	95	14	6	0
FIN	590	22	99.1	22	9	1
FRA	983	21.2	96.2	34.8	5	1
GER	795	56.5	98	40.4	11	0
GRE	390	31.1	59.2	28.1	10	0
HUN	424	36.3	85	21.6	13	0
IRE	662	25	95	14.5	5	1
ITA	517	31.4	72.1	29.6	9	0
NET	1008	78.8	99.9	39.3	2	1
POL	350	37	76.9	11.2	21	0
POR	320	15.3	38	23.1	19	0
ROM	331	21.9	61.8	12.2	7	0
SPA	367	43	55.6	25.5	12	0
SWE	897	34	99.9	32.3	6	1
UK	1038	74	99.9	49.9	4	1

Labels for conditions: same as Table 3.2, plus a fifth condition:

GOVSTAB: Governmental stability (number of cabinets in period)

(Case abbreviations and sources: same as Table 3.2.)

Table 3.6 Lipset's Indicators, Dichotomized Data, Plus a Fifth Condition

CASEID	GNPCAP	URBANIZA	LITERACY	INDLAB	GOVSTAB	SURVIVAL
AUS	1	0	1	1	0	0
BEL	1	1	1	1	1	1
CZE	0	1	1	1	1	1
EST	0	0	1	0	1	0
FIN	0	0	1	0	1	1
FRA	1	0	1	1	1	1
GER	1	1	1	1	0	0
GRE	0	0	0	0	0	0
HUN	0	0	1	0	0	0
IRE	1	0	1	0	1	1
ITA	0	0	0	0	1	0
NET	1	1	1	1	1	1
POL	0	0	1	0	0	0
POR	0	0	0	0	0	0
ROM	0	0	0	0	1	0
SPA	0	0	0	0	0	0
SWE	1	0	1	1	1	1
UK	1	1	1	1	1	1

This truth table (Table 3.7) is "richer" than the previous one (Table 3.4): By adding a condition, we move from 6 to 10 configurations, so indeed we have added diversity across the cases. This has enabled us to resolve most contradictions. Consider, for instance, the three cases of Austria, Sweden, and France, which formed a contradictory configuration when we considered only the four Lipset conditions (see first row in Table 3.4). By adding the [GOV-STAB] condition, we can now differentiate Austria (first row in Table 3.7), which has a [0] value on [GOVSTAB], from Sweden and France (fifth row in

Table 3.7 Truth Table of the Boolean Configurations (4 + 1 Conditions)

CASEID	GNPCAP	URBANIZA	LITERACY	INDLAB	GOVSTAB	SURVIVAL
AUS	1	0	1	1	0	0
BEL, NET, UK	1	1	1	1	1	1
CZE	0	1	1	1	1	1
EST, FIN	0	0	1	0	1	C
FRA, SWE	1	0	1	1	1	1
GER	1	1	1	1	0	0
GRE, POR, SPA	0	0	0	0	0	0
HUN, POL	0	0	1	0	0	0
IRE	1	0	1	0	1	1
ITA, ROM	0	0	0	0	1	0

Table 3.7), which have a [1] value on [GOVSTAB]. Some other contradictions have been resolved in the same way.

However, there still is *one* contradictory configuration, embracing two cases: Estonia and Finland. Even with the addition of a fifth condition, those two cases still share the same values on all conditions, and yet they display different outcomes: Estonia is a "breakdown" case ([0] outcome), whereas Finland is a "survivor" case ([1] outcome). In such a situation, we now envisage three possible options. The first one would be to further reexamine the model, which could—possibly—lead to the inclusion of a sixth condition ("good practice" strategy 1 in Box 3.6). The problem, however, is that the model becomes more complex with the addition of each condition and less clear for the pedagogical purpose of this textbook. The second option is simply to accept that those two cases deserve some specific qualitative-historical interpretation and that hence they should be left out for the next steps of the csQCA.

The third option ("good practice" strategy 3 in Box 3.6) is to reexamine the way in which the various conditions included in the model have been operationalized, with a particular focus on the cases of Finland and Estonia. Doing this, we discover that if we move the threshold of the GNPCAP condition from $600 to $550 (actually this latter threshold is located near a natural "gap" in the data[11]), this allows us to differentiate between Finland ($590) and Estonia ($468). Incidentally, note that this modification of the threshold also changes the score for Czechoslovakia ($586: from a [0] to a [1] value). More important, it allows us to produce a contradiction-free truth table,[12] as is shown in the next two tables (Tables 3.8 and 3.9).

Table 3.8   Lipset's Indicators, Dichotomized Data,
Plus a Fifth Condition (and GNPCAP Recoded)

CASEID	GNPCAP	URBANIZA	LITERACY	INDLAB	GOVSTAB	SURVIVAL
AUS	1	0	1	1	0	0
BEL	1	1	1	1	1	1
CZE	1	1	1	1	1	1
EST	0	0	1	0	1	0
FIN	1	0	1	0	1	1
FRA	1	0	1	1	1	1
GER	1	1	1	1	0	0
GRE	0	0	0	0	0	0
HUN	0	0	1	0	0	0
IRE	1	0	1	0	1	1
ITA	0	0	0	0	1	0
NET	1	1	1	1	1	1
POL	0	0	1	0	0	0
POR	0	0	0	0	0	0
ROM	0	0	0	0	1	0
SPA	0	0	0	0	0	0
SWE	1	0	1	1	1	1
UK	1	1	1	1	1	1

Table 3.9   Truth Table of the Boolean Configurations
(4 + 1 Conditions, GNPCAP Recoded)

CASEID	GNPCAP	URBANIZA	LITERACY	INDLAB	GOVSTAB	SURVIVAL
AUS	1	0	1	1	0	0
BEL, CZE, NET, UK	1	1	1	1	1	1
EST	0	0	1	0	1	0
FRA, SWE	1	0	1	1	1	1
GER	1	1	1	1	0	0
GRE, POR, SPA	0	0	0	0	0	0
HUN, POL	0	0	1	0	0	0
FIN, IRE	1	0	1	0	1	1
ITA, ROM	0	0	0	0	1	0

Table 3.9 can also be grasped more visually, through a Venn diagram (Figure 3.3). This five-dimensional diagram is a bit less easy to grasp than the previous, four-dimensional Venn diagram (Figure 3.2, above), but it is built on the same premises: Each condition still splits the logical space into two equal parts (of 16 basic zones each). Graphically, what is new is that the visualization of the fifth condition (GOVSTAB) requires two separate "patches" (two horizontal squares, each one comprising 8 basic zones, in which this condition has a [1] value). Note also that many more basic zones of the logical property space are left empty (as compared with the previous, four-dimensional diagram; Figure 3.2)—a reminder that the more conditions we include in the model, the more limited the observed empirical diversity (see p. 27).

Indeed the revised, contradiction-free truth table (Table 3.9) now places Finland and Estonia in two separate configurations. More precisely: Estonia is now alone in a specific configuration, and Finland has joined Ireland in another configuration. Note also that Czechoslovakia has also moved and joined the

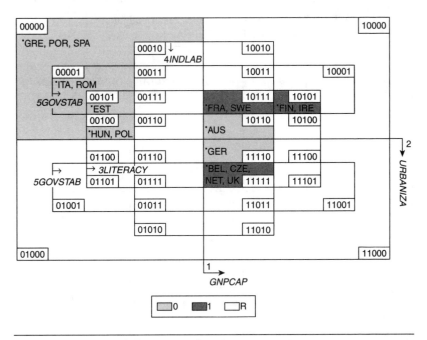

Figure 3.3   Venn Diagram (5 Conditions; GNPCAP Recoded)*

* Venn diagram produced by the "visualizer" tool, TOSMANA 1.3.0.0 software.

configuration of "perfect" survivor cases ([1] values on all conditions, leading to a [1] value on the outcome): Belgium, the Netherlands, and the UK.

STEP 4: BOOLEAN MINIMIZATION

For this key operation of csQCA, the material used by the software is the truth table (Table 3.9) with its nine configurations: three configurations with a [1] outcome (corresponding to 8 cases), and six configurations with a [0] outcome (corresponding to 10 cases). As is obvious by looking at Table 3.9, each configuration may correspond to one or more empirical cases (or to none—the "logical remainder" configurations; see p. 59). What is important to mention here is that the software does not recognize cases but rather the *configurations* specified in the truth table. Thus the number of cases in each configuration will not be relevant in the course of the minimization process. After the minimization, however, it will be possible to connect each of the cases to the minimal formula that is obtained.

The software minimizes these configurations, using the Boolean minimization algorithms (see Box 3.2), considering *separately* the [1] configurations and the [0] configurations. One must thus apply the minimization procedure twice, first for the [1] configurations, and then for the [0] configurations. The sequence is not important, as long as both are carried out. It is important to minimize both types of configurations, because we do not expect to find some form of perfect "causal symmetry" in social phenomena (see p. 9). In other words, we should not deduce the minimal formula for the [0] outcome from that of the [1] outcome, or vice versa, although it would be technically feasible in some circumstances to do so by applying the De Morgan's law.[13]

Minimization of the [1] Configurations (Without Logical Remainders)

First, we ask the software to minimize the [1] configurations, *without* including some non-observed cases. We obtain the following minimal formula (*Formula 1*):

GNPCAP * LITERACY * INDLAB * GOVSTAB	+	GNPCAP * urbaniza * LITERACY * GOVSTAB	→	SURVIVAL
(BEL, CZE, NET, UK FRA, SWE)	+	(FIN, IRE + FRA, SWE)		

This is called a "descriptive" formula, because it does not go much beyond the observed, empirical cases. In consists of two *terms*, each one of which is a combination of conditions linked with the « 1 » outcome value. Following the Boolean notation (see Box 3.1), it can be read as follows:

"The '1' outcome (survival of democracy) is observed:

- In countries that combine high GNP per capita [GNPCAP] *AND* high literacy rates [LITERACY] *AND* high percentage of industrial labor forces [INDLAB] *AND* high governmental stability [GOVSTAB]

OR

- In countries that combine high GDP per capita [GNPCAP] *AND* low urbanization [urbaniza] *AND* high literacy rates [LITERACY] *AND* high governmental stability [GOVSTAB]"

The first *term* of the minimal formula corresponds to six countries: on the one hand Belgium, Czechoslovakia, the Netherlands, and the UK (which share the same configuration—i.e., with all five conditions) and on the other hand[14]

France and Sweden. The second term corresponds to four countries: on the one hand Finland and Ireland and on the other hand France and Sweden. Note that concerning France and Sweden, we thus have two partly "concurrent" explanations. In such a situation—which is quite often met with csQCA—the researcher has to make a choice, using his or her case knowledge. This is part of the phase of interpretation of the minimal formula (see Step 6, p. 65).

This descriptive minimal formula is still quite complex, as each term still includes four out of the five conditions of the model. Only a small measure of parsimony has been achieved. The formula does allow some first interpretations, however. For instance, we could interpret the fact that the [URBANIZA] condition does not play a role in the survival of democracy in Belgium, Czechoslovakia, the Netherlands, and the UK.

Note that the two terms of the formula share the [GNPCAP * LITERACY * GOVSTAB] combination of conditions. Thus, this combination can be made more visible by manually modifying the minimal formula (this is not done by the software). We simply treat the formula as a conventional algebraic expression, a sum of products, and factor out the common conditions. This will produce a more structured version of the formula—*not* a more parsimonious one, because no further conditions are eliminated by this operation. Thus, Formula 1 can be rewritten as follows (*Formula 2*):

$$\text{GNPCAP * LITERACY * GOVSTAB *} \left\{ \begin{array}{l} \text{INDLAB} \\ \\ \text{urbaniza} \end{array} \right. \rightarrow \quad \text{SURVIVAL}$$

This rewriting of the formula shows quite clearly what is common to all the "survivor" cases (the left-hand side of Formula 2)—once again, this could be subject to interpretation by the researcher, as indeed this core combination of three conditions is shared by all "survivor" cases. The rewritten formula also shows what is specific to each one of the two clusters of cases (the two different "paths" on the right-hand side of Formula 2).

Minimization of the [0] Configurations
(Without Logical Remainders)

Secondly, we perform exactly the same procedure, this time for the [0] configurations and also without including some non-observed cases. We obtain the following minimal formula (*Formula 3*):

gnpcap * urbaniza * indlab	+	GNPCAP * LITERACY *	$\rightarrow$	survival
(EST + GRE, POR, SPA	+	INDLAB * govstab		
HUN, POL + ITA, ROM)		(AUS + GER)		

As the previous one, this minimal formula is also quite complex. Reading this formula (following the same conventions as explained above), we see that csQCA provides us with two "paths" to the [0] outcome. The first one corresponds to many cases: Estonia; Greece, Portugal, and Spain; Hungary and Poland; Italy and Romania. These eight cases of democracy breakdown all share the [gnpcap * urbaniza * indlab] combination—i.e., the combination [0] values on three conditions—which is quite consistent with the theory. The second one is specific to Austria and Germany—note that this result could have been guessed by looking at the Venn diagram (Figure 3.3, p. 56), in which those two cases are "distant" from the eight above-mentioned cases. This formula cannot be rewritten in a "shorthand" manner, because the two *terms* have nothing in common.

STEP 5: BRINGING IN THE "LOGICAL REMAINDERS" CASES

Why Logical Remainders Are Useful

The problem with Formulas 1 to 3 is that they are still quite complex: Relatively little parsimony has been achieved. To achieve more parsimony, it is necessary to allow the software to include non-observed cases, called "logical remainders." In this example, remember that there is a large "reservoir" of logical remainders, as is seen in the Venn diagram (Figure 3.3, p. 56). Only a tiny proportion of the logical property space is occupied by empirical cases: Out of the 32 potential configurations (= 2^5, as there are 5 conditions; see p. 27), only 9 correspond to observed cases. Thus, the 23 logical remainders (= 32 minus 9) constitute a pool of potential cases that can be used by the software to produce a more parsimonious minimal formula.

Why does the inclusion of logical remainders produce more parsimonious minimal formulas? This can be explained visually, using the Venn diagram and eight concrete cases: all those cases with a [0] outcome, which also happen to be situated on the left-hand side of the Venn diagram (Estonia; Greece, Portugal and Spain; Hungary and Poland; Italy and Romania).

First, note that the simpler (the "shorter") a Boolean expression, the larger the number of configurations it covers:

- A combination of all five conditions covers only one configuration (e.g., the [00000] zone, which contains the Greece, Portugal, and Spain cases).

- A combination of four conditions covers two configurations: If we want to "cover" not only the Greece, Portugal, and Spain cases but also the zone right near it that contains the Italy and Romania cases (the [00001] zone), we only need to have information about four conditions. Indeed, we don't need to know about the [GOVSTAB] condition: It has a [1] value for the Italy and Romania cases and a [0] value for the Greece, Portugal, and Spain cases.

- Likewise, a combination of three conditions covers four configurations.

- A combination of two conditions covers eight configurations.

- And a statement containing only 1 condition covers 16 configurations—i.e., half of the Boolean property space. For instance, the zone corresponding to a [0] value on the [GNPCAP] condition is the whole left half of the Venn diagram, corresponding to 16 configurations (only 4 of which, incidentally, contain some observed cases—those 8 cases that all happen to have a [0] outcome).

Following this logic, the usefulness of logical remainders is quite straight-forward: To express those eight cases in a simpler way, it suffices to express them as part of a broader zone, also comprising some logical remainders.

Hence what we can do is to make a "simplifying assumption" regarding the 12 logical remainders on the left-hand side of the Venn diagram: Let us *assume* that, if they existed, they would also have a [0] outcome, just like the 8 observed cases. If this assumption is correct, then we have produced a much larger zone (the whole left-hand side of the Venn diagram, comprising 16 configurations) sharing the [0] outcome, and thus the 8 observed cases can be expressed in a much more parsi-monious way: simply [gnpcap]—i.e., [0] value for the [GNPCAP] condition.

This is exactly what the software does: It selects *some* logical remainders (only those that are useful to obtain a shorter minimal formula), adds them to the set of observed cases, and makes "simplifying assumptions" regarding these logical remainders. This then produces a simpler *term* in the minimal formula.

Minimization of the [1] Outcome (With Logical Remainders)

Running again the minimization procedure, this time allowing the software to include some of the logical remainders, we obtain the following minimal formula (*Formula 4*):

GNPCAP * GOVSTAB → SURVIVAL

(BEL, CZE, NET, UK + FIN, IRE + FRA, SWE)

It is read as follows: "For all these countries, a high GDP per capita, combined with governmental stability, has led to the survival of democracies in the inter-war period." Comparing this formula with Formula 1 (see p. 57), we see that a more parsimonious solution has been achieved, thanks to the simplifying assumptions made by the software regarding some of the logical remainders. We can obtain a list of these simplifying assumptions from the software and lay them out in the report of the analysis—in this instance five of them were used[15]:

1/ GNPCAP{1}URBANIZA{0}LITERACY{0}INDLAB{0}GOVSTAB{1}

2/ GNPCAP{1}URBANIZA{0}LITERACY{0}INDLAB{1}GOVSTAB{1}

3/ GNPCAP{1}URBANIZA{1}LITERACY{0}INDLAB{0}GOVSTAB{1}

4/ GNPCAP{1}URBANIZA{1}LITERACY{0}INDLAB{1}GOVSTAB{1}

5/ GNPCAP{1}URBANIZA{1}LITERACY{1}INDLAB{0}GOVSTAB{1}

These simplifying assumptions can be visualized in the Venn diagram (through the TOSMANA software). In Figure 3.4, the minimal formula (the "solution") is represented by the horizontal stripes. This area corresponds to the three configurations with observed cases displaying a [1] outcome, plus five logical remainder configurations.

Minimization of the [0] Outcome (With Logical Remainders)

Likewise, we obtain the following minimal formula (*Formula 5*):

gnpcap	+	govstab	→	survival
(EST + GRE, POR, SPA HUN, POL + ITA, ROM)	+	(AUS + GER + GRE, POR, SPA + HUN, POL)		

It is read as follows:

- "In eight countries (Estonia, . . . and Romania), low GNP per capita 'explains' the breakdown of democracy in the inter-war period.
- In seven countries (Austria, . . . and Poland), governmental instability 'explains' the breakdown of democracy in the inter-war period."

There are thus two alternative paths toward the [0] outcome. Note that for five countries (Greece, Portugal, and Spain; Hungary and Poland), both paths

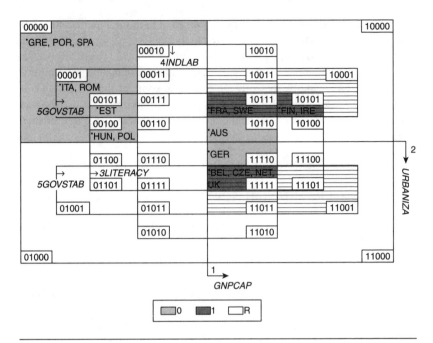

Figure 3.4   Venn Diagram: Solution for the [1] Outcome (With Logical
                     Remainders)*

* Venn diagram produced by the "visualizer" tool, TOSMANA 1.3.0.0 software.

are valid. In such a situation, the researcher must choose, country by country,
and relying on his or her case knowledge, which path makes more sense.

Comparing this formula with Formula 2 (see p. 58), we see that substantial
parsimony—even more[16] than in Formula 4—has been gained, thanks to the
"simplifying assumptions" made, by the software, regarding some of the logical remainders. We can also obtain a list of these simplifying assumptions and
lay them out in the report of the analysis. In this case, many more have been
used (18 in all). This can be visualized through a Venn diagram (Figure 3.5;
same conventions as Figure 3.4).

Examining Figures 3.4 and 3.5, it is clear that the minimal formula for the
[0] outcome (including 18 logical remainders) and the minimal formula for
the [1] outcome (including five logical remainders) are the perfect *logical
complement* of one another. In other words, the software has used up all the
available "empty space" of logical remainders, so as to produce the most

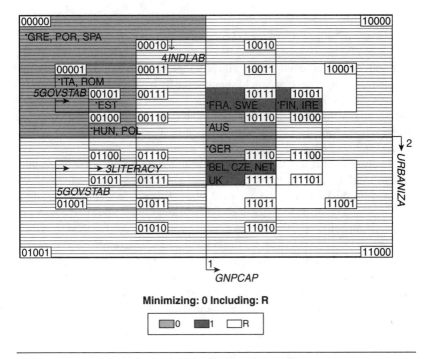

Figure 3.5   Venn Diagram: Solution for the [0] Outcome (With Logical
Remainders)*

* Venn diagram produced by the "visualizer" tool, TOSMANA 1.3.0.0 software.

parsimonious minimal formulas possible. Thus, the two minimal formulas
completely fill up the Boolean property space, well beyond the observed cases.

This use of logical remainders raises a concern and also an important technical issue. First the concern: Isn't it altogether audacious to make assumptions about non-observed cases? One way to frame this debate is to question
the relative plausibility of those simplifying assumptions. This issue is
addressed in detail in Ragin and Sonnett (2004; see also Ragin, 2008), in our
review of the critiques of QCA (see p. 152) and of applications (see p. 135),
and is exemplified in the fsQCA application below (see pp. 110–118).
For reasons of space, we cannot engage here in a full discussion of this issue,
using this inter-war project data. The key point to remember is that it is always
possible to *restrict* the choice of logical remainders used by the software. If we
do this, we obtain somewhat less parsimonious minimal formulas.

Second, the issue: What if the software uses the *same* logical remainders both for the minimization of the [1] configurations and for the minimization of the [0] configurations? If it does, it will produce "contradictory simplifying assumptions," because indeed it would be a logical contradiction to assume that a given (non-observed) case would simultaneously have a [1] outcome *and* a [0] outcome. Gladly, in this example, it is not the case. The comparison of Figures 3.4 and 3.5 shows that the two minimal formulas (with logical remainders) do not overlap. If we had encountered such a difficulty, it would have been possible to address it, using more advanced technical steps (see p. 136).

Finally, note that it is useful at this stage to assess the *coverage* of the minimal formulas—that is, the way the respective terms (or "paths") of the minimal formulas "cover" the observed cases. This is a second measure of the "fit" of the model, as the measure of consistency (see p. 47) at a previous stage. Technically, one should make three measures, both for the [1] and [0] outcome values. For instance, for the [1] outcome value: (a) *raw coverage:* the proportion of [1] outcome cases that are covered by a given term; (b) *unique coverage:* the proportion of [1] outcome cases that are uniquely covered by a given term (no other terms cover those cases); (c) *solution coverage:* the proportion of cases that are covered by all the terms.[17]

Box 3.7
"Good Practices" (6): Four Complete Minimization Procedures to Be Run and Made Explicit

Checklist for the minimization procedure(s), using the computer software:

- Perform the minimization both with and without inclusion of logical remainders. Each of these approaches may yield information of some interest.
- Thus: Four complete minimization procedures must be run:
  ○ [1] configurations, without logical remainders
  ○ [1] configurations, with logical remainders
  ○ [0] configurations, without logical remainders
  ○ [0] configurations, with logical remainders
- Ask the software to list the "simplifying assumptions" and display those in your research report.
- Check for possible "contradictory simplifying assumptions" and, insofar as possible, solve them (see p. 136).

- Present all your minimal formulas (including the case labels), and if needed use visual displays (e.g., Venn diagrams) to make the minimal formulas more understandable for the reader.

- If it is useful for your interpretation, factor (by hand) some conditions, to make the key regularities in the minimal formulas more apparent.

- Assess the "coverage" of the minimal formulas—i.e., the connection between the respective terms of the minimal formulas and the observed cases.

STEP 6: INTERPRETATION

Remember that, as a formal data analysis technique, but even more so because it is a "case-oriented" technique (see p. 6), csQCA (the formal, computer-run part of it), as well as the other QCA techniques, is not an end in itself; rather, it is a tool to enhance our comparative knowledge about cases in small- and intermediate-N research designs.

This means that the final step of the procedure is a crucial one: The researcher interprets the minimal formulas. The emphasis can be laid more on theory or on the cases, or on both, depending on the research goals. Obviously this requires a "return to the cases" using the minimal formula(s) that is (are) considered most relevant. In the inter-war project example we have unfolded in this chapter, some case-based interpretations could follow from questions such as the following: What is the "narrative" behind the fact that, according to the minimal formula, high GNP per capita combined with governmental stability has lead to survival (or non-breakdown) of democracy in countries such as Belgium, Czechoslovakia, the Netherlands, and the UK? Is the "causal" story the same in these four countries? What distinguishes them from other countries also covered by this same minimal formula, such as France and Sweden? Why does low GNP per capita, as a single factor, seem to play a more prominent role in the breakdown of democracy in countries such as Estonia, Italy, and Romania? Conversely, why does a more directly "political" factor (governmental instability) come out as the single key determinant in democracy breakdown in countries such as Greece, Portugal, and Spain, even though these are also relatively poor countries (low GNP per capita as well)? To what extent is the "narrative" behind the German and Austrian cases of democracy breakdown really comparable? And so on.

To sum up: csQCA minimal formulas allow the researcher to ask more focused "causal" questions about ingredients and mechanisms producing (or not) an outcome of interest, with an eye on both within-case narratives and cross-case patterns. Note that unless individual conditions can be clearly singled out (e.g., the condition is clearly a necessary condition or comes close to being a necessary and sufficient condition), it is important to refrain from interpreting relations between singular conditions and the outcome. At the interpretation stage, do not lose sight of the fact that the richness of csQCA minimal formulas resides precisely in the combinations and "intersections" of conditions. It would be a pity to lose a chance to gain some "configurational knowledge" (Nomiya, 2004) at this crucial stage. Note, finally, that these rules and 'good practices' of interpretation also apply to mvQCA and fsQCA.

Key Points

- csQCA is based on a specific language, Boolean algebra, which uses only binary data ([0] or [1]) and is based on a few simple logical operations. As any language, its conventions must be properly used. It is a formal, but non-statistical, language.

- It is important to follow a sequence of steps, from the construction of a binary data table to the final "minimal formulas."

- Two key challenges in this sequence, before running the minimization procedure, are: (1) implementing a useful and meaningful dichotomization of each variable and (2) obtaining a "truth table" (table of configurations) that is free of "contradictory configurations."

- The key csQCA procedure is "Boolean minimization." One must run the minimization procedures both for the [1] and the [0] outcomes, and both with and without "logical remainders" (non-observed cases).

- The use of "logical remainders"—and the "simplifying assumptions" that are made on them by the software—raises some principal and technical difficulties, but the latter can be addressed.

- Obtaining minimal formulas is only the end of the computer-aided part of csQCA. It marks the beginning of a key final step: case- and/or theory-informed *interpretation*, which should be focused on the link between key *combinations* of conditions and the outcome.

Key Complementary Readings

Caramani (2008), De Meur & Rihoux (2002), Ragin (1987, 2000), Schneider & Wagemann (2007, forthcoming).

NOTES

1. Note that, in most publications so far, the equal symbol [=] has been used. Following Schneider and Wagemann's (2007) suggestion, we recommend using the arrow symbol [→] instead. One of the key reasons therefore is that, by using this symbol, the Boolean formula can not be mistaken with a standard statistical (e.g., regression) equation.

2. Actually, in this example, we can't tell, because we should also examine the (combinations of) conditions leading to the absence ([0] value) of the outcome.

3. A *condition* corresponds to an "independent variable" in statistical analysis. However, it is *not* an "independent" variable in the statistical sense. There is no assumption of independence between the conditions—quite the contrary; we would expect combinations to be relevant (see Chapter 1).

4. For more detailed justifications, see Berg-Schlosser and De Meur, 1994.

5. Typically, one should not use the median or the mean if this locates the dichotomization threshold in an area of the data distribution where many cases are situated (this would give opposite scores [0 or 1] to cases that display quite proximate raw values).

6. Actually the software (e.g., TOSMANA) can already be used in the prior stages—for example, for the clustering of cases (dichotomization) if one uses more technical criteria.

7. It is also a problem for further QCA software treatment. Each time the software meets a "don't care" configuration, it will produce *two distinct configurations*: one with a [0] outcome and one with a [1] outcome. This might not make sense from an empirical perspective. In practice, the "don't care" outcome is rarely used, and even then it is used simply to signal a combination of conditions that is empirically impossible (e.g., pregnant males).

8. It is actually more complex—depending on whether or not the cases involved in those contradictory configurations are left (by the researcher) in the data table, this will have an impact on the size of the "reservoir" of non-observed "logical remainder" cases that can be used by the software in the minimization procedure (see note 10, below).

9. See also further discussion on p. 132.

10. Note that if one chooses to include logical remainders, these two sub-options will have a different influence on the end result (the minimal formula). If the cases involved in contradictions are deleted outright, the logical space they used to occupy will be left "open," and the software will have the possibility to use this "free space" in its search for useful logical remainders—this is likely to generate a shorter, more parsimonious minimal formula. Conversely, if one keeps those cases in the data table, the logical space will be "occupied" by those cases, and the reservoir of potential "logical remainders" will be a little more constrained—this is likely to generate a less parsimonious minimal formula. Probably it is advisable to prefer the second, more cautious option, because we cannot assume that the logical space occupied by these contradictory cases is "empty empirical space."

11. This can be visualized using the "thresholdssetter" function in TOSMANA (see p. 79).

12. This key suggestion has been made by Svend-Erik Skaaning.

13. For many reasons, one of which being that social phenomena display limited diversity (for a more detailed discussion, see De Meur & Rihoux, 2002). See also pp. 8–10 on the issue of causal complexity. However, under some very specific circumstances, De Morgan's law can be meaningfully applied (see Wagemann & Schneider, 2007, p. 26).

14. In the TOSMANA output, the "+" sign in between (groups of) cases separates cases with different configurations (in the truth table).

15. The notation used here is that of the TOSMANA software for simplifying assumptions. GNPCAP{1} simply means [1] value on the GNPCAP condition; and so on (see Box 4.1).

16. This is simply because even more logical remainders have been included by the software for the minimization procedure.

17. For more details, see Ragin (2006b, 2008), Goertz (2006b), and Schneider & Wagemann (2007, forthcoming). Note that this operation is also implemented in mvQCA and fsQCA.

4

Multi-Value QCA (mvQCA)

Lasse Cronqvist

Dirk Berg-Schlosser

Goals of This Chapter

After reading this chapter, you should be able to do the following:

- Reflect on the limitations of using dichotomized conditions and on the potential advantages of using multi-value conditions

- Read and use the specific mvQCA notation; grasp the basics of multi-value minimization

- Make informed choices regarding threshold values

- Replicate a standard mvQCA procedure, step by step, using the software (TOSMANA)

- Reflect on the respective strengths and limitations of both csQCA and mvQCA for your own research

WHY mvQCA?

Some Problems in the csQCA Example

Remember that in the previous chapter on csQCA we quickly bumped into a first difficulty: the presence of many contradictory configurations. To solve these, as a technical solution, we had to add a fifth condition related to governmental stability.

However this technical solution still leaves some problems unresolved, or at least is not fully satisfactory, in at least three respects. First, by adding this fifth condition, we have moved beyond the simple testing of Lipset's theory, because we have included in the model a condition that is outside the realm of that theory. Second, to obtain sufficiently parsimonious minimal formulas, we included a very large number of "logical remainders," some of which could be questioned in terms of plausibility. Third, when we chose *not* to consider the logical remainders, we obtained more "descriptive" minimal formulas that, with csQCA at least, were not sufficiently parsimonious.

Actually, all these limitations may stem in part from the fact that the conditions had to be dichotomized from the outset. Aren't there ways to keep the logic and fundamental intention of csQCA, but at the same time to move beyond such stringent dichotomies? This is the key question that spurred the development of mvQCA.

Further Limitations of Dichotomous Variables . . . and Why mvQCA

Multi-value QCA, as the name suggests, is an extension of csQCA. It retains the main principles of csQCA, namely to perform a synthesis of a data set, with the result that cases with the same outcome value are "covered" by a parsimonious solution (the minimal formula). As in csQCA, the minimal formula contains one or more terms, each of which covers a number of cases with the outcome, while no cases with a different outcome are explained by any of the terms in the minimal formula.

The key difference is that whereas csQCA allows only dichotomous variables, mvQCA also allows multi-value variables. In fact, mvQCA is a generalization of csQCA, because indeed a dichotomous variable is a specific subtype of multi-value variables—it is simply a multi-value variable with only two possible values. Therefore, data sets analyzed with csQCA also can be processed using mvQCA.

As explained above, one problem in applying csQCA is the compulsory use of dichotomous variables, which bears the risk of information loss and may create a large number of contradictory configurations. The compulsory use of dichotomized variables can lead to instances where two cases with somewhat different raw values are assigned the same Boolean value and/or two cases with quite similar raw values are assigned different Boolean values. This may be the result of an inadequate choice of thresholds by the researcher, but in some situations the structure of the data simply does not allow a sensible choice of one single threshold value.

In Figure 4.1, for instance, the use of Threshold A would assign the two cases c2 and c4 the same Boolean value although they indeed have very different raw data scores. On the other hand, the use of Threshold B would put together the cases c1 and c3, which also have very different values. In this example, therefore, it would be of advantage to be able to use *two* thresholds to create more homogenous subsets. It is not only possible to use multi-value

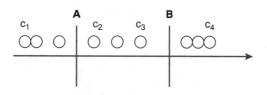

Figure 4.1   Data Distribution Not Allowing a Simple Dichotomization

categories in mvQCA for refined coding of ordinal or interval data, but multi-valued categories also can be used advantageously to represent multi-categorical nominal-scale conditions such as regions (Africa, Latin America, Europe, etc.), religion (Christian, Muslim, Jewish, etc.) or family status (single, married, civil union, divorced, etc.).

Do we need a new method to use multi-value variables? Technically speaking, it would be possible, instead, to code a multi-value variable into multiple binary variables, using "dummies," and then to use the standard csQCA technique. However, transforming multi-value data into binary data does raise problems. As an example, let us consider a traffic light with three possible values: red light, yellow light, and green light. Transforming the multi-value variable *Light* with $P_{Light}=$ *{red, yellow, green}* into three binary dummy variables (red, yellow, green) would result in Table 4.1.

The problem is not only that the three combinations displayed in Table 4.1 will be created, but also that, if logical remainders are included, then all other logical possibilities will be created as well (in this example: five more logical remainders).[1] However, in empirical reality, a combination such as red=1 and green=1 will never occur in regular traffic light usage, but this combination still occurs in the truth table when including logical remainders in csQCA.

Table 4.1   Dichotomous Coding of a 3-Value Traffic Light

MV Value	Red	Yellow	Green
Red	1	0	0
Yellow	0	1	0
Green	0	0	1

This means that a high number of non-observed configurations will be created and combined with the other conditions, resulting in many superfluous iterations of the minimization algorithm.

Another problem is that, by using such dummy variables, the total number of conditions in the model will be increased.[2] This is of course a disadvantage in small- and intermediate-N research designs, where the number of conditions needs to be kept relatively low (see Box 2.3).

These practical problems and limitations have led to the development of mvQCA. It can be viewed as an *extension* of csQCA and has been included in the TOSMANA software (Cronqvist 2007a, 2007b). The key additional feature, as compared with csQCA, is that it allows the use of "real" (i.e., observed) multi-value conditions.

DIFFERENCES BETWEEN mvQCA AND csQCA

As mentioned above, mvQCA is an extension of csQCA and shares most of its features and procedures. In fact, there are only two major differences between the two techniques: the notation and the minimization rule.

Notation in mvQCA

As multi-value variables can have more than two values, lowercase and uppercase letters (as in csQCA; see Box 3.1) can no longer be used to denote different values. In mvQCA, therefore, set notation is used to represent the logical configurations of the cases, as well as the prime implicants. Each logical configuration consists of one or more expressions $X\{S\}$, where X is the condition and S is the set of possible values of X. Binary conditions can be converted directly from csQCA notation, as cases with the value [0] for a condition (and thus written with lowercase letters in csQCA notation) are assigned the value [0] for the value set of this conditions, and cases with the value [1] (uppercase letters in QCA) are assigned the value [1] for the value set of this condition. If, for instance, the condition *[MALE]* indicates whether a student is male or female, male students would be represented with *MALE{1}* in mvQCA (*MALE* in csQCA), whereas female students would be *MALE{0}* in mvQCA (*male* in csQCA).

The values of a multi-valued condition can be obtained in different ways. For multi-categorical conditions based on nominal data, each value represents a specific category. For the condition *region*, one could use a multi-categorical scale with three values: Africa (value [0]), Latin America (value [1]), and Europe (value [2]). In this scheme, the case of France would be denoted as *REGION{2}*, as the value of Europe for this condition is [2]. Equally, Brazil would be assigned *REGION{1}*, whereas Togo is represented by *REGION{0}*.

Although each case can have only one value for each condition, mvQCA does contract values of conditions in logical expressions to ease the interpretation of prime implicants and minimal formulas. For instance, I=*REGION{0,1}* indicates that the prime implicant *I* represents all cases with the value [0] or [1] for *REGION* (all cases in Africa or Latin America). Subscript notation can be used as well: *REGION{1}* can be written as $REGION_1$. In the same way, *REGION{0,1}* can be written as $REGION_{0,1}$.

If an interval-scale variable is transformed into a multi-value condition, the process is similar to the process of dichotomization in csQCA (see p. 42), except for the fact that more than one threshold may be used. To obtain a multi-valued condition, a set of thresholds is used to create subsets of the cases. In Table 4.2, a four-value scale is shown for classifying children according to age. A newly born child would be declared a baby (value [0]), whereas a 12-year-old girl is classified as a teenager (value [3]). Although there is still a loss of information involved in creating this multi-valued condition, difficult dichotomizations (as in csQCA) can be avoided by the use of multiple thresholds (see more on the selection of thresholds below). Due to technical reasons relating to the software, the scale of multi-valued conditions always has to begin with the value [0].

Box 4.1
mvQCA Notation: Main Conventions

- The Boolean operators are identical to those in csQCA (see Box 3.1).

- Multi-valued conditions can be obtained from a multi-categorical nominal, ordinal scale, or by the use of multiple thresholds for interval data.

- The value for a condition is represented in a bracket next to the condition label (e.g., *REGION{0}*) or with subscripts (e.g., $REGION_1$).

- Multiple values can be contracted into one bracket in prime implicants (e.g., *REGION {0,1}*).

- The scale of a multi-valued condition must begin with the value [0] (then [1], [2], [3], [4], etc.).

Table 4.2   Multi-Valued Scale Classifying Children's Ages

Description	Range in years	mvQCA value
Baby	0–1	0
Toddler	2–5	1
Young child	6–10	2
Teenager	>11	3

Minimization in mvQCA

As in csQCA, the purpose of mvQCA is to extract a parsimonious explanation of an outcome by minimizing (synthesizing) a complex data set. Remember that in csQCA, minimization is straightforward: If two expressions differ by only one condition and yet produce the same outcome, this condition can be excluded to obtain a combined, reduced expression (see Box 3.2).

Multi-value synthesis is a generalization of Boolean synthesis: A number of expressions can be replaced by a reduced expression only if all expressions in the data set including the reduced expression share the same outcome.

In other words, the fundamental Boolean minimization rule (see Box 3.2) can be rewritten for multi-value reduction: "If all n multi-value expressions $(c_0\Phi, \ldots, c_{n-1}\Phi)$ differ only in the causal condition C and all n possible values of C produce the same outcome, then the causal condition C that distinguishes these n expressions can be considered irrelevant and can be removed to create a simpler, combined expression Φ" (Rule 1). Actually, the rule for Boolean (i.e., dichotomous) reduction is a special case of the rule for multi-value reduction, and thus the rule for multi-value reduction also is valid for strictly dichotomous expressions.

Box 4.2
The mvQCA Minimization Rule

The minimization rule in mvQCA is a generalization of the minimization rule in csQCA (see Box 3.2). A condition can be considered irrelevant if a number of logical expressions differ in only this condition and produce the same outcome, and if all possible values of this condition are included in these logical expressions.

Let us consider a data set with a dichotomous condition A, a three-valued condition B and the outcome O. All possible combinations of these conditions are present in the truth table and the outcome O is present in the cases with the configurations A_0B_0, A_0B_1 and A_0B_2:

$A_0B_0 + A_0B_1 + A_0B_2 \rightarrow O$

A can be reduced by the multi-value minimization rule only if all three values of B are combined with the same value for A, and if all three of those combinations produce the same outcome, then $(A_1B_0 + A_1B_1 + A_1B_2)$ can be reduced to A_1. In other words, as the outcome O is present in all cases with A_1, no matter what value B has, this means that condition B is superfluous and the expression can be simplified.

Including Logical Remainders in the Minimization Rule

The problems arising from limited diversity in csQCA (see p. 27) are also relevant to mvQCA. As in csQCA, only a tiny subset of all logically possible configurations are found in the empirical cases, and given the higher complexity of the data sets with multi-valued conditions, this problem is much more acute than in strictly Boolean csQCA: To reduce a condition with three possible values, we already need three cases with the same outcome. It might be possible to reduce one or a few conditions in this way. But, as in csQCA, the goal of mvQCA is to produce a solution as parsimonious as possible, which seems difficult when using multi-valued conditions: To reduce two conditions with three values, nine cases are needed with the same outcome, and these have to share the identical values for the rest of the conditions.[3]

Thus, due to the higher complexity of the data, the number of logically possible configurations is higher in mvQCA. In csQCA, the number of possible configurations is given by the formula $|k| = 2^n$ where n is the number of conditions, and $|k|$ is the number of possible configurations. In mvQCA, the number of configurations is given by the formula, $|k| = \prod_{i=0}^{n} v_i$ where v_i is the number of possible values for condition c_i. In other words, to obtain the number of logical configurations in an mvQCA data set, the numbers of possible values for all conditions are multiplied. So if we have a data set with four conditions, two of them dichotomous and two of them with three possible values, the number of possible configurations is $2 * 2 * 3 * 3 = 36$.[4]

Similar to csQCA, *simplifying assumptions* can be included in mvQCA to obtain more parsimonious solutions (see simple example on the resource Web page listed in the Appendix). The software created for mvQCA calculations (TOSMANA, see Cronqvist, 2007a, 2007b) can select those logical remainders that result in more parsimonious minimal formulas.

> ## Box 4.3
> ### Inclusion of Logical Remainders in mvQCA Minimization
>
> - *Simplifying assumptions* can be included in mvQCA, similarly to csQCA.
> - Due to the higher complexity of mvQCA data sets, the logical remainders have to be included in larger data sets to obtain meaningful results.

DECIDING THRESHOLD VALUES

If interval-level data are used in an mvQCA analysis, they must be transformed to ordinal scales before the minimization can proceed. As with csQCA, the results derived *might* depend on the thresholds selected, and therefore the thresholds should be selected with care (see details in Cronqvist, 2007c, pp. 88–91). As the result can be dependent on the choice made by the researcher, it is very important that all thresholds are discussed transparently and that a check is performed to see whether a small change of a threshold produces substantially different results. In any case, thresholds should not be manipulated to produce a desired solution.

Although it is possible to change the results of an mvQCA analysis by changing one or multiple threshold(s), this should not be considered as a general weakness of mvQCA. Rather, it should be considered as an opportunity to assess the impact of selecting different thresholds. On the one hand, it could be interesting, for example, to differentiate between large and small countries in a data set. On the other hand, it could also be of interest to check how very large countries differ from other countries in a specific setting. Two different thresholds would allow including different theoretical emphases in the analysis. Nonetheless, it is always necessary to justify why a specific threshold (or set of thresholds) has been used, so as to make the analysis both comprehensible and replicable.

In general, there is no fixed rule regarding how thresholds should be set. As with csQCA, if an empirical or theory-based justification can be found to create the relevant subsets, this should be used. If, for example, we would like to include the degree of success of a party in elections to the German Parliament, a threshold of 5% would be adequate, as this is the official hurdle for gaining seats.

mvQCA permits any number of thresholds; therefore, it is also important to determine the number of thresholds to be used for each condition. As a rule of thumb, the partitioning should be as fine as is needed to take account of the different meaningful clusters in the data, but the subgroups also should be as large as possible to obtain as parsimonious solutions as possible. In most applications the use of difficulties three- or four-valued condition has been sufficient to overcome the difficulties caused by the problem of forced dichotomization, especially the generation of contradictory configurations (see, e.g., Cronqvist, 2007c; Cronqvist & Berg-Schlosser, 2006; Herrmann & Cronqvist, 2008).

In any case, thresholds that artificially divide cases with proximate values in the original data should be avoided. Statistical measures such as the arithmetic mean or the median should never be used mechanically (see also Box 3.3), as such values might easily place cases with similar values in two different groups. In Figure 4.2, for example (see next section), the use of the median (thick vertical line) as a threshold to create a dichotomous *GNPCAP* condition would separate Czechoslovakia (value $586) from France ($590), although these two cases obviously display very proximate values on this condition (raw values: see Table 3.2).

To consider a threshold a "good threshold," it should make sense theoretically and no artificial cuts should be generated. For example, for *LITERACY* in the inter-war project data (see Table 3.2), one can argue that the threshold should be set very high (at 95%) to separate countries with a very high rate from those at a lower level.

Nonetheless, it is often not possible to select an indisputable theoretical threshold, and thus a subdivision of data based on the evidence itself has to be performed. More advanced statistical tools, such as cluster analysis (see also p. 130), can be used to better define thresholds, but in any case the distribution of data should also be inspected visually to ensure that no misleading groupings have been made.

Thresholds that create very differently sized subgroups should be avoided as well. Let us consider an mvQCA of 18 cases (as in the inter-war project example) for which, on a given condition, only 2 cases are singled out following the threshold-setting—for example, 2 thresholds generate 3 subgroups, consisting respectively of 2 larger groups (8 cases each) and a smaller group (only 2 cases). This could lead to the situation that those 2 cases in the smaller group, if they share the same outcome, will be explained by this given condition only, and that this given condition will explain these cases exclusively. If many conditions with unequally sized subsets exist, this could thus lead to a highly individualized solution, where most cases are accounted for by their own, case-specific explanation. This undercuts some of the key goals of csQCA and mvQCA—to generate parsimonious explanations and to identify cross-case "causal" patterns.

Box 4.4
"Good Practices" (7): Threshold-Setting With mvQCA

- NB: The "good practices" specified for dichotomization in csQCA are also valid for mvQCA (see Box 3.3).

- In most cases, only three or four values per condition should be used with mvQCA.

- It is best to limit the number of multi-valued conditions, maintaining a preponderance of dichotomous conditions.

EMPIRICAL EXAMPLE: LIPSET'S THEORY

Let us now pursue the inter-war project empirical example (see Chapter 3) to demonstrate the use of mvQCA and the limitations of csQCA. Remember that it proved impossible, with csQCA, to fully test Lipset's theory. One of the major problems, with the four-conditions model extracted from Lipset's theory, is that 11 out of 18 cases yielded contradictory configurations. For that reason, the test of Lipset's theory could not be pursued further with csQCA, and a fifth condition was added.

As explained above (see p. 70), this problem was largely due to the necessity of dichotomizing conditions. Indeed, dichotomization is sometimes very crude and can entail a considerable loss of information. In Figure 4.2 it is very difficult to set the threshold without losing some original information regarding *GNPCAP*. If we use the threshold of $600 as in the initial csQCA analysis (see Tables 3.2 and 3.3), some cases close to the threshold are assigned different dichotomized values, even though they have similar values for this condition.[5] By contrast, countries with very different *GNPCAP* values were assigned the same Boolean value (e.g., Ireland with a *GNPCAP* of $655 as well as Belgium with a value of $1,098 are assigned [1] for this condition). Although this misspecification cannot be avoided completely in mvQCA, homogeneity can be greatly increased using multi-valued conditions, as shown below.

In the mvQCA analysis we keep three conditions unchanged: *URBANIZA, LITERACY,* and *INDLAB*. However, we divide *GNPCAP* into three categories instead of two, as follows: G_0=below $550, G_1= $550 to $850, G_2= above $850 (see Figure 4.2). This recalibration is chosen because of the more "spread out" and continuous distribution of data between the minimum and the maximum values of the interval data. The use of a non-dichotomous subdivision here allows us to achieve more homogenous groupings.

Note that the selection of the optimal number of thresholds is a tradeoff between the wish to obtain homogenous groups on the one hand and the fact, on the other hand, that a very fine fragmentation leads to highly individualized results, where each case or group of very few cases is explained by an individual prime implicant. As the use of more than two thresholds would result in very small subgroups, the use of two thresholds is considered most useful here. The thresholds are first calculated using the cluster algorithm included in TOSMANA (technically, it performs an *average linkage* cluster analysis; see details in Cronqvist, 2007b). The thresholds obtained by the cluster analysis are, respectively, $550 and $750. Reviewing these thresholds with the "thresholdssetter" function of TOSMANA actually shows that the middle group of cases with a GNPCAP value between $550 and $750 is very small, which breaches the rule that small groups should be avoided, so we decide to use the thresholds of $550 and $850 instead, which seems appropriate, as similarly sized subgroups emerge using these thresholds, and no artificial cuts are made.

Using the software, we obtain a truth table (Table 4.3).

When we examine the truth table, a more differentiated picture emerges. The number of contradictions is drastically reduced, as only one contradictory configuration remains. It contains only two cases: Czechoslovakia and Germany. Even though there is still one contradictory configuration, this is a much more favorable situation than the one we had with the four binary conditions in csQCA (see Table 3.4).[6]

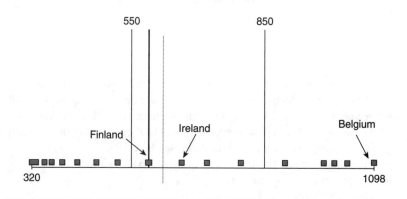

Figure 4.2   Using Two Thresholds for the GNPCAP Condition*

(bold vertical line: median; dotted line: threshold of $600 as used with csQCA, Chapter 3)

*Output from the TOSMANA software, using the "thresholdssetter" function.

Table 4.3 Lipset's Indicators, Multi-Value Truth Table (4 Conditions)

CASEID	GNPCAP	URBANIZA	LITERACY	INDLAB	OUTCOME
SWE, FRA	2	0	1	1	1
FIN, IRE	1	0	1	0	1
BEL, NET, UK	2	1	1	1	1
CZE, GER	1	1	1	1	C
AUS	1	0	1	1	0
ITA, ROM, POR, SPA, GRE	0	0	0	0	0
HUN, POL, EST	0	0	1	0	0

Thresholds:

GNPCAP = 0: gross national product/capita (ca. 1930) below \$550; 1if above \$550 but below \$850; 2 if above \$850

URBANIZA = 0: urbanization (population in towns with 20,000 and more inhabitants) below 50%; 1 if above

LITERACY = 0: literacy below 50%; 1 if above

INDLAB = 0: industrial labor force (incl. mining) below 30% of active population; 1 if above

We can now proceed with the minimization procedure on the remaining 16 cases (the cases of Czechoslovakia and Germany are thus excluded for the next steps; see note 6 above), following the same sequence as with csQCA, in four separate rounds (for the [1] outcome, then for the [0] outcome; at first without the logical remainders, then including them; see Box 3.7).

The minimal formula for the [1] outcome (survival), without the inclusion of logical remainders (*Formula 1*) is:

$GNPCAP_2 * LITERACY_1 * INDLAB_1$ + $GNPCAP_1 * URBANIZA_0 * LITERACY_1 * INDLAB_0$ → $OUTCOME_1$

(SWE, FRA + BEL, UK, NET)   (FIN, IRE)

This formula is relatively complex. The second term, especially, is simply a description (without any gain in parsimony) of the two cases of Finland and Ireland. Thus we rerun the mvQCA minimization procedure for the [1] outcome, this time *with* the inclusion of logical remainders.[7]

We obtain the following formula (*Formula 2*):

$$GNPCAP_2 \quad + \quad GNPCAP_1 * INDLAB_0 \quad \rightarrow \quad OUTCOME_1$$

(SWE, FRA + BEL, UK, NET)   (FIN, IRE)

Thus the inclusion of logical remainders produces a considerably more parsimonious solution. The formula indicates that either a high level of income (Lipset's "classic" cases), or a *medium* income level combined with low industrialization, is conducive to the survival of democracy. The latter result points to a different theoretical explanation—for example, Vanhanen's (1984) emphasis on the positive impact of family farms and the rural middle class in terms of democratic solidity in still largely agricultural countries. The consequences of included logical remainders can be seen in Figure 4.3, where an adapted Venn diagram shows the high number of simplifying assumptions included to produce the parsimonious solution.[8] Here, thanks to mvQCA, we have derived a solution relevant to middle-income countries, which would have been difficult using csQCA.

Next, we compute the minimal formula for the [0] outcome ("non-survival"—i.e., breakdown of democracy), first without inclusion of logical remainders (*Formula 3*):

$$GNPCAP_0 * URBANIZA_0 * \quad + \quad GNPCAP_1 * URBANIZA_0 \quad \rightarrow \quad OUTCOME_0$$
$$INDLAB_0 \qquad\qquad\qquad\qquad LITERACY_1 * INDLAB_1$$

(POR, ROM, GRE, ITA,   (AUS)
SPA+EST, HUN, POL)

As with Formula 1, this solution is relatively complex. The second term, especially, is simply a description (without any gain in parsimony) of the case of Austria. Similarly, we run again the mvQCA minimization procedure, *with* the inclusion of logical remainders. We obtain the following formula (*Formula 4*)[9]:

$$GNPCAP_0 \quad + \quad GNPCAP_1 * URBANIZA_0 * \quad \rightarrow \quad OUTCOME_0$$
$$\qquad\qquad\qquad\qquad INDLAB_1$$

(POR, ROM, GRE, ITA,
SPA+EST, HUN, POL)   (AUS)

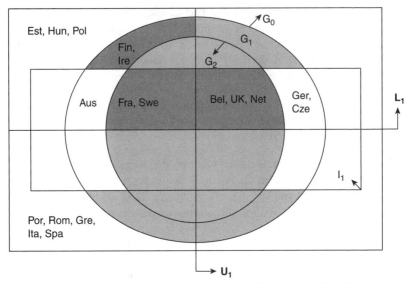

Configurations with existing cases for the outcome [1] are filled dark gray. Simplifying assumptions are filled light gray.

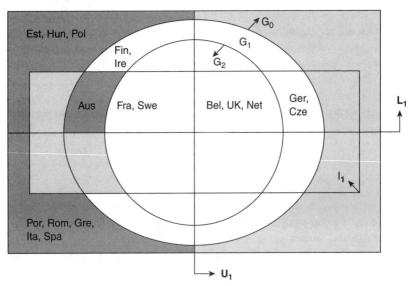

Configurations with existing cases for the outcome [0] are filled dark gray. Simplifying assumptions are filled light gray.

Figure 4.3. Venn Diagrams Adapted for a Multi-Value Data Set

Again, the "classic" low-income countries are separated from the more mixed and controversial case of Austria. This can serve as a hint for specialists of this case and period to further investigate such conditions (see also Gerlich & Campbell, 2000). Once again, we have learned something new about middle-income countries by using mvQCA.

All in all, thus, a modification of the original rather sweeping Lipset hypothesis is found to be more appropriate for the cases considered, especially considering some intermediate values with regard to income (GNP per capita). In addition, mvQCA allows us to pinpoint some specific "conjunctural" patterns (see the Austrian case, above) that are characteristic for the "case-oriented" focus of QCA (see p. 6). One drawback of this mvQCA analysis, of course, is that the most dramatic and historically significant case of breakdown, Germany, has been excluded due to its membership in a contradictory configuration.

CONCLUSION

This chapter has demonstrated that mvQCA can bring added value to the standard csQCA technique, by allowing the processing of multi-value conditions rather than merely dichotomous ones. In the example given, the number of contradictions was reduced considerably from three contradicting configurations representing 11 out of the 18 cases in the first analysis in Chapter 3. With the use of just one recalibrated multi-valued condition, only one contradiction with two cases remained in the analysis using mvQCA. Unlike the csQCA analysis, which added a condition to resolve the contradictions, the differentiation of countries with a low, middle, and high GNP per capita generated a meaningful, alternate explanation, as the results for both outcomes do in fact confirm Lipset's arguments: The wealth of a nation has a substantial influence on the stability of democracy, as all cases with a high GNP per capita (value [2] for *GNPCAP*) sustained democracy, while all cases with a low GNP per capita (value [0]) did not. In other words, a high *GNPCAP* was a *sufficient* condition for a positive outcome, while a low *GNPCAP* was a *sufficient* condition for a negative outcome. By contrast, the outcome for cases with a medium GNP per capita cannot be determined, and thus for these cases other explanations must be sought.

An additional feature in TOSMANA, facilitating the use of such conditions, is the "thresholdssetter," which allows for an easy and plausible illustration of the transformation of various types of raw data into ordinal multi-value scales. If the threshold cannot be set by the use of a theoretically based argument, this tool allows an inductive selection of threshold values. The thresholdssetter plots the values of all cases for the condition examined, and thus groups of cases can be detected either visually or using the simple built-in average distance clustering feature (see Cronqvist, 2007b, for details). Furthermore, the thresholdssetter is an especially useful tool when it comes to avoiding poor thresholds (e.g., thresholds that divide cases with close raw values into different categories or that create very differently sized subsets). Such problems can be directly identified in the graphical presentation of the data using this tool.

The possibility of using multi-valued conditions within the logic of csQCA opens up the possibility of a more flexible analysis. Nevertheless, some limitations must be noted. First, although there is no technical limit on the number of categories to be used per condition (except for the fact that complex calculations might take a long time even on high-speed computers), the use of fine-graded conditions should be avoided. This practice would lead to a singularization of cases, resulting in non-parsimonious solutions not consistent with the goals of csQCA and mvQCA (see p. 10). In most situations with a small- or intermediate-N of cases, the use of a few multi-value conditions with three or four categories each should suffice to gain an adequate representation of the cases on the one hand and to avoid singularization of cases on the other. Second, it is important to note that, at the current stage of development of mvQCA, multi-valued *outcomes* cannot be used and hence must be transformed into dichotomous outcomes.[10]

Box 4.5
"Good Practices" (8): Specific to mvQCA

All "good practices" for csQCA (see Chapter 3) are also valid for mvQCA. In addition, here are some more specific ones for mvQCA:

- If justifiable from an empirical and/or theoretical perspective, use a preponderance of dichotomous conditions.

- Multi-value conditions can be used to create a more genuine representation of multi-categorical nominal data, ordinal data, and interval data.

- Include multi-value conditions "à la carte," when needed. If at all possible, keep the number of values low (e.g., if you have the choice between three or four categories, use three); more than five categories should be avoided.

- Use the "thresholdssetter" function (TOSMANA) more systematically, to check visually the meaningfulness of the thresholds.

NOTES

1. As 3 binary variables are created, the number of logically possible configurations amounts to $2^3 = 8$. As there are 3 observed configurations, 5 logical remainders (8 minus 3) can be listed as well.

2. See Brayton and Khatri (1999) on the problem of dummy variables in general and of a large number of conditions in this context in particular.

3. A simple example should clarify this: Let us take a simple data set with four conditions. Two of these conditions are dichotomous (A,B) and the other two conditions (C,D) are multi-valued with three possible values $(0,1,2)$. To obtain the logical expression A_0B_0 we need the following nine logical configurations to perform the needed minimizations:

$$A_0B_0C_0D_0 + A_0B_0C_0D_1 + A_0B_0C_0D_2 \rightarrow A_0B_0C_0$$
$$A_0B_0C_1D_0 + A_0B_0C_1D_1 + A_0B_0C_1D_2 \rightarrow A_0B_0C_1$$
$$A_0B_0C_2D_0 + A_0B_0C_2D_1 + A_0B_0C_2D_2 \rightarrow A_0B_0C_2$$

After this first minimization (which "eliminates" the D condition), the derived logical configurations can be further reduced to the logical configuration A_0B_0, as follows:

$$A_0B_0C_0 + A_0B_0C_1 + A_0B_0C_2 \rightarrow A_0B_0$$

4. By contrast, the number of possible logical configurations in a csQCA data set with four conditions is $2^4 = 16$. Although a data set with two 3-valued conditions seems

only slightly more complex than the strictly dichotomous data set, the number of logical configurations is already more than doubled.

    5. Finland was assigned the value "0" for GNPCAP, indicating it is a country with a low GNP per capita, whereas Ireland was assigned the value "1," indicating it is a country with a high GNP per capita, although their original values were rather close (Finland: $560, Ireland: $655).

    6. A change of the threshold for URBANIZA from 50% to 65% would in fact solve this last contradiction, but the use of this threshold cannot be justified regarding the criteria for "good" thresholds mentioned above. Such a threshold would indeed create very unequal subdivision of cases, leaving only three cases in the group with high urbanization, whereas all other cases are assigned the value [0] for this condition. Furthermore, the subgroups created with the 65% threshold are more heterogeneous than those created with the 50% threshold, also creating an artificial cut between Belgium and Germany (values 56.5% and 60.5%) on the one hand and Czechoslovakia (65%) on the other. Therefore, it seems more appropriate to keep this contradictory configuration in the analysis and to perform a closer case study (outside of mvQCA proper) on the contradicting cases to find further evidence on the different outcome in Germany and Czechoslovakia.

    7. With three dichotomous and one 3-valued condition, there are $2 * 2 * 2 * 3 = 24$ possible logical configurations. Of those, 8 configurations are represented in Table 4.3, resulting in 16 potential logical remainders. Nine of these are included in the solution here.

    8. As the current software (TOSMANA) can draw Venn diagrams only on Boolean (i.e., dichotomous) data sets, this diagram was made by hand and cannot be considered a proper Venn diagram, as not all fields differing in only one value are found next to each other, as would be the case in a true Venn diagram.

    9. Seven simplifying assumptions were included.

    10. Further information on the use of multi-valued outcomes can be found in Cronqvist (2006).

5

Qualitative Comparative Analysis Using Fuzzy Sets (fsQCA)

Charles C. Ragin

Goals of This Chapter

After reading this chapter, you should be able to:

- Understand key differences between crisp set and fuzzy set logics

- Calibrate in an informed way the fuzzy-set membership scores for the different conditions

- See the connection between the multidimensional vector space defined by fuzzy-set conditions and a conventional truth table

- Gain a deeper understanding of the fuzzy subset relationship and of how to calculate and evaluate its consistency

- Relate fuzzy subset relations to the concepts of causal sufficiency and necessity

- Understand the different steps in a fuzzy-set analysis, especially the importance of frequency thresholds and consistency thresholds when creating a crisp truth table summarizing the results of multiple fuzzy-set analyses

One apparent limitation of the truth table approach is that it is designed for conditions that are simple presence/absence dichotomies (i.e., Boolean or "crisp" sets—see Chapter 3) or multichotomies (mvQCA—see Chapter 4). Many of the conditions that interest social scientists, however, vary by level or degree. For example, while it is clear that some countries are democracies and some are not, there is a broad range of in-between cases. These countries are not fully in the set of democracies, nor are they fully excluded from this set.

Fortunately, there is a well-developed mathematical system for addressing partial membership in sets, fuzzy-set theory (Zadeh, 1965; Klir, Clair, & Yuan, 1997). This chapter first provides a brief introduction to the fuzzy-set approach, building on Ragin (2000). Fuzzy sets are especially powerful because they allow researchers to calibrate partial membership in sets using values in the interval between [0] (nonmembership) and [1] (full membership) without abandoning core set theoretic principles such as, for example, the subset relation. As Ragin (2000) demonstrates, the subset relation is central to the analysis of causal complexity.

While fuzzy sets solve the problem of trying to force-fit cases into one of two categories (membership versus nonmembership in a set) or into one of three or four categories[1] (mvQCA), they are not well suited for conventional truth table analysis. With fuzzy sets, there is no simple way to sort cases according to the combinations of conditions they display because each case's array of membership scores may be unique. Ragin (2000) circumvents this limitation by developing an algorithm for analyzing configurations of fuzzy-set memberships that bypasses truth table analysis altogether. While this algorithm remains true to fuzzy-set theory through its use of the containment (or inclusion) rule, it forfeits many of the analytic strengths that follow from analyzing evidence in terms of truth tables. For example, truth tables are very useful for investigating "limited diversity" and the consequences of different "simplifying assumptions" that follow from using different subsets of "logical remainders" to reduce complexity (see Chapters 3 and 4, and also Ragin, 1987, 2008; Ragin & Sonnett, 2004). Analyses of this type are difficult when not using truth tables as the starting point.

A further section of this chapter thus builds a bridge between fuzzy sets and truth tables, demonstrating how to construct a conventional Boolean truth table from fuzzy-set data. It is important to point out that this new technique takes full advantage of the gradations in set membership central to the constitution of fuzzy sets and is not predicated upon a dichotomization of fuzzy membership scores. To illustrate these procedures, the same data set is used as in the previous chapters. However, the original interval-scale data are converted into fuzzy membership scores (which range from 0 to 1), thereby avoiding dichotomizing or trichotomizing the data (i.e., sorting the cases into crude categories). Of course, the important qualitative states of full membership (fuzzy membership = 1.0) and full nonmembership (fuzzy membership = 0.0) are retained, which makes fuzzy sets simultaneously qualitative and quantitative. It is important to point out that the analytic approach sketched in this chapter offers a new way to conduct fuzzy-set analysis of social data. This new analytic strategy is superior in several respects to the one sketched in *Fuzzy-Set Social Science* (Ragin, 2000). While both approaches have strengths and weaknesses, the one presented here uses the truth table as the key analytic device. As shall be demonstrated, a further advantage of the fuzzy-set truth-table approach is that it is more transparent. Thus, the researcher has more direct control over the process of data analysis. This type of control is central to the practice of case-oriented research.

FUZZY SETS: A BRIEF PRESENTATION

In many respects fuzzy sets are simultaneously qualitative and quantitative, for they incorporate both kinds of distinctions in the calibration of degree of set membership. Thus, fuzzy sets have many of the virtues of conventional interval-scale variables, especially their ability to make fine-grained distinctions, but at the same time they permit set theoretic operations. Such operations are outside the scope of conventional variable-oriented analysis.

Fuzzy Sets Defined

As explained in Chapter 3, csQCA was developed originally for the analysis of configurations of crisp-set memberships (i.e., conventional Boolean sets). With crisp sets, each case is assigned one of two possible membership scores in each set included in a study: "1" (membership in the set) or "0" (non-membership in the set). In other words, an object or element (e.g., a country) within a domain (e.g., members of the United Nations) is either in or out of the various sets within this domain (e.g., membership in the UN Security Council). Crisp sets establish distinctions among cases that are wholly qualitative in nature (e.g., membership versus nonmembership in the UN Security Council).

Fuzzy sets extend crisp sets by permitting membership scores in the interval between [0] and [1]. For example, a country (e.g., the United States) might receive a membership score of [1] in the set of rich countries but a score of only 0.9 in the set of democratic countries, especially in the wake of the 2000 presidential election. The basic idea behind fuzzy sets is to permit the scaling of membership scores and thus allow partial membership.

> ## Box 5.1
> ## Fuzzy-Set Membership Scores: What Are They?
>
> Fuzzy membership scores address the varying degree to which different cases belong to a set (including two qualitatively defined states: full membership and full nonmembership), as follows:
>
> • A fuzzy membership score of [1] indicates full membership in a set; scores close to [1] (e.g., 0.8 or 0.9) indicate strong but not quite full membership in a set; scores less than 0.5 but greater than [0] (e.g., 0.2 and 0.3) indicate that objects are more "out" than "in" a set, but still weak members of the set; and finally a score of [0] indicates full nonmembership in the set.
>
> • Thus, fuzzy sets combine qualitative and quantitative assessment: [1] and [0] are qualitative assignments ("fully in" and "fully out," respectively); values between [0] and [1] indicate partial membership. The 0.5 score is also qualitatively anchored, for it indicates the point of maximum ambiguity (fuzziness) in the assessment of whether a case is more "in" or "out" of a set.

Note that fuzzy set membership scores do not *simply* rank cases relative to each other. Rather, fuzzy sets pinpoint qualitative states while at the same time assessing varying degrees of membership between full inclusion and full exclusion. In this sense, a fuzzy set can be seen as a continuous variable that has been purposefully calibrated to indicate degree of membership in a well-defined set. Such calibration[2] is possible only through the use of theoretical and substantive knowledge, which is essential to the specification of the three qualitative breakpoints: full membership (1), full nonmembership (0), and the crossover point, where there is maximum ambiguity regarding whether a case is more "in" or more "out" of a set (0.5).

For illustration of the general idea of fuzzy sets, consider a simple three-value set that allows cases to be in the gray zone between "in" and "out" of a set. As shown in Table 5.1, instead of using only two scores, [0] and [1], this three-value logic adds a third value, 0.5, indicating objects that are neither fully in nor fully out of the set in question (compare columns 1 and 2). This three-value set is a rudimentary fuzzy set. A more elegant but still simple fuzzy set uses four numerical values, as shown in column 3. The four-value scheme uses the numerical values 0, 0.33, 0.67, and 1.0 to indicate "fully out," "more out than in," "more in than out," and "fully in," respectively. Such a scheme is especially useful in situations where researchers have a substantial amount of information about cases, but the nature of the evidence is not identical across cases. A more fine-grained fuzzy set uses six values, as shown in column 4.

Table 5.1   Crisp Versus Fuzzy Sets

Crisp set	Three-value fuzzy set	Four-value fuzzy set	Six-value fuzzy set	"Continuous" fuzzy set
1 = fully in	1 = fully in	1 = fully in	1 = fully in	1 = fully in
0 = fully out	0.5 = neither fully in nor fully out	0.67 = more in than out	0.9 = mostly but not fully in	Degree of membership is more "in" than "out": $0.5 < X_i < 1$
	0 = fully out	0.33 = more out than in	0.6 = more or less in	0.5 = cross-over: neither in nor out
		0 = fully out	0.4 = more or less out	Degree of membership is more "out" than "in": $0 < X_i < 0.5$
			0.1 = mostly but not fully out	0 = fully out
			0 = fully out	

Like the four-value fuzzy set, the six-value fuzzy set utilizes two qualitative states ("fully out" and "fully in"). The six-value fuzzy set inserts two intermediate levels between "fully out" and the crossover point ("mostly out" and "more or less out") and two intermediate levels between the crossover point and "fully in" ("more or less in" and "mostly in"). The number of levels in fuzzy sets of this type is determined by the researcher. For example, a researcher might construct a fuzzy set with five or eight levels, instead of four or six. Also, it is not necessary to use equal intervals between the levels. For example, based on substantive knowledge a researcher might develop a five-value scheme using the scores 0, 0.2, 0.4, 0.6, and 1.0. This scheme would signal that while there are cases that are fully in the set (1.0), there are no cases that are "mostly but not fully in" (e.g., with fuzzy membership scores of 0.8).

At first glance, the four-value and six-value fuzzy sets might seem equivalent to ordinal scales. In fact, however, they are qualitatively different from such scales. An ordinal scale is a mere ranking of categories, usually without reference to such criteria as set membership. When constructing ordinal scales, researchers do not peg categories to degree of membership in sets; rather, the categories are simply arrayed relative to each other, yielding a rank order.

For example, a researcher might develop a six-level ordinal scheme of country wealth, using categories that range from destitute to super rich. It is unlikely that this scheme would translate automatically to a six-value fuzzy set, with the lowest rank set to 0, the next rank to 0.1, and so on (see column 4 of Table 5.1). Assume the relevant fuzzy set is the set of *rich countries*. The lower two ranks of the ordinal variable might both translate to "fully out" of the set of rich countries (fuzzy score = 0). The next rank up in the ordinal scheme might translate to 0.2 rather than 0.1 in the fuzzy set scheme. The top two ranks might translate to "fully in" (fuzzy score = 1.0), and so on. In short, the specific translation of ordinal ranks to fuzzy membership scores depends on the fit between the content of the ordinal categories and the researcher's conceptualization of the fuzzy set. The bottom line is that researchers must calibrate membership scores using substantive and theoretical knowledge when developing fuzzy sets. Such calibration should not be mechanical.

Finally, a continuous fuzzy set permits cases to take values anywhere in the interval from [0] to [1], as shown in the last column of Table 5.1. The continuous fuzzy set, like all fuzzy sets, utilizes the two qualitative states (fully out and fully in) and also the crossover point. As an example of a continuous fuzzy set, consider membership in the set of rich countries, based on GNP per capita. The translation of this variable to fuzzy membership scores is neither automatic nor mechanical. It would be a serious mistake to score the poorest country [0], the richest country [1], and then to array all the other countries between [0] and [1], depending on their positions in the range of GNP per capita values. Instead, the first task in this translation would be to specify three important qualitative anchors: the point on the GNP per capita distribution at which full membership is reached (i.e., definitely a rich country, membership score = 1), the point at which full nonmembership is reached (i.e., definitely not a rich country, membership score = 0), and the point of maximum ambiguity in whether a country is "more in" or "more out" of the set of rich countries (a membership score of 0.5, the crossover point). When specifying these qualitative anchors, the investigator should present a rationale for each breakpoint.

Qualitative anchors make it possible to distinguish between relevant and irrelevant variation. Variation in GNP per capita among the unambiguously rich countries is *not* relevant to membership in the set of rich countries, at least from the perspective of fuzzy sets. If a country is unambiguously rich, then it is accorded full membership, a score of [1]. Similarly, variation in GNP per capita among the unambiguously not-rich countries is also irrelevant to degree of membership in the set of rich countries because these countries are uniformly and completely out of the set of rich countries. Thus, in research using fuzzy sets it is not enough simply to develop scales that show the relative positions of cases in distributions (e.g., a conventional index of wealth such as GNP per capita). It is also necessary to use qualitative anchors to map the links between specific scores on continuous variables (e.g., an index of wealth) and fuzzy set membership (see Ragin, 2008).

In a fuzzy-set analysis both the outcome and the conditions are represented using fuzzy sets. Crisp sets also may be included among the causal conditions. Table 5.2 shows a simple data matrix containing fuzzy membership scores. The data are the same used in the two previous chapters and show the five conditions relevant to the breakdown/survival of democracy in inter-war Europe (see Table 3.5).

In this example, the outcome of interest is the degree of membership in the set of countries with democracies that survived the many economic and political upheavals of this period (SURVIVED). Degree of membership in the set of countries experiencing democratic breakdown (BREAKDOWN) is simply the negation of degree of membership in SURVIVED (see discussion of negation below). The conditions are degrees of membership in the set of developed countries (DEVELOPED), of urbanized countries (URBAN), of industrialized countries (INDUSTRIAL), of literate countries (LITERATE), and of countries that experienced political instability during this period (UNSTABLE; the fuzzy scores for this condition have been reversed so that they indicate *stability* rather than instability). The table shows both the original data (interval-scale values or ratings) and the corresponding fuzzy membership scores (denoted with "FZ" suffixes). The fuzzy membership scores were calibrated using a procedure detailed in Ragin (2008). The original interval-scale data were rescaled to fit the fuzzy-set metric using the FSQCA software (see Ragin, 2008). For the crossover point (fuzzy membership = 0.50), these fuzzy sets use the same value selected for dichotomizing these conditions in Chapter 3, including the revised value for the development indicator (a GNP/capita of $550 instead of $600).

Box 5.2
"Good Practices" (9): Specific to the Calibration of Fuzzy Sets

Similarly with dichotomization in csQCA (see Box 3.3) and thresholds setting in mvQCA (see Box 4.4), the calibration of fuzzy sets is a key operation, to be performed with great care. Some good practices—for example, being transparent or justifying the cutoff points on substantive and/or theoretical grounds—are common to all three operations. Here are some *specific* good practices for the calibration of fuzzy sets:

- Carefully identify and define the target category using set theoretic language (e.g., the set of "less developed countries" or the set of "more urbanized countries").

(Continued)

(Continued)

> - Based on theoretical and substantive knowledge, specify what it takes to warrant "full membership" in this set (a fuzzy score of 1.0) and full exclusion from this set (a fuzzy score of 0).
> - Make sure that extraneous or irrelevant variation is truncated (e.g., variation in an index variable like GNP/capita among the countries that are unquestionably fully in or fully out of the target set; for example, the set of less developed countries).
> - Evaluate what constitutes maximum ambiguity in whether a case is more in or out of the target set (e.g., the GNP/capita score that is at the border between countries that are more in versus more out of the set of "less developed countries"). This evaluation provides the basis for establishing the crossover point (0.50).
> - If you are basing your fuzzy membership scores on an index variable that is interval or ratio scale, use FSQCA's "calibrate" procedure to create the fuzzy set. To do this, you will need to be able to specify threshold values for full membership, full nonmembership, and the crossover point (see Ragin, 2008).
> - Always examine carefully the fuzzy scores that result from any procedure you use to calibrate membership scores. Make sure that the scores make sense at the case level, based on your substantive and theoretical knowledge.

Operations on Fuzzy Sets

There are three common operations on fuzzy sets: negation, logical *and*, and logical *or*. These three operations provide important background knowledge for understanding how to work with fuzzy sets.

Negation

Like conventional crisp sets, fuzzy sets can be negated. With crisp sets, negation switches membership scores from [1] to [0] and from [0] to [1]. The negation of the crisp set of democracies that survived, for example, is the crisp set of democracies that collapsed. This simple mathematical principle holds in fuzzy algebra as well, but the relevant numerical values are not restricted to the Boolean values [0] and [1]; instead, they extend to values between [0] and [1].

To calculate the membership of a case in the *negation* of fuzzy set A (i.e., *not-A*), simply subtract its membership in set A from [1], as follows:

(membership in set *not-A*) = [1] − (membership in set A)

or

$$\sim A = [1] - A$$

(The tilde sign ["~"] is used to indicate negation.)

Table 5.2 Data Matrix Showing Original Variables and Fuzzy-Set Membership Scores

Country	Outcome		Conditions									
	SURVIVED	SURVIVED-FZ	DEVELOPED	DEVELOPED-FZ	URBAN	URBAN-FZ	LITERATE	LITERATE-FZ	INDUSTRIAL	INDUSTRIAL-FZ	UNSTABLE	STABLE-FZ
Austria	−9	0.05	720	0.81	33.4	0.12	98	0.99	33.4	0.73	10	0.43
Belgium	10	0.95	1098	0.99	60.5	0.89	94.4	0.98	48.9	1	4	0.98
Czechoslovakia	7	0.89	586	0.58	69	0.98	95.9	0.98	37.4	0.9	6	0.91
Estonia	−6	0.12	468	0.16	28.5	0.07	95	0.98	14	0.01	6	0.91
Finland	4	0.77	590	0.58	22	0.03	99.1	0.99	22	0.08	9	0.58
France	10	0.95	983	0.98	21.2	0.03	96.2	0.99	34.8	0.81	5	0.95
Germany	−9	0.05	795	0.89	56.5	0.79	98	0.99	40.4	0.96	11	0.31
Greece	−8	0.06	390	0.04	31.1	0.09	59.2	0.13	28.1	0.36	10	0.43
Hungary	−1	0.42	424	0.07	36.3	0.16	85	0.88	21.6	0.07	13	0.13
Ireland	8	0.92	662	0.72	25	0.05	95	0.98	14.5	0.01	5	0.95
Italy	−9	0.05	517	0.34	31.4	0.1	72.1	0.41	29.6	0.47	9	0.58
Netherlands	10	0.95	1008	0.98	78.8	1	99.9	0.99	39.3	0.94	2	0.99
Poland	−6	0.12	350	0.02	37	0.17	76.9	0.59	11.2	0	21	0
Portugal	−9	0.05	320	0.01	15.3	0.02	38	0.01	23.1	0.11	19	0.01
Romania	−4	0.21	331	0.01	21.9	0.03	61.8	0.17	12.2	0	7	0.84
Spain	−8	0.06	367	0.03	43	0.3	55.6	0.09	25.5	0.21	12	0.2
Sweden	10	0.95	897	0.95	34	0.13	99.9	0.99	32.3	0.67	6	0.91
United Kingdom	10	0.95	1038	0.98	74	0.99	99.9	0.99	49.9	1	4	0.98

Thus, for example, Finland has a membership score of 0.77 in SURVIVED; therefore, its degree of membership in BREAKDOWN is 0.23. That is, Finland is more out than in the set of democracies that collapsed.

Logical AND

Compound sets are formed when two or more sets are combined, an operation commonly known as set intersection. A researcher interested in the fate of democratic institutions in relatively inhospitable settings might want to draw up a list of countries that combine being "democratic" with being "poor." Conventionally, these countries would be identified using crisp sets by cross-tabulating the two dichotomies, poor versus not-poor and democratic versus not-democratic, and seeing which countries are in the democratic/poor cell of this 2 x 2 table. This cell, in effect, shows the cases that exist in the intersection of the two crisp sets.

With fuzzy sets, logical *AND* is accomplished by taking the minimum membership score of each case in the sets that are combined. The minimum membership score, in effect, indicates degree of membership of a case in a combination of sets. Its use follows "weakest link" reasoning. For example, if a country's membership in the set of poor countries is 0.7 and its membership in the set of democratic countries is 0.9, its membership in the set of countries that are both poor *and* democratic is the smaller of these two scores, 0.7. A score of 0.7 indicates that this case is more in than out of the intersection.

For further illustration of this principle, consider Table 5.3. The last two columns demonstrate the operation of logical *AND*. The penultimate column shows the intersection of DEVELOPED and URBAN, yielding membership in the set of countries that combine these two traits. Notice that some countries (e.g., France and Sweden) with high membership in DEVELOPED but low membership in URBAN have low scores in the intersection of these two sets. The last column shows the intersection of DEVELOPED, URBAN, and UNSTABLE (the negation of STABLE). Note that only one country in interwar Europe, Germany, had a high score in this combination. In general, as more sets are added to a combination of conditions, membership scores either stay the same or decrease. For each intersection, the *lowest* membership score provides the degree of membership in the combination.

Logical OR

Two or more sets also can be joined through logical *OR*—the union of sets. For example, a researcher might be interested in countries that are "developed" *or* "democratic" based on the conjecture that these two conditions might offer equivalent bases for some outcome (e.g., bureaucracy-laden government).

Table 5.3   Illustration of Logical *AND* (Intersection)

Country	*DEVELOPED*	*URBAN*	*UNSTABLE*	*DEVELOPED and URBAN*	*DEVELOPED, URBAN, and UNSTABLE*
Austria	0.81	0.12	0.57	0.12	0.12
Belgium	0.99	0.89	0.02	0.89	0.02
Czechoslovakia	0.58	0.98	0.09	0.58	0.09
Estonia	0.16	0.07	0.09	0.07	0.07
Finland	0.58	0.03	0.42	0.03	0.03
France	0.98	0.03	0.05	0.03	0.03
Germany	0.89	0.79	0.69	0.79	0.69
Greece	0.04	0.09	0.57	0.04	0.04
Hungary	0.07	0.16	0.87	0.07	0.07
Ireland	0.72	0.05	0.05	0.05	0.05
Italy	0.34	0.1	0.42	0.1	0.1
Netherlands	0.98	1	0.01	0.98	0.01
Poland	0.02	0.17	1	0.02	0.02
Portugal	0.01	0.02	0.99	0.01	0.01
Romania	0.01	0.03	0.16	0.01	0.01
Spain	0.03	0.3	0.8	0.03	0.03
Sweden	0.95	0.13	0.09	0.13	0.09
United Kingdom	0.98	0.99	0.02	0.98	0.02

When using fuzzy sets, logical *OR* directs the researcher's attention to the *maximum* of each case's memberships in the component sets. That is, a case's membership in the set formed from the *union* of two or more fuzzy sets is the *maximum* value of its memberships in the component sets. Thus, if a country has a score of 0.3 in the set of democratic countries and a score of 0.9 in the set of developed countries, it has a score of 0.9 in the set of countries that are "democratic *or* developed."

For illustration of the use of logical *OR*, consider Table 5.4. The last two columns of Table 5.4 show the operation of logical *OR*. The penultimate

Table 5.4   Illustration of Logical *OR* (Union)

Country	DEVELOPED	URBAN	UNSTABLE	DEVELOPED or URBAN	DEVELOPED or URBAN or UNSTABLE
Austria	0.81	0.12	0.57	0.81	0.81
Belgium	0.99	0.89	0.02	0.99	0.99
Czechoslovakia	0.58	0.98	0.09	0.98	0.98
Estonia	0.16	0.07	0.09	0.16	0.16
Finland	0.58	0.03	0.42	0.58	0.58
France	0.98	0.03	0.05	0.98	0.98
Germany	0.89	0.79	0.69	0.89	0.89
Greece	0.04	0.09	0.57	0.09	0.57
Hungary	0.07	0.16	0.87	0.16	0.87
Ireland	0.72	0.05	0.05	0.72	0.72
Italy	0.34	0.1	0.42	0.34	0.42
Netherlands	0.98	1	0.01	1	1
Poland	0.02	0.17	1	0.17	1
Portugal	0.01	0.02	0.99	0.02	0.99
Romania	0.01	0.03	0.16	0.03	0.16
Spain	0.03	0.3	0.8	0.3	0.8
Sweden	0.95	0.13	0.09	0.95	0.95
United Kingdom	0.98	0.99	0.02	0.99	0.99

column shows countries that are DEVELOPED *or* URBAN. Notice that the only countries that have low membership in this union of sets are those that have low scores in both component sets (e.g., Estonia, Greece, Portugal, and Romania). The last column shows degree of membership in the union of three sets, DEVELOPED, URBAN, or UNSTABLE. Only Estonia and Romania have low scores in this union.

Box 5.3
Three Main Operations on Fuzzy Sets

- Negation: reverses scores so that scores close to [1], after negation, are close to [0], and the reverse. The 0.5 score (maximum ambiguity) does not change. The label attached to the set is also negated or reversed (e.g., the negation of the set of "developed" countries is the set of "not-developed" countries).

- Logical *AND*: is the same as *set intersection*. The minimum score (or weakest link) in the component sets is the degree of membership of each case in an intersection of sets.

- Logical *OR*: is the same as *set union*. The maximum score in the component sets is the degree of membership of each case in their union.

Fuzzy Subsets

The key set theoretic relation in the study of causal complexity is the subset relation. As discussed in Ragin (2000), if cases sharing several causally relevant conditions uniformly exhibit the same outcome, then these cases constitute a subset of instances of the outcome. Such a subset relation signals that a specific combination of causally relevant conditions may be interpreted as *sufficient* for the outcome. If there are other sets of cases sharing other causally relevant conditions, and if these cases also agree in displaying the outcome in question, then these other combinations of conditions also may be interpreted as sufficient for the outcome.

The interpretation of *sufficiency*, of course, must be grounded in the researcher's substantive and theoretical knowledge; it does not follow automatically from the demonstration of the subset relation. Regardless of whether the concept of sufficiency is invoked, the subset relation is the key device for pinpointing the different combinations of conditions linked in some way to an outcome (e.g., the combinations of conditions linked to democratic survival or breakdown in inter-war Europe).

With crisp sets it is a simple matter to determine whether the cases sharing a specific combination of conditions constitute a subset of the outcome. The researcher simply examines cases sharing each combination of conditions (i.e., *configurations*) and assesses whether or not they agree in displaying the outcome. In crisp-set analyses, researchers use truth tables to sort cases according to the conditions they share, and the investigator assesses whether or not the cases in each row of the truth table agree on the outcome. The assessment specific to each row can be conceived as a 2×2 cross-tabulation of the presence/absence of the outcome against the presence/absence of the combination of conditions specified in the row. The subset relation is indicated when the cell corresponding to the presence of the combination of conditions and the *absence* of the outcome is empty, and the cell corresponding to the presence of the causal combination and the *presence* of the outcome is populated with cases, as shown in Table 5.5.

Obviously, these procedures cannot be duplicated with fuzzy sets. There is no simple way to isolate the cases sharing a specific combination of conditions because each case's array of fuzzy membership scores may be unique. Cases also have different degrees of membership in the outcome, complicating the assessment of whether they "agree" on the outcome. Finally, with fuzzy sets cases can have partial membership in every logically possible combination of causal conditions, as illustrated in Table 5.6.

Table 5.6 shows the membership of countries in three of the five conditions used in this example (DEVELOPED, URBAN, and LITERATE) and in the eight combinations that can be generated using these three fuzzy sets. These eight combinations also can be seen as eight logically possible causal arguments, as fuzzy sets representing causal conditions can be understood as a multi-dimensional vector space with 2^k corners, where k is the number of conditions (Ragin, 2000). The number of corners in this vector space is the same as the number of rows in a crisp truth table with k conditions. Empirical cases can be plotted within this multidimensional space, and the membership of each case in each of the eight corners can be calculated using fuzzy algebra, as shown in Table 5.6. For example, the membership of Austria in the corner of the vector space corresponding to DEVELOPED, URBAN, and LITERATE (D * U * L, the

Table 5.5 Cross-Tabulation of Outcome
Against Presence/Absence of a Causal Combination

	Causal combination absent	*Causal combination* present
Outcome *present*	1. not directly relevant	2. cases here
Outcome *absent*	3. not directly relevant	4. no cases here

Table 5.6 Fuzzy-Set Membership of Cases in Causal Combinations

Country	Membership in causal conditions			Membership in corners of vector space formed by causal conditions							
	DEVELOPED (D)	URBAN (U)	LITERATE (L)	~D*~U*~L	~D*~U*L	~D*U*~L	~D*U*L	D*~U*~L	D*~U*L	D*U*~L	D*U*L
Austria	0.81	0.12	0.99	0.01	0.19	0.01	0.12	0.12	**0.81**	0.01	0.12
Belgium	0.99	0.89	0.98	0.01	0.01	0.01	0.01	0.01	0.11	0.02	**0.89**
Czechoslovakia	0.58	0.98	0.98	0.02	0.02	0.02	0.42	0.02	0.02	0.02	**0.58**
Estonia	0.16	0.07	0.98	0.02	**0.84**	0.02	0.07	0.07	0.16	0.02	0.07
Finland	0.58	0.03	0.99	0.01	0.42	0.01	0.03	0.03	**0.58**	0.01	0.03
France	0.98	0.03	0.99	0.01	0.02	0.01	0.02	0.02	**0.97**	0.01	0.03
Germany	0.89	0.79	0.99	0.01	0.11	0.01	0.11	0.11	0.21	0.01	**0.79**
Greece	0.04	0.09	0.13	**0.87**	0.13	0.09	0.09	0.09	0.04	0.04	0.04
Hungary	0.07	0.16	0.88	0.12	**0.84**	0.12	0.16	0.16	0.07	0.07	0.07
Ireland	0.72	0.05	0.98	0.02	0.28	0.02	0.05	0.05	**0.72**	0.02	0.05
Italy	0.34	0.1	0.41	**0.59**	0.41	0.1	0.1	0.1	0.34	0.1	0.1
Netherlands	0.98	1	0.99	0	0	0.01	0.02	0	0	0.01	**0.98**
Poland	0.02	0.17	0.59	0.41	**0.59**	0.17	0.17	0.17	0.02	0.02	0.02
Portugal	0.01	0.02	0.01	**0.98**	0.01	0.02	0.01	0.02	0.01	0.01	0.01
Romania	0.01	0.03	0.17	**0.83**	0.17	0.03	0.03	0.03	0.01	0.01	0.01
Spain	0.03	0.3	0.09	**0.7**	0.09	0.3	0.09	0.3	0.03	0.03	0.03
Sweden	0.95	0.13	0.99	0.01	0.05	0.01	0.05	0.05	**0.87**	0.01	0.13
United Kingdom	0.98	0.99	0.99	0.01	0.01	0.01	0.02	0.01	0.01	0.01	**0.98**

last column of Table 5.6) is the minimum of its memberships in developed (0.81), urban (0.12), and literate (0.99), which is 0.12. Austria's membership in the not-developed, not-urban, and not-literate (~D * ~ U * ~L) corner is the minimum of its membership in not-industrial (1 − 0.81 = 0.19), not-urban (1 − 0.12 = 0.88), and not-literate (1 − 0.99 = 0.01), which is 0.01. The link between fuzzy-set vector spaces and crisp truth tables is explored in greater depth below.

While these properties of fuzzy sets make it difficult to duplicate crisp-set procedures for assessing subset relationships, the fuzzy subset relation can be assessed using fuzzy algebra. With fuzzy sets, a subset relation is indicated when membership scores in one set (e.g., a condition or combination of conditions) are consistently less than or equal to membership scores in another set (e.g., the outcome). If, for example, memberships scores in a combination of conditions are consistently less than or equal to their corresponding membership scores in the outcome ($X_i \leq Y_i$), then a subset relation exists, which in turn supports an argument of sufficiency. For illustration, consider Figure 5.1, the plot of degree of membership in BREAKDOWN (the negation of SURVIVED) against degree of membership in the ~D * ~U * ~L (not developed, not urban, not literate) corner of the three-dimensional vector space. (The negation of the fuzzy membership scores for SURVIVED in Table 5.2 provides the BREAKDOWN membership scores.)

This plot shows that almost all countries' membership scores in this corner of the vector space (~D * ~ U * ~L) are less than or equal to their corresponding scores in BREAKDOWN. The characteristic upper-left triangular plot indicates that the set plotted on the horizontal axis is a subset of the set plotted on the vertical axis. The (almost) vacant lower triangle in this plot corresponds to Cell 4 of Table 5.5. Just as cases in Cell 4 of Table 5.5 are inconsistent with the crisp subset relation, cases in the lower-right triangle of Figure 5.1 are inconsistent with the fuzzy subset relation. Thus, the evidence in Figure 5.1 supports the argument that membership in ~D * ~U * ~L is a subset of membership in BREAKDOWN ($X_i \leq Y_i$), which in turn provides support for the argument that this combination of conditions (not developed, not urban, and not literate) is sufficient for democratic breakdown.

Note that when membership in the causal combination is high, membership in the outcome also must be high. However, the reverse does not have to be true. That is, the fact that there are cases with relatively low membership in the causal combination but substantial membership in the outcome is not problematic from the viewpoint of set theory because the expectation is that there may be several different conditions or combinations of conditions capable of generating high membership in the outcome. Cases with low scores in the condition or combination of conditions but high scores in the outcome indicate the operation of alternate conditions or alternate combinations of conditions.

Figure 5.1 illustrates the fuzzy subset relation using only one corner of the three-dimensional vector space shown in Table 5.6. As shown below, this same assessment can be conducted using degree of membership in the other seven corners (causal combinations) shown in the table. These eight assessments establish which causal combinations formed from these three causal conditions are subsets of the outcome (BREAKDOWN), which in turn signals which combinations of conditions might be considered *sufficient* for the outcome.

USING CRISP TRUTH TABLES
TO AID FUZZY-SET ANALYSIS

The bridge from fuzzy-set analysis to truth tables has three main pillars. The first pillar is the *direct correspondence* that exists between the rows of a crisp truth table and the corners of the vector space defined by fuzzy-set conditions (Ragin, 2000). The second pillar is the assessment of the *distribution of cases* across the logically possible combinations of conditions (i.e., the distribution of cases within the vector space defined by the conditions). The cases included in a study have varying degrees of membership in each corner of the vector

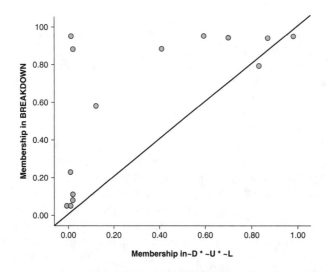

Figure 5.1   Plot of Degree of Membership in BREAKDOWN Against Degree of Membership in the ~D * ~U * ~L Combination (Corner of Vector Space)

space, as shown in Table 5.6 for a three-dimensional vector space. Some corners of the vector space may have many cases with strong membership; other corners may have no cases with strong membership. When using a crisp truth table to analyze the results of multiple fuzzy-set assessments, it is important to take these differences into account. The third pillar is the fuzzy set assessment of the *consistency of the evidence* for each causal combination with the argument that it is a subset of the outcome. The subset relation is important because it signals that there is an explicit connection between a combination of conditions and an outcome. Once these three pillars are in place, it is possible to construct a crisp truth table summarizing the results of multiple fuzzy-set assessments and then to analyze this truth table using Boolean algebra.

The Correspondence Between Vector Space Corners and Truth Table Rows

A multidimensional vector space constructed from fuzzy sets has 2^k corners, just as a crisp truth table has 2^k rows (where k is the number of conditions). There is a one-to-one correspondence between causal combinations, truth table rows, and vector space corners (Ragin, 2000). The first four columns of Table 5.7 show the correspondence between truth table rows and corners of the vector space. In crisp-set analyses, cases are sorted into truth table rows according to their specific combinations of presence/absence scores on the conditions. Thus, each case is assigned to a unique row, and each row embraces a unique subset of the cases included in the study. With fuzzy sets, however, each case has varying degrees of membership in the different corners of the vector space and thus varying degrees of membership in each truth table row (as illustrated in Table 5.6).

When using a truth table to analyze the results of fuzzy-set assessments, the truth table rows do not represent subsets of cases, as they do in crisp-set analyses. Rather, they represent the 2^k causal arguments that can be constructed from a given set of causal conditions. In this light, the first row of the crisp truth table is the causal argument that ~D * ~U * ~L is a subset of the outcome (democratic BREAKDOWN in this example); the outcome for this row is whether the argument is supported by the fuzzy-set evidence. The second row addresses the ~D * ~U * L causal combination, and so on. If both arguments (~D * ~U * ~L and ~D * ~U * L) are supported, then they can be logically simplified to ~D * ~U, using Boolean algebra. Thus, in the translation of fuzzy-set analyses to crisp truth tables, the rows of the truth table specify the different causal arguments based on the logically possible combinations of conditions as represented in the corners of the vector space of conditions. As will be explained in the next two sections of this chapter, two pieces of

Table 5.7 Correspondence Between Truth Table Rows and Vector Space Corners

Developed	Urban	Literate	Corresponding Vector Space Corner (Table 5.6)	N of cases with membership in causal combination > 0.5	Consistency with subset relation vis-à-vis the outcome (N = 18 in each assessment)	Outcome code (based on consistency score)
0	0	0	~D * ~U * ~L	5	0.98	1
0	0	1	~D * ~U * ~L	3	0.84	1
0	1	0	~D * ~U * ~L	0	(too few cases with scores > 0.5)	remainder
0	1	1	~D * ~U * ~L	0	(too few cases with scores > 0.5)	remainder
1	0	0	~D * ~U * ~L	0	(too few cases with scores > 0.5)	remainder
1	0	1	~D * ~U * ~L	5	0.44	0
1	1	0	~D * ~U * ~L	0	(too few cases with scores >0.5)	remainder
1	1	1	~D * ~U * ~L	5	0.34	0

information about these corners are especially important: (1) the *number* of cases with strong membership in each corner (i.e., in each combination of conditions) and (2) the *consistency* of the empirical evidence for each corner, with the argument that degree of membership in the corner (i.e., causal combination) is a subset of degree of membership in the outcome.

Specifying Frequency Thresholds for Fuzzy-Set Assessments

The distribution of cases across causal combinations is easy to assess when conditions are represented with crisp sets, for it is a simple matter to construct a truth table from such data and to examine the number of cases crisply sorted into each row. Rows without cases are treated as "logical remainders" (see p. 59). When causal conditions are fuzzy sets, however, this analysis is less straightforward because each case may have partial membership in every truth table row (i.e., in every corner of the vector space), as Table 5.6 demonstrates with three causal conditions. Still, it is important to assess the distribution of cases' membership scores across causal combinations in fuzzy-set analyses because some combinations may be empirically trivial. If all cases have very low membership in a combination, then it is pointless to conduct a fuzzy-set assessment of that combination's link to the outcome.[3]

Table 5.6 shows the distribution of the membership scores of the 18 countries across the eight logically possible combinations of the three causal conditions. In essence, the table lists the eight corners of the three-dimensional vector space that is formed by the three fuzzy sets and shows the degree of membership of each case in each corner.

This table demonstrates an important property of combinations of fuzzy sets—namely, that each case can have only *one* membership score greater than 0.5 in the logically possible combinations formed from a given set of conditions (shown in bold type).[4] A membership score greater than 0.5 in a causal combination signals that a case is more in than out of the causal combination in question. It also indicates which corner of the multidimensional vector space formed by conditions a given case is closest to. This property of fuzzy sets makes it possible for investigators to sort cases according to corners of the vector space, based on their degree of membership. The fifth column of Table 5.7 shows the number of cases with greater than 0.5 membership in each corner, based on the evidence presented in Table 5.6. For example, Table 5.6 shows that five countries have greater than 0.5 membership in ~D * ~U * ~L (not developed, not urban, and not literate) and thus are good instances of this combination. These are the five cases with greater than 0.5 membership in row 1 of Table 5.7.

The key task in this phase of the analysis is to establish a number-of-cases threshold for assessing fuzzy subset relations. That is, the investigator must formulate a rule for determining which combinations of conditions are relevant, based on the number of cases with greater than 0.5 membership in each combination. If a combination has enough cases with membership scores greater than 0.5, then it is reasonable to assess the fuzzy subset relation, as in Figure 5.1. If a combination has too few cases with membership scores greater than 0.5, then there is no point in conducting this assessment.

The number-of-cases threshold chosen by the investigator must reflect the nature of the evidence and the character of the study. Important considerations include the total number of cases included in the study, the number of conditions, the degree of familiarity of the researcher with each case, the degree of precision that is possible in the calibration of fuzzy sets, the extent of measurement and assignment error, whether the researcher is interested in coarse versus fine-grained patterns in the results, and so on. The data set used in this simple demonstration comprises only 18 cases and 8 logically possible combinations of conditions. In this situation, a reasonable frequency threshold is at least one case with greater than 0.5 membership in a combination. Thus, the four combinations of conditions lacking a single case with greater than 0.5 membership (see Rows 3, 4, 5, and 7 in Table 5.7) are treated as "logical remainders" in the analysis that follows, for there are no solid empirical instances of any of them.

When the number of cases is large (e.g., hundreds of cases), it is important to establish a higher frequency threshold. In such analyses, some corners may have several cases with greater than 0.5 membership due to measurement or coding errors. In these situations, it is prudent to treat low-frequency causal combinations in the same way as those lacking strong empirical instances altogether (number of cases with greater than 0.5 membership = 0). When the total number of cases in a study is large, the issue is not which combinations have instances (i.e., at least one case with greater than 0.5 membership) but which combinations have enough instances to warrant conducting an assessment of their possible subset relation with the outcome. For example, a researcher's rule might be that there must be at least 5 or at least 10 cases with greater than 0.5 membership in a causal combination in order to proceed with the assessment of the fuzzy subset relation. By contrast, when the total number of cases is small, it is possible for the researcher to gain familiarity with each case, which in turn mitigates the measurement and coding errors that motivate use of a higher threshold.

Assessing the Consistency of Fuzzy Subset Relations

Once the empirically *relevant* causal combinations have been identified using the procedures just described, the next step is to evaluate each combination's *consistency* with the set theoretic relation in question. Which causal combinations are subsets of the outcome? Social science data are rarely perfect, so it is important to assess the *degree* to which the empirical evidence is consistent with the set theoretic relation in question. Ragin (2006b) described a measure of set theoretic consistency based on fuzzy membership scores (see also Kosko, 1993; Smithson & Verkuilen, 2006). The formula is:

Consistency $(X_i \leq Y_i) = \Sigma(\min(X_i, Y_i))/\Sigma(X_i)$

where "min" indicates the selection of the lower of the two values, X_i represents membership scores in a combination of conditions, and Y_i represents membership scores in the outcome. When all of the X_i values are less than or equal to their corresponding Y_i values, the consistency score is 1.00; when there are only a few near misses, the score is slightly less than 1.00; when there are many inconsistent scores, with some X_i values greatly exceeding their corresponding Y_i values, consistency drops below 0.5.[5] This measure of consistency prescribes substantial penalties for *large* inconsistencies but small penalties for near misses (e.g., an X_i score of 0.85 and a Y_i score of 0.80).

Box 5.4
The Criterion of Consistency in Fuzzy Sets, in a Nutshell

The consistency of a fuzzy subset relation, in simple terms, is the degree to which one set is contained within another (all X_i are less than or equal to their corresponding Y_i). When the values of X_i exceed the value of Y_i, then not all of X_i is contained within Y_i. The formula for fuzzy-set consistency takes this into account by not counting the portion of X_i values that exceeds their corresponding Y_i values in the numerator of the formula, while counting these values in the denominator, which is simply the sum of the membership scores in X.

The penultimate column of Table 5.7 reports fuzzy subset consistency scores, using the formula just presented. The assessment is conducted for the four combinations that meet the frequency threshold—the combination must have at least one case with greater than 0.5 membership (see Table 5.6). All 18 cases were included in each consistency assessment, following the pattern shown in Figure 5.1. That is, the assessment of each row (each configuration) uses fuzzy scores for all 18 cases, not just those cases with greater than 0.5 membership in that row. Thus, the evidentiary bases for consistency assessments are much broader in fuzzy-set analyses than in crisp and multi-value analyses. In essence, the consistency scores assess the degree to which the evidence for each combination conforms to the upper triangular pattern shown in Figure 5.1. Note that the consistency of the evidence in Figure 5.1 with the subset relation is 0.98, indicating near perfect consistency.

Constructing the Truth Table

It is a short step from tables like Table 5.7 to crisp-set truth tables appropriate for the Quine–McCluskey minimization procedure (as conducted in Chapter 3 with csQCA). The key determination that must be made is the consistency score to be used as a cutoff value for determining which causal combinations pass fuzzy set theoretic consistency and which do not. Causal combinations with consistency scores at or above the cutoff value are designated fuzzy subsets of the outcome and are coded [1]; those below the cutoff value are not fuzzy subsets and are coded [0].[6]

In effect, the causal combinations that are fuzzy subsets of the outcome delineate the kinds of cases in which the outcome is consistently found (e.g., the kinds of countries that experienced democratic breakdown). It is important to point out, however, that some cases displaying the outcome may be found among configurations with low consistency. This situation corresponds roughly to the existence of "contradictory configurations" in crisp-set analysis, and the same strategies for addressing contradictions discussed in Chapter 3 can be applied in fuzzy-set analyses. Indeed, simple inspection of the consistency values in Table 5.7 reveals that there is a substantial gap in consistency scores between the second consistency score reported (0.84) and the third highest score (0.44). This gap provides an easy basis for differentiating consistent causal combinations from inconsistent combinations, as shown in the last column of Table 5.7, which shows the coding of the outcome for truth table analysis.[7] Together, the first three columns plus the last column of Table 5.7 form a simple truth table appropriate for standard (crisp set) truth table analysis using the Quine–McCluskey algorithm. The results of this truth table analysis are not presented here. Instead, an analysis of a more fully specified truth table is presented below, using five conditions.

The Fuzzy-Set Analysis of Necessary Conditions

One issue not addressed in the preceding discussion is the fuzzy-set analysis of necessary conditions. A necessary condition is a condition that must be present for the outcome to occur, but its presence does not guarantee that occurrence (see also Box 1.3). For example, "state breakdown" is considered by some to be a necessary condition for "social revolution," but the occurrence of state breakdown does not ensure that a social revolution will occur. Indeed, social revolutions are not nearly as common as state breakdowns.

With fuzzy sets, a possible necessary condition is signaled whenever it can be demonstrated that instances of the outcome in question constitute a subset of instances of a condition, as would be the case, for example, with state breakdowns and social revolutions. In formal terms, the consistency of the fuzzy subset relation indicating necessity can be assessed using this formula:

Consistency $(Yi \leq Xi) = \Sigma(\min(Xi,Yi))/\Sigma(Yi)$

which states simply that the consistency of set Y as a subset of set X is their intersection expressed as a proportion of set Y. If all Y values are less than or equal to their corresponding X values, the formula returns a score of 1.0. If many Y values exceed their corresponding X values, then the score returned is substantially less than 1.0. The formula also applies to crisp sets, where the numerator is simply the number of cases where both X and Y are found; the denominator is the number of cases of Y.

It is often useful to check for necessary conditions before conducting the fuzzy truth table procedure. Any condition that passes the test and that "makes sense" as a necessary condition can be dropped from the truth table procedure, which, after all, is essentially an analysis of sufficiency. (This is true for all varieties of QCA—crisp set, multi-value, and fuzzy set.) Of course, the condition identified in this way would be retained for discussion as a necessary condition and should be considered relevant to any sufficient combination of conditions identified through the truth table analysis. In general, a necessary condition can be interpreted as a superset of the outcome, while sufficient conditions (usually, sufficient combinations of conditions) constitute subsets of the outcome.

It is important to point out as well that if a necessary condition is included in a truth table analysis, it is often eliminated from solutions that include logical remainders (i.e., necessary conditions are often eliminated from parsimonious solutions). For example, it is clear from a simple inspection of Table 3.9 that SURVIVAL is a subset of LITERACY (indeed: every time SURVIVAL displays a [1] value ("present"), LITERACY also displays a [1] value ("present")), which in turn might suggest that LITERACY is a necessary condition for SURVIVAL. However, the solution for SURVIVAL (based on Table 3.9) that includes logical remainders (see Formula 4, p. 60) eliminates LITERACY altogether and presents instead a solution with GNPCAP and STABILITY as joint conditions. Thus, it is important to use logical remainders consciously and wisely—to evaluate their appropriateness in any analysis.

Ragin and Sonnett (2004; see also Ragin, 2008) developed a procedure that limits the use of logical remainders, so that only those that are consistent with the researcher's theoretical and substantive knowledge are incorporated into solutions. This procedure is now implemented in FSQCA and can be used for both crisp-set and fuzzy-set analyses. Three solution are produced for each analysis: a "complex" solution (no logical remainders used), a "parsimonious" solution (all logical remainders may be used, without any evaluation of their plausibility), and an "intermediate" solution (only the logical remainders that "make sense" given the researcher's substantive and theoretical knowledge are incorporated into the solution). An important benefit of intermediate solutions is that they will not allow removal of necessary conditions—any condition that is a superset of the outcome and that makes sense as a necessary condition. In general, "intermediate" solutions are superior to both the "complex" and "parsimonious" solutions and should be a routine part of any application of any version of QCA. It is important to point out that whenever researchers evaluate the logical remainders incorporated into a solution (one of the most important "good practices" involved in using QCA) and decide that a logical remainder is implausible and should be excluded from a solution, they are, in effect, deriving an intermediate solution.

APPLICATION OF THE PROCEDURE

To facilitate comparison of the fuzzy-set analysis with the analyses presented in Chapters 3 (csQCA) and 4 (mvQCA), the analysis presented in this section uses all five fuzzy-set conditions shown in Table 5.2: DEVELOPED, URBAN, INDUSTRIAL, LITERATE, and STABLE (they basically correspond, with a few changes in labels, to the raw data initially presented in Table 3.5, p. 51). Two separate analyses will be demonstrated: first using SURVIVED as the outcome, and then using BREAKDOWN as the outcome. The analysis presented below uses all five conditions to enhance comparison with the results of the csQCA analysis.

Analysis With SURVIVED as the Outcome

With five causal conditions, there are 32 (i.e., 2^5) corners to the vector space formed by the fuzzy set causal conditions. These 32 corners correspond to the 32 rows of the crisp truth table formed from the dichotomous versions of these conditions (see Table 3.4, p. 45) and also to the 32 logically possible arguments that can be constructed using five dichotomous causal conditions (see p. 27). While the 18 cases all have some degree of membership in each of the 32 causal combinations, they are, of course, unevenly distributed within the five-dimensional vector space. Table 5.8 shows the distribution of cases across the causal combinations (which also constitute corners of the vector space).

The penultimate column of this table shows the number of cases with greater than 0.5 membership in each combination (causal combinations that fail to meet this frequency threshold of at least one case are not shown). Altogether, this means that there are good instances (i.e., countries with greater than 0.5 membership) of 9 of the 32 logically possible combinations of conditions. The remaining 23 are logical remainders and thus are available as potential counterfactual cases for further logical simplification of the truth table (see Ragin & Sonnett, 2004; Ragin, 2008; and p. 59). Recall that in most fuzzy-set analyses, all cases have some degree of membership in each row. Thus, while it is possible to report which rows have strong instances, as in the first column of the table, it is not possible to assign cases strictly to rows, as is common in csQCA and mvQCA.

The last column of Table 5.8 shows the degree of consistency of each causal combination with the argument that it is a subset of the outcome SURVIVED. In short, this column shows the truth value of the following statement: "Membership in the combination of conditions in this row is a subset of membership in the outcome." The rows have been sorted to show the distribution of consistency scores, which range from 0.22 to 0.90. To prepare this evidence for conventional truth table analysis, it is necessary simply to select a cutoff value for consistency and recode it as a dichotomy.

To derive a solution that is as compatible as possible with the previous analyses (especially the csQCA presented in Chapter 3), a very low cutoff value is first used. If the consistency of the combination as a subset of the outcome is at least 0.70, it is coded as consistent (outcome = [1]); otherwise it is coded inconsistent (outcome = [0]). As in the csQCA, this truth table is first minimized without including logical remainders, which yields the following results (*Formula 1*):

| DEVELOPED * urban * LITERATE * STABLE | + | DEVELOPED * LITERATE * INDUSTRIAL * STABLE | → | SURVIVED |

Cases with strong membership in the first combination: FIN, FRA, IRE, SWE

Cases with strong membership in the second combination: BEL, CZE, NET, UK

This is the same solution that was obtained in the final crisp-set analysis (without logical remainders) presented in Chapter 3 (see Formula 1, p. 57). The two paths to survival share a high level of development, high literacy, and political stability. In essence, the countries with democracies that survived were in the advanced areas of Europe that avoided political instability.

Table 5.8 Distribution of Cases Across Causal Combinations and
Set-Theoretic Consistency of Causal Combinations as Subsets of SURVIVED

Best Instances	DEVELOPED	URBAN	LITERATE	INDUSTRIAL	STABLE	N of cases with > 0.5 membership	Consistency as a subset of SURVIVED
BEL, CZE, NET, UK	1	1	1	1	1	4	0.90
FIN, IRE	1	0	1	0	1	2	0.80
FRA, SWE	1	0	1	1	1	2	0.71
EST	0	0	1	0	1	1	0.53
HUN, POL	0	0	1	0	0	2	0.52
GER	1	1	1	1	0	1	0.45
AUS	1	0	1	1	0	1	0.38
ITA, ROM	0	0	0	0	1	2	0.28
GRE, POR, SPA	0	0	0	0	0	3	0.22

The parsimonious solution (which allows the incorporation of logical remainders, without evaluating their plausibility, into the solution) is as follows (*Formula 2*):

DEVELOPED * STABLE → SURVIVED

Cases with strong membership in this combination: BEL, CZE, FIN, FRA, IRE, NET, SWE, UK

Note that the formula is also the same as the results of the final crisp-set analysis presented in Chapter 3 (with the inclusion of logical remainders; see Formula 4, p. 60). In general, this should not be surprising because the fuzzy sets have been crafted to reflect the dichotomizations used in that analysis, and the threshold for consistency has been set at a very low level, in order to demonstrate continuity with the crisp-set analysis.

As noted previously, it is also possible to derive an intermediate solution, situated in between the complex and the parsimonious solutions, using the researcher's theoretical and substantive knowledge to guide the incorporation of logical remainders (see Ragin, 2008; see also discussion on p. 135). The intermediate solution is (*Formula 3*):

DEVELOPED * LITERATE * STABLE → SURVIVED

Cases with strong membership in this combination: BEL, CZE, FIN, FRA, IRE, NET, SWE, UK

The intermediate solution adds a third condition, LITERACY, to the parsimonious solution. This third condition is included because (a) it can be seen as a necessary condition (SURVIVED is a subset of LITERATE, with a fuzzy set consistency score of 0.99) and (b) the logical remainders that are needed to remove LITERACY (in order to produce the parsimonious solution) run counter to theoretical and substantive knowledge (i.e., which indicates that high levels of literacy should enhance the survival of democracy).

While it is reassuring that the results of the crisp-set analysis can be reproduced using fuzzy sets, it is important to note that that has been possible only by using a relatively low cutoff value (0.70) for set theoretic consistency (the last column of Table 5.8). As explained in Ragin (2008), the fuzzy-set test of consistency is more exacting than its crisp-set counterpart. A case can be more in than out of both the condition and the outcome but still be substantially inconsistent when considered from the viewpoint of fuzzy sets. For example, assume that the score on the condition is 0.95, while the score on the outcome is 0.55. In a crisp-set analysis, both scores would be recoded (via dichotomization) to [1] and thus be considered consistent with a subset relation, while from a fuzzy-set perspective, the outcome score greatly exceeds the condition scores (by a margin of 0.40), which in turn would be considered substantially *inconsistent* with the subset relation.

Applying a more stringent cutoff value to Table 5.8 produces a more narrowly circumscribed formula. For comparison purposes, consider this same analysis using 0.80 as the cutoff value, which accords only the top two rows the 1 outcome. The "intermediate" solution using this more stringent cutoff value is (*Formula 4*):

DEVELOPED * LITERATE * STABLE * (URBAN + industrial) → SURVIVED

In short, using a more stringent cutoff value for fuzzy-set theoretic consistency adds a fourth condition to the intermediate solution derived previously. This fourth condition can be satisfied by having either strong membership in the set of urbanized countries or weak membership in the set of industrial countries.

Analysis With BREAKDOWN as the Outcome

Table 5.9 shows the results of the analysis of the same 5 causal conditions with BREAKDOWN as the outcome. Because the 5 causal conditions are the same, the vector space of causal conditions is unchanged, and the distribution of cases within the vector space also is unchanged. Once again, there are 9 causal combinations with "good instances" (i.e., at least one case with greater than 0.5 membership) and 23 causal combinations lacking good empirical instances.

The key difference between tables 5.9 and 5.8 is in the last column, which in Table 5.9 shows the degree of consistency of each causal combination with the following statement: "Membership in the combination of conditions in this row is a subset of membership in the outcome (BREAKDOWN)." Again the rows have been sorted to show the distribution of the consistency scores. Applying the same cutoff criterion that was applied to the second analysis of Table 5.8 (at least 0.80 consistent; see above on this page) results in a coding of the first six rows as [1] (true) and bottom three rows as [0] (false).

First, we minimize the truth table *without* including the logical remainders, which produces the following minimal formula (*Formula 5*):

developed * urban +   DEVELOPED *   →   BREAKDOWN
* industrial   LITERATE *
                         INDUSTRIAL * stable

Table 5.9 Distribution of Cases Across Causal Combinations and Set-Theoretic Consistency of Causal Combinations as Subsets of BREAKDOWN

Best Instances	DEVELOPED	URBAN	LITERATE	INDUSTRIAL	STABLE	N of cases with >.5 membership	Consistency as a subset of BREAKDOWN
ITA, ROM	0	0	0	0	1	2	1.00
GRE, POR, SPA	0	0	0	0	0	3	0.98
GER	1	1	1	1	0	1	0.98
AUS	1	0	1	1	0	1	0.97
HUN, POL	0	0	1	0	0	2	0.86
EST	0	0	1	0	1	1	0.86
FRA, SWE	1	0	1	1	1	2	0.50
FIN, IRE	1	0	1	0	1	2	0.49
BEL, CZE, NET, UK	1	1	1	1	1	4	0.25

Cases with strong membership in the first combination: EST, GRE, POR, SPA, HUN, POL, ITA, ROM

Cases with strong membership in the second combination: GER, AUS

This minimal formula indicates two paths to democratic breakdown. The first path combines three conditions: low level of development, low urbanization, and low industrialization. In short, this path reveals that democratic breakdown in the inter-war period occurred in some of the least advanced areas of Europe. Countries with very strong membership in this combination include Hungary, Poland, Portugal, and Romania. The second path is quite different; it combines four conditions: high level of development, high literacy, high industrialization, and political instability. Countries with strong membership in this combination are Austria and Germany. These results are not altogether surprising. The conditions used in this illustration are very general and not based on detailed case-oriented study. Still, it is important to point out that the analysis reveals there were two very different paths, thus demonstrating the utility of the method for the investigation of causal complexity.

Next, we minimize again this truth table, this time *with* the inclusion of some logical remainders (see p. 59). This produces the following minimal formula (*Formula 6*), which is much more parsimonious than the previous one:

developed + stable → BREAKDOWN

Cases with strong membership in the first combination: EST, GRE, POR, SPA, HUN, POL, ITA, ROM

Cases with strong membership in the second combination: GER, AUS, GRE, POR, SPA, HUN, POL

Again, there are two paths, but this time the paths are quite simple. Note also that this is the same as the final crisp-set solution presented in Chapter 3 (see Formula 5, p. 61). However, this solution may be considered "too parsimonious" because some of the simplifying assumptions that it incorporates are theoretically or empirically untenable. Using the procedures detailed in Ragin and Sonnett (2004; see also Ragin, 2008, and the discussion on p. 135), it is possible to derive the following intermediate solution (*Formula 7*):

developed * urban * industrial + stable → BREAKDOWN

Cases with strong membership in the first combination: EST, GRE, POR, SPA, HUN, POL, ITA, ROM

Cases with strong membership in the second combination: GER, AUS, GRE, POR, SPA, HUN, POL

The intermediate solution just presented is preferred because it incorporates only the logical remainders that are consistent with theoretical and substantive knowledge. While more complex than the parsimonious solution that precedes it, the intermediate solution gives, in essence, a more complete account of the first group of BREAKDOWN cases. Not only are they less developed, but they combine this aspect with low levels of industrialization and urbanization.

Box 5.5
"Good Practices" (10): Specific to fsQCA

- It is crucially important to use theoretical and substantive (empirical) knowledge, rather than mechanical criteria, to calibrate degree of membership in sets; assigning fuzzy membership scores is interpretive and involves both theoretical knowledge and case-oriented research, based on available data.

- Researchers should develop an explicit rationale for their specifications of full membership (1), full nonmembership (0), and the crossover point (0.5).

- If converting interval or ratio-scale data to fuzzy sets, use the calibration procedure that is built into the software (see Ragin, 2008).

- When examining the truth table spreadsheet showing consistency scores (as in Tables 5.8 and 5.9), remember that instances of the outcome may be included in rows with low consistency; treat these as contradictory configurations and use the procedures for resolving them, as presented in this book (see Chapters 3 and 4, and especially Box 3.6).

- If you explicitly hypothesize necessary conditions, test for them before conducting truth table analysis; set a high consistency threshold for necessary conditions and eliminate any condition that is found to be necessary from the truth table analysis (i.e., address such conditions separately, as necessary conditions).

- When selecting frequency thresholds, take into account not only total number of cases, but also the nature and quality of the evidence; generally, the larger the total N, the higher the frequency threshold.

- When selecting consistency thresholds, choose a threshold as close to 1.0 as is feasible, given the nature of the data; look for gaps in the distribution of consistency scores; avoid using a threshold below 0.75.

- Derive all three solutions in each analysis—"complex" (no logical remainders used), "parsimonious" (logical remainders used without evaluating their plausibility), and "intermediate" (logical remainders restricted to those that are most plausible).

CONCLUSION

By using fuzzy sets, researchers can address a key limitation of csQCA—namely, the necessity to dichotomize conditions. Beyond solving this fundamental limitation, the use of fuzzy sets offers a number of additional benefits.

First, with fuzzy sets researchers are able to implement a more precise and demanding assessment of set theoretic consistency (and thus of sufficiency and necessity) than is possible using crisp sets or multi-value sets. With fuzzy sets, the calculation of consistency takes into account degree of membership, and thus many cases that would be defined as consistent using crisp sets or multi-value sets are defined as inconsistent using fuzzy sets. For example, a case with a score of 0.95 on a condition and 0.55 on the outcome is considered consistent from a crisp-set point of view because dichotomization would recode both scores to [1] and thus this case would satisfy $X_i \leq Y_i$ (X is a subset of Y). From a fuzzy-set perspective, however, the two scores are dramatically inconsistent with $X_i \leq Y_i$ because 0.95 is 0.40 units greater than 0.55—a substantial gap (X is not a subset of Y). Because of this higher consistency standard, the results of a fuzzy-set analysis will generally be more empirically circumscribed than the results of a crisp-set or a multi-value analysis.

Second, not only is the fuzzy-set assessment of consistency more demanding, but it is also more encompassing. In crisp-set and multi-value analyses, a causal combination is assessed using only those cases that exactly conform to it—the cases that reside in a specific row of the truth table. If the cases in a given row all agree in displaying the outcome, then the sufficiency of that combination for the outcome is established. With fuzzy sets, by contrast, each case can have partial membership in every row of the truth table (because each row represents a different combination of conditions). Thus, the assessment of the consistency of each row with sufficiency involves all cases included in the analysis and focuses on the degree to which the plot of membership in the outcome against membership in a row (again, using all cases) produces the upper triangular pattern that is characteristic of the subset relationship. Thus, in fsQCA the assessment of each combination of conditions is based on the pattern observed across all cases, not on a small subset of cases (as in csQCA and mvQCA).

Third, in contrast to mvQCA, the use of fuzzy sets does not exacerbate the problem of limited diversity. While useful, mvQCA's key drawback is that it greatly expands the number of logically possible combinations of conditions as each new category is added. For example, four conditions conceptualized as dichotomies yields 16 ($= 2^4$) logically possible combinations. These same four conditions converted to trichotomies, a seemingly modest step, yields 81 ($= 3^4$) logically possible combinations. Converting these four dichotomies to fuzzy sets, however, yields the same 16 logically possible combinations of conditions generated in their use as dichotomous conditions. The key difference between fuzzy sets and crisp sets is that these 16 combinations are the 16 corners of a four-dimensional property space. At an analytic level, however, the number of relevant causal combinations is the same. Each corner of the vector space constitutes, in effect, a different ideal-typical combination of conditions.

Key Points

- fsQCA retains key aspects of the general QCA approach, while allowing the analysis of phenomena that vary by level or degree.

- The fsQCA procedure presented in this chapter provides a bridge between fuzzy sets and conventional truth table analysis by constructing a Boolean truth table summarizing the results of multiple fuzzy-set analyses; this procedure differs from the fuzzy-set procedure described in Ragin (2000).

- Fuzzy membership scores (i.e., the varying degree to which cases belong to sets) combine qualitative and quantitative assessment.

- The key set theoretic relation in the study of causal complexity is the *subset relation*; cases can be precisely assessed in terms of their degree of consistency with the subset relation, usually with the goal of establishing that a combination of conditions is sufficient for a given outcome.

- The assessment of sufficiency is especially stringent in fsQCA, as it involves a more exacting standard and a more encompassing approach, involving all cases in the assessment of each combination of conditions.

- "Logical remainders" are important in fsQCA; they can be avoided altogether ("complex" solution), used without explicit evaluation of their plausibility ("parsimonious" solution), or used selectively, based on the researcher's substantive and theoretical knowledge ("intermediate" solution).

Key Complementary Readings

Klir et al. (1997), Ragin (2000, 2006b, 2008); Schneider & Wagemann (2007, forthcoming), Smithson & Verkuilen (2006).

NOTES

1. The typical mvQCA application involves a preponderance of dichotomous conditions and one or two trichotomous conditions—see Box 4.4 and p. 78.

2. For more details on the calibration of fuzzy sets, see Ragin (2007, 2008), Schneider and Wagemann (2007, forthcoming), and Verkuilen (2005).

3. If the membership scores in a causal combination are all very low, then it is very easy for that combination to satisfy the subset relation signaling sufficiency (where scores in the causal combination must be less than or equal to scores in the outcome). However, the consistency with the subset relation in such instances is meaningless, for the researcher lacks good instances of the combination (i.e., cases with greater than 0.5 membership in the causal combination).

4. Note that if a case has 0.5 membership in any condition, then its maximum membership in a causal combination that includes that condition is only 0.5. Thus, any case coded 0.5 will not be "closest" to any single corner of the vector space defined by the conditions.

5. NB: when the formula for the calculation of fuzzy-set theoretic consistency is applied to crisp-set data, it returns the simple proportion of consistent cases. Thus, the formula can be applied to crisp and fuzzy data alike.

6. Rows not meeting the frequency threshold selected by the investigator (based on the number of cases with greater than 0.5 membership) are treated as "logical remainder" rows. Designating such rows as logical remainders is justified on the grounds that the evidence relevant to these combinations is not substantial enough to permit an evaluation of set theoretic consistency.

7. Ragin (2000) demonstrates how to incorporate probabilistic criteria into the assessment of the consistency of subset relations, and these same criteria can be modified for use here. The probabilistic test requires a benchmark value (e.g., 0.80 consistency) and an alpha (e.g., 0.05 significance). In the interest of staying close to the evidence, it is often useful simply to sort the consistency scores in descending order and observe whether a substantial gap occurs in the upper ranges of consistency scores. In general, the cutoff value should not be less than 0.75; a cutoff value of 0.80 or higher is generally recommended. While the measure of consistency used here can range from 0.0 to 1.0, scores between 0.0 and 0.75 indicate the existence of substantial inconsistency.

6

A Commented Review of Applications

Sakura Yamasaki

Benoît Rihoux

Goals of This Chapter

After reading this chapter, you should:

- Understand how key steps of QCA techniques have been dealt with, and concrete difficulties solved, in some selected "real life" applications.

- Have a more precise view of both "good practices" and inventive ways of using QCA techniques.

- Be able to read published applications and assess their quality with regard to the key practical steps.

While the majority of QCA applications are csQCA, its two sibling techniques, fuzzy sets and mvQCA, have been rapidly catching up since their respective launchings in 2000 and 2004. The structure of this chapter follows the chronological link between the three techniques. The review of applications using csQCA emphasizes some crucial aspects of the technique, such as dichotomization, the handling of contradictory configurations, and the inclusion of logical remainders. As for fuzzy sets and mvQCA, we have selected both "standard" and technically creative applications. In doing so, our goal is to expose how various scholars have dealt, in practice, with the issues discussed in the previous chapters (see Chapters 2–5).

csQCA

Several hundred studies have thus far applied csQCA in a wide range of disciplines, from sociology and political science (most applications), to the life sciences going through economics, management, criminology, psychology, geography, and others (see p. 179). This section is framed along a number of issues that are perceived, for anyone who has gone through the challenge of using csQCA, as particularly crucial and delicate, because much of the quality of the analysis depends on how these issues are addressed and resolved: case and condition selection, dichotomization, contradictory configurations, logical remainders, and contradictory simplifying assumptions.

Case Selection

As cases constitute the fundamental focus of any comparative analysis, the case selection process requires more attention in comparative analyses than in large-N statistical applications or in single case studies (Geddes, 2003; Collier, Mahoney, & Seawright, 2004; Griffin, Botsko, Wahl, & Isaac, 1991). Indeed, given the case-sensitivity of any comparative analysis, the rigor of this preliminary step is of primary importance for the interpretation of the results (see also p. 20 and p. 155).

Scouvart (2006; Scouvart et al., 2007) sought to uncover regularities in the causes of the Brazilian rainforest deforestation along roads. Her method of case selection involved a three-step process. First, she identified the area of investigation by gradually narrowing it down, from the larger Brazilian Amazonian Basin to the specific "agricultural borders of the deforestation arch" in the Brazilian Amazonian forest. These border areas witness the most acute forms of deforestation and share several characteristics, such as the presence of human activities (migrants and settlers) and the existence of long structuring roads, while differing in their ecosystems. Scouvart also justified the delineation of her area of investigation through the abundance of existing scientific sources, which were central to her meta-analysis, the homogeneity of the political and socioeconomic context, the homogeneity of human activities, and the omnipresence of roads whose role could thus be controlled for.

In a second step, Scouvart layered the area of investigation through three historical periods. This temporal sequencing is necessary due to the "important evolution of human context" and the changes in "governmental policies, macro-economic and political contexts, and the interests and motivations of various groups of actors" (2006, p. 99). She then explained why the selected periods constitute three different phases of the deforestation contexts in Brazil.

Finally, Scouvart operationalized her theoretical, geographical, and temporal area of investigation by providing an exact definition of what she saw as a *case* in her analysis:

> a zone situated on the agricultural border of the deforestation arch in the Brazilian Amazon, along a national road or a State, observed during a given period in relation to the general context of the study (Brazilian political context) and having been

the object of active research by a multidisciplinary team of experts who are reachable and willing to collaborate. (2006, p. 101)

Eventually, seven zones were selected as cases. Scouvart insisted on the fact that these cases had been *constructed* and not randomly selected as is often the case in formalized geographical science. The seven selected zones carefully cover the geographical diversity of the deforestation process. This is in line with the general emphasis of QCA: "beyond the issues of relative frequencies, of distribution and of case representativeness, QCA emphasizes the diversity of situations and of causal structures" (2006, p. 104, fn7). Scouvart added a diachronic aspect to her study by considering these seven cases through three different time periods.

All in all, Scouvart's detailed description of her case selection process reminds us how crucial this step is in any comparative design, let alone in a formalized technique such as csQCA. Cases are not "given" or randomly selected as in statistical techniques but carefully defined and chosen so as to maximize diversity on factors of interest and to minimize variation on contextual conditions.

Selection of Conditions

In an oft-cited article, Amenta and Poulsen (1994) identified five approaches to the selection of conditions in csQCA—actually their arguments can be expanded to the other QCA techniques as well.

Box 6.1
Six[1] Approaches to Selection of Conditions in QCA

- The *comprehensive* approach, where the full array of possible factors are considered in an iterative process

- The *perspective* approach, where a set of conditions representing two or three theories are tested in the same model

- The *significance* approach, where the conditions are selected on the basis of statistical significance criteria

- The *second look* approach, where the researcher adds one or several conditions that are considered as important although dismissed in a previous analysis[2]

- The *conjunctural* approach (advocated by Amenta & Poulsen), where conditions are selected on the basis of "theories that are conjunctural or combinatorial in construction and that predict multiple causal combinations for one outcome" (1994, p. 29)

- The *inductive* approach, where conditions are mostly selected on the basis of case knowledge and not on existing theories

Below, we exemplify each of these strategies with selected published applications.

Rihoux (2001) looked at factors influencing major organizational change among 14 Green political parties in 12 Western European countries. Condition selection followed an iterative process, starting with an open model of organizational change and taking into account 26 potential conditions. This clearly exemplifies the *comprehensive* approach. Actually, in a prior step, Rihoux had tested two of the most authoritative theories with csQCA, but these tests produced a very high proportion of contradictory configurations. This led him to combine the conditions from both theories (implementing, in fact, the *perspective* approach as well), plus some other conditions from the main theories and models drawn from the literature in order to perform csQCA.

Through many preliminary tests, in which he had to redefine and re-operationalize many conditions, Rihoux eventually obtained an "operational model" that was both parsimonious enough and free of contradictory configurations. Six out of the 13 initial conditions were kept in the model: a major electoral success, a major electoral defeat, access to governing institutions (Parliament or government), a shift in the dominant faction in favor of a "modernizing" orientation, an increase in organizational size, and, conversely, a decrease in organizational size. Some of these conditions (the last one, for instance) are aggregates of some of the initial 26 conditions. The limitation of such a comprehensive approach to variable selection is that it can be (very) time-consuming. However, it has the advantage of lowering the risk of omitted variables.

Schneider and Wagemann's (2006) approach was slightly different from a perfect illustration of Amenta and Poulsen's *statistical significance* approach.[3] They used a formalized discrimination technique, but since they used fsQCA in a two-step process (see below), their approach was more endogenous and therefore more in compliance with the fundamental ontological differences between statistical and configurational approaches.

Given that the number of possible combinations increases exponentially in QCA as the number of conditions increase, "limited diversity" is a recurring issue (see p. 27). Schneider and Wagemann divide the Boolean minimization into two steps, based on the distinction between "remote" and "proximate" conditions. Remote conditions are "relatively stable over time" (p. 760, for all quotes in this paragraph) and "their origin is often also remote in the time and/or space from the outcome to be explained," while proximate conditions "vary over time and are subject to changes introduced by actors." The distinction between remote versus proximate conditions is "not only related to space and time, but, first and foremost, to the causal impact that is assumed." The conceptual distinction thus keeps some degree of flexibility and "depends on various factors, such as the research question, the research design, or the way the dependent variable is framed." In a first step, only the remote conditions are analyzed, including the logical remainders. The (underspecified) broad combinations of conditions that are derived in this manner are then "mixed" with proximate factors for a second step analysis, which does not include logical remainders.

Schneider and Wagemann applied their two-step approach to the analysis of factors leading to the consolidation of democracy in 32 relatively "new" democracies. They considered six remote conditions: level of economic development, level of education, degree of ethnolinguistic homogeneity, distance from the West, degree of previous democratic experience, and extent of communist past. The 32 cases were coded as combinations of fuzzy membership scores on each of the remote conditions and on the outcome variable, the presence of a consolidated democracy. After a transformation of the fuzzy score truth table into a crisp truth table (see Chapter 5), Schneider and Wagemann ran the Boolean minimization. The minimal formula including logical remainders produced a set of three conditions, each one of which was sufficient on its own: a high level of economic development, a high degree of ethnolinguistic homogeneity, and the absence of a communist past. The other three remote conditions were thus removed since they could be considered "logically redundant." The second step of the analysis called for three analyses: Each of the retained remote condition was "mixed" with the three proximate conditions—namely, the executive format, the type of electoral law, and the degree of party fragmentation. Each set of four conditions was then minimized, this time without the inclusion of logical remainders.

This two-step analysis thus provided a parsimonious but theoretically rich and solid model to be tested. If the analysis had been conducted in a single step—i.e., including all 10 conditions—there would have been 1,024 (i.e., 2^{10}) logically possible combinations, whereas this two-step analysis limited them to only 16 (i.e., 2^4) for each of the three analyses in the second step. This approach thus proceeded with the selections of conditions in a way very similar to the significance approach identified by Amenta and Poulsen (1994), but with the merit of avoiding the danger of "fail[ing] to observe QCA's epistemology of combinations" (p. 28).

Osa and Corduneanu-Huci's (2003) study of social movements in authoritarian regimes exemplifies the "second look" approach. They explored whether the Political Opportunity Structure (POS) (Eisinger, 1973; Kitschelt, 1986; Tarrow, 1994) can be successfully applied to non-democratic states. They test this concept on 24 cases of occurrence/non-occurrence of mobilization in 15 authoritarian countries. Four conditions were selected to represent the POS, based on Tarrow's formulation (1994): level of state repression, elite divisions, presence of influential allies, and media access/information flow.

However, the truth table built on this model displayed many contradictory configurations and the minimized formulas did not allow coherent interpretations. Consequently, the authors decided to incorporate the dimension of social networks into the concept of the POS in order to consolidate their model. The new model with five conditions reduced the number of contradictory configurations from nearly half the total number of configurations to just one configuration. In the final minimal formula, the role of the level of repression and of social networks came to the fore. More specifically, increasing and decreasing state repressions provoke opposite effects on mobilization depending on their temporal concordance with protest cycles, and social networks are seen as having a stronger mobilizing effect on people in authoritarian countries than in democratic countries.

In the same way as the endogenous "significance approach" avoided some of the pitfalls identified by Amenta and Poulsen (1994), this endogenous "second look approach" also safely bypassed the warning that "unless specific combinational effects are expected beforehand, logic dictates that this strategy will degenerate into the comprehensive approach" (p. 29).

Amenta and Poulsen's fifth, *conjunctural theory* approach, has the merit of "taking seriously QCA as a method, exploiting its ability to produce conjunctural results that are causally heterogeneous" (1994, p. 29). It is also in line with the recent debate in comparative historical analysis according to which there is a need to bridge the theoretical complexity inherent in macro-comparative studies of social phenomena and the methodology used to analyze it (Hall, 2003).

Amenta, Caren, and Olasky (2005) followed this approach in their application of csQCA to the study of the impact of social movements on the generosity of old age pension schemes in 48 U.S. states. They selected six conditions based on their theoretical hypothesis that social movements can have an impact on social policy only when combined with a favorable political and institutional situation or with assertive action on the part of social movement organizations. The institutional characteristics were represented by two conditions, POLLTAX and ADMIN, the political situation by two other conditions, PATRONAGE and DEMOCRATIC, and the social movements' action by two last conditions, MOBILIZED and ASSERTIVE. Following the authors' conjunctural hypothesis about movement impact on generous social programs, "in structurally conducive and politically favorable short-term situations, only challenger mobilization is needed to produce collective benefits. When short-term political conditions are less favorable, more assertive action is the best strategy. This type of activity is sufficient to bring results" (p. 528). This conjunctural hypothesis was also expressed in Boolean terms, a required step for a hypothesis testing using Boolean algorithms:

H = polltax * patronage (MOBILIZED * (DEMOCRAT + ADMIN) + ASSERTIVE)

However, the authors did not proceed to the formalized hypothesis testing and instead evaluated the evidence in a non-formalized way, assessing the fit between their obtained minimized formula and their hypothesis. They exploited the potential of csQCA to address conjunctural research questions that were otherwise difficult to answer through inferential statistical techniques. Since csQCA evaluates the combinations of conditions that are linked to an outcome, they were careful when formulating their research question: "Instead of asking whether movements are generally influential or whether certain aspects of movements are always influential, ... we ask *under what conditions* are social movements likely to be influential" (2005, p. 517, emphasis is ours).

Finally, in qualitative analysis, researchers are sometimes confronted by a paucity of existing theories concerning a particular dimension of their cases. In this context, conditions cannot be selected solely through a deductive approach but rather through an *inductive approach,* based on the in-depth case knowledge of the researcher. This knowledge adds an "edge" to the general knowledge offered by preexisting theories and allows the construction of a more articulated explanatory model, specific to the pool of cases considered.

Several applications have explicitly adopted such an iterative (inductive–deductive) approach to guide their selection of conditions. Clément (2003, 2005a, 2005b) began her analysis of the process of state collapse by observing that there is no appropriate single theory that could be called upon to explain state collapse in former Yugoslavia, Lebanon, and Somalia. She then "casted the net wide to include related theories of state instability (e.g., war, revolutions, social mobilization, secession)" (p. 8), and based on her in-depth knowledge of the historical process leading to a state collapse in each of the three countries, she built a model of four conditions that are individually insufficient to produce state collapse: "It takes their combination to reach that outcome" (p. 8). These four conditions are an inconsistent international environment, a sharp economic decline or substantial growth, mobilized advanced groups, and an improper cooptation of the political elite. As such, the occurrence of *all* four conditions *together* was hypothesized to trigger state collapse.

This sixth approach to the selection of conditions comes closest to the comprehensive approach of Amenta et al., but the former appears to be more appropriate when the number of cases to be analyzed is relatively low. On the one hand, existing theories relevant to the small number of cases under investigation might prove more difficult to identify than when a larger number of cases representing a more general population is studied. On the other hand, it is easier to extract fine-grained hypotheses when the case knowledge is deeper and hence when the number of cases is relatively small. Finally, the inductive approach to the selection of conditions partly joins the conjunctural theory approach advocated by Amenta et al. As in the case of Clément's (2005a, 2005b) analysis of state collapse, conjunctural relationships among conditions can be more intuitively hypothesized based on case knowledge than on the basis of existing theories.

Threshold Setting (Dichotomization)

Besides the methodological debate around the issue of dichotomization (see p. 148), there are basically two ways to set a threshold for a condition in QCA: mechanically and theoretically (see also pp. 42, 76, 89). The following applications illustrate each of these approaches to threshold setting.

Redding and Viterna (1999) attempted to explain the relative success of Left-Libertarian parties in 18 Western democracies during the 1980s and the 1990s, operationalized as an index of electoral success. They extracted five potential conditions from the existing literature: material wealth, measured by the GDP per capita; economic security, measured by a high degree of social security expenditure; a high degree of labor corporatism; a high degree of national government formation by leftist parties; and the presence of a proportional system of representation.

To dichotomize the conditions, values for each case were assigned using a clustering technique suggested by Ragin (1994). In short, this technique builds a five-dimensional (as there are five conditions) space with 32 corners (i.e., 2^5 possible combinations). After having standardized the measurement of the conditions, the values for each case represent the point coordinates within that five-dimensional space, and "the clustering algorithm is used to measure the distance between these point coordinates and the pre-established cluster corners" (Redding & Viterna, p. 497). The cases are then scored on each condition according to their closest cluster corner.

Such a mechanical technique of threshold setting is not based in either theoretical or substantive knowledge. However, Redding and Viterna argued that this method represents a "considerable improvement over strategies that rely on the median or some 'natural' breaks in the data to establish what counts as a 0 or a 1 for each variable" (p. 498). And indeed, many existing csQCA applications dichotomize interval-level conditions using the median or mean values as cutoff points. Moreover, Redding and Viterna argued that compared to theoretically informed dichotomization procedures, "cases are assigned their dichotomous values through precise, replicable calculations of the relative fit of individual case values to a particular row of the truth table" (p. 498).

By contrast, Varone, Rothmayr, and Montpetit (2006) adopted a purely qualitative approach to threshold setting. They examined 11 countries in which biopolicies range from restrictive to permissive in their design. They defined three outcome variables: restrictive policy design, intermediary policy design, and permissive policy design. For example, Germany, Norway, and Switzerland are classified as having a restrictive Assisted Reproductive Technology (ART) policy, because

> in these countries, many techniques are prohibited or, at the very least, strictly regulated with requirements for licensing and reporting. . . . They also prohibit several techniques—namely egg donation, pre-implantation diagnostics and embryo donation. . . . Embryo research is fully or almost prohibited. (p. 320)

On the other hand, countries such as Belgium, Canada, Italy, and the United States presented cases of a permissive policy design in terms of ART policy, since

> almost everything is permitted when some procedural rules are respected. . . . A very broad range of techniques may be practiced. Research is restricted insofar as reproductive cloning is prohibited in Italy and in some states in the United States, and is discouraged by a voluntary moratorium in Canada. . . . Governance of ART is mainly left to private regulation—that is, the self-regulation of physicians and health care providers. (p. 321)

The other four countries (France, the Netherlands, the United Kingdom, and Spain) were tagged as "intermediary" along the permissive–restrictive continuum of ART policy design. From this, it is already obvious that no single numerical variable had been used to dichotomize each of the outcome variables. Rather, the many existing regulations and their strength had been examined in a country-by-country manner, and this qualitative assessment formed the basis of their trichotomization.

Their five explanatory conditions were also dichotomized through a similar qualitative strategy. However, for matter of space, it was not possible for the authors to justify the coding of a condition for each country separately.[4] Hence, for each condition, Varone et al. selected two cases that stand closest to some "ideal–typical" category of that condition and explicated their coding justification based upon these two cases. For instance, the "Mobilization of interest groups" condition indicated "the degree of organization and mobilization of the various final beneficiaries of the policy design" (p. 328). They expected the ART policy design to be permissive in countries in which there was little or no mobilization from these interest groups, and by contrast, they expected to see a restrictive policy design to be in place in those countries that experienced substantial mobilization from these interest groups. The two cases Varone et al. chose as their ideal types were Switzerland (very strong mobilization; coded 0) and Spain (almost no mobilization; coded 1). The (non-)mobilization of interest groups and the reasons for this were then described for each country in an in-depth historical manner. In Switzerland, the use of popular direct democracy in order to counter the government's more permissive policy lines resulted in a restrictive ART federal law in 1998. By contrast, and quite surprisingly, Spain, in spite of a strong religious basis in its population, implemented one of the most liberal ART policies and experienced almost no protest from the church or other interest groups. The authors attributed this to historical and contextual reasons, where the Catholic community "failed to adopt a coherent strategy and could not mobilize sufficient resources" (p. 329) because of an overloaded agenda (anti-abortion, religion in education issues, etc.) and the complexity of the policy itself. The political parties with a Catholic basis were also described as having been stymied by their lack of capacity at the time the law was passed.

Once again, as for the outcome variables, there were no quantitative measures to identify a clear threshold for the dichotomization of the conditions: Instead, Varone et al. adopted qualitative and historical knowledge-based criteria for the dichotomization procedure. Although this type of strategy indeed does not ensure replicability (see p. 14), it offers a much stronger empirical justification, given its anchor in case knowledge, and this added value might be most useful when the link between the csQCA minimal formulas and the cases is reestablished at the end of the analysis.

Dealing With Contradictory Configurations

As explained previously, contradictory configurations occur when cases with identical values on relevant conditions display different values on the outcome variable (see p. 48). Eight strategies were identified to address this issue (see Box 3.6). Here, we pursue this discussion by revisiting some of these strategies and examining other options, as well.

First, let us examine again the "probabilistic" strategy (strategy 8 in Box 3.6), in which the value of the outcome variable is recoded into the value that is more frequent. This option, which has often been applied (e.g., Amenta et al., 2005; Chan, 2003), has the merit of being the most intuitive and quick one where there is no possibility to go back to the cases or to theory, but it runs counter to the main argument of QCA that the relative frequency of cases within a configuration should not be the main focus.

Also in the vein of a more probabilistic approach, another way to treat contradictions has been developed by Roscigno and Hodson (2004; Hodson & Roscigno, 2004), in their meta-analysis of organizational ethnographies. For each configuration of observed cases, they consider the relative frequency of the cases with [1] and with [0] outcomes, respectively, and then use a conventional statistical method (t-tests) to make comparisons between the distribution of outcomes for that configuration on the one hand and that of the outcomes for cases not captured by the configuration on the other hand. With this technique, they are able to demonstrate that, from a statistical—i.e., probabilistic—perspective, some of the contradictory configurations that would otherwise be excluded from a standard csQCA minimization procedure can be resolved, at least to a certain extent.

There are still other strategies, not listed in Box 3.6 because, as far as we know, they have so far not been tested in real-life applications. One of them consists in including all contradictory configurations in the minimization procedure. For example, to explain the occurrence of coup d'états, configurations that led to both occurrence and nonoccurrence of coup d'états will be included in the minimization, and vice versa for the minimization of nonoccurrence of coup d'états. This logic of full inclusion is to be employed when *all* possible causes of the outcome are to be identified, as opposed to when *all* possible causes *minus* those leading to the nonoccurrence of the outcome are sought. Ragin (1987) qualifies this strategy as one of full inclusion of complexity, since every single possible explanatory path is taken into consideration (pp. 116–117). Yet another strategy, suggested by Ragin (1987), consists in coding all contradictory configurations as logical remainders and then letting the software code them either [0] outcome cases or [1] outcome cases according to their minimizing capacities.

A most fruitful way to solve contradictory configurations is to *combine* the strategies outlined above. For instance, in his study of causes of Japanese peasant revolutions, Nomiya (2001) identified three contradictory configurations. One of them corresponded to 6 cases of occurrence of a peasant revolution and 57 cases of nonoccurrence. Based on the intensity of the imbalance between positive and negative cases, Nomiya decided to code this row as a [0] outcome configuration. Hence, he used the probabilistic approach for the resolution of the contradictory configuration. The two remaining contradictory configurations, however, called for a less intuitive resolution, since the number of cases leading respectively to a positive outcome and to a negative outcome were more or less similar. In these cases, Nomiya tested both possibilities—i.e., he minimized the truth table with these configurations coded as [1] on the outcome and then with these same configurations coded [0]. Nomiya clarified the different meanings of both strategies as follows: The exclusion of the contradictory configurations from the [1] outcome minimization (i.e., they are coded as [0] outcome configurations) yields a minimal formula that identifies conditions that *strictly* lead to peasant revolutions, while the inclusion of the contradictory configurations in the [1] outcome minimization (i.e., they are coded as [1] outcome configurations) yields a minimal formula that identifies conditions that *possibly* lead to peasant revolutions (see also Ragin, 1995, on this method of addressing contradictions). In short, the first formula offered a rather exclusive set of explanatory factors, while the second formula offered a more inclusive perspective on explanatory factors. Indeed, Nomiya obtained two slightly different minimal formulas and confronted them with his research hypotheses. He had hypothesized a joint effect of two conditions (economic shift and political instability) on the occurrence of peasant revolutions. However, neither formula included the necessity of these two joint conditions for peasant revolutions. Consequently, he rejected the hypothesis that both economic and political shifts are simultaneously necessary for the occurrence of peasant revolutions.

Nomiya's combination of strategies illustrates the need and possibility of flexible resolution by the user according to the "type" of the contradictory configurations. His testing of both ways of coding the contradictions can also be viewed as a test of robustness. Moreover, since both coding choices (inclusion with and exclusion from the [1] outcome minimization) are conceptually clarified, the interpretation of the two diverging formulas is facilitated.

Using another combination of strategies, Fischer et al. (2006) ended up removing the two [1] outcome cases from the contradictory configuration of their truth table, hence leaving a "clean" row with 24 [0] outcome cases. Thus at first sight it seems they were simply applying the "probabilistic" strategy. However, the authors proceeded to a very careful and thorough disentanglement of the possible sources of the contradiction and identified the most probable causes before casting the final decision to remove the two positive cases. First, they eliminated the possibility that the contradiction was due to a coding error by checking the cases again. Second, they went back to the two problematic cases, into their specific historical context, and identified what differentiates these two cases from the other 24 cases. The two cases were thoroughly described and analyzed in search for any omitted variables. As a result, Fischer et al. uncovered a potential omitted variable: the intensity of a crisis in terms of number of aggravating events within a period of time (leading to the resignation of a minister, the outcome variable). Moreover, they also stressed the "stunning likeness of the first and the second [cases] with respect to cause and content" (p. 727). They then considered including a time dimension in the analysis, in the hope that this might discriminate the two problematic cases from the 24 other cases of the contradiction, but they "did not find any general evidence for a threshold effect. The simple inclusion of a variable 'time' thus does not resolve our problem" (p. 728). It is only at the end of this meticulous process of contradiction solving that the authors decided to remove the two problematic cases from the analysis: "Although this is only the second-best option, we consider it justifiable because the number of dropped cases is very small and the theoretical anomaly cannot be eliminated by going back to them" (p. 728).

In conclusion, contradictory configurations are one of the most challenging features of csQCA because they force the user to stop and think about the robustness of the model. That is why contradictions are also one of the self-strengthening tools of csQCA. Dealing with contradictions in the most thorough and transparent way possible not only enhances the scientific quality of the analysis but also is a sign of a real understanding of the purpose of csQCA (see also Chapter 7).

Inclusion of Logical Remainders

As explained above (p. 59), logical remainders lie at the core of the Boolean minimization procedure. The purpose of this section is to present csQCA applications that discuss the "nuts and bolts" of logical remainders with regard to different degrees of inclusion but also vis-à-vis statistical techniques and more qualitative methods.

Stokke (2004) made a strong case of csQCA and its treatment of "assumptions about the non-existing combinations of the modeled conditions" compared to how they are handled in classical statistical techniques and in more qualitative methods such as narrative analysis. By contrast to statistical analyses, which "often make strong assumption about homogeneity, additivity and linearity," "simplifying assumptions are not made at the outset" in QCA and "when such assumptions are introduced, the researcher is able to *specify* them in substantive terms and thus evaluate their plausibility" (p. 107, emphasis in original). On the other hand, "narrative comparativists would never be able to conduct thought experiments of the type . . . with the same level of accuracy and transparency" as in QCA (p. 108).

To demonstrate this, Stokke showed how it is possible to have varying degrees of inclusion of logical remainders. Since he had 5 conditions for 10 cases, he admitted that "the limitations on diversity in the present data is considerable," even if they were "hardly greater than in most narratively structured comparison" (p. 107). After a first analysis without the inclusion of any logical remainders, he produced the minimal formula in which all logical remainders are potentially considered for inclusion—i.e., the most parsimonious minimal formula. Stokke examined the theoretical implications of this minimal formula, which appeared to be coherent. However, he noted that several assumptions needed to be accepted in order to jump from the formula before inclusion of logical remainders to the one after their inclusion. He listed the simplifying assumptions (see p. 61) that have been included in the minimization procedure and assessed their theoretical plausibility vis-à-vis the outcome. This led him to identify some assumptions whose value on one specific condition could cast some doubts on their causal relationship with the outcome. Hence, he decided that "a more prudent approach would then be to remove those simplifying assumptions that harbour the claim that success [outcome variable] is possible without commitments [absence of a condition]" (p. 108). By doing so, he obtained a minimal formula that was less general than the one with full inclusion of logical remainders but still more general than the one with full exclusion of logical remainders. Stokke thus arrived at an "intermediate" generalization with a stronger theoretical basis than that of a generalization with full inclusion of logical remainders.

This theoretically informed inclusion of logical remainders joins the idea developed in Ragin and Sonnett (2004; see also Ragin & Rihoux, 2004a; Ragin, 2008) where the authors differentiated between logical remainders for which it is relatively "easy" to assign a given outcome value (because of clear theoretical expectations) and logical remainders for which it is "difficult" to assign a given outcome value (see illustration: pp. 110–118). This strategy of informed inclusion/exclusion of logical remainders has the advantage of strengthening QCA's claim to generalization because it avoids a major pitfall of both case-oriented and variable-oriented research by requiring the specification of the assumptions that are made regarding non-observed cases (see, however, an opposite argument on p. 152). Real-life applications of this strategy have been made by Grassi (2004), in his analysis of democratic consolidation in Latin American political systems, and by Clément (2004) in her exploration on the causes of state collapse in Somalia, Lebanon, and former Yugoslavia.

Dealing With Contradictory Simplifying Assumptions

Recall that a contradictory simplifying assumption (CSA) occurs when the same logical remainder is used both in the minimization of the [1] outcome configurations *and* in the minimization of the [0] outcome configurations, thereby making contradictory assumptions regarding the outcome value of that logical remainder (see p. 64).

At the logical level, the presence of CSAs in an analysis is a flaw that should be corrected. In many applications of QCA, the [0] outcome minimal formula can be interpreted just as the [1] outcome minimal formula—i.e., as the (causal) relationship between several conditions in the presence or absence of which a social phenomenon (outcome) is observed or not observed. However, this implies the assumption that the presence and the absence of a phenomenon (outcome) can be explained with identical conditions. In that case, CSAs become a problem when the same logical remainders are assumed to *explain* both cases with a [1] outcome and cases with a [0] outcome.

Only a few published applications have tackled this issue (Rihoux, 2001; Scouvart, 2006; Scouvart et al., 2007, Skaaning, 2006; Vanderborght & Yamasaki, 2004). The basic strategy for resolving CSAs is to add "theoretical cases" to the truth table. First, the CSA(s) must be identified. This can be done either with the software, by intersecting the [1] outcome minimal formula including logical remainders with the [0] outcome minimal formula including logical remainders, or by comparing the respective lists of logical remainders used. Second, the identified CSAs need to be assigned a specific outcome value, based on empirical and/or theoretical knowledge. For example, if the combination of conditions A.B.c (presence of A with presence of B with absence of C) is one of the CSAs, the user must judge whether it makes a stronger theoretical case that A.B.c leads to the presence or to the absence of the outcome. The created theoretical configuration is then added to the truth table. This assigns a fixed outcome value to the configuration of conditions, hence preventing it from becoming contradictory. If there are more than one CSA configurations, all should be replaced by theoretical cases and added to the truth table. Third, the new truth table can be minimized, but one should check again for the possible presence of other CSAs generated by the software. If they exist, then the second and third steps need to be repeated, in an iterative way, until no CSAs remain.

When there are only a couple of CSAs, the procedure highlighted above is appropriate. In Vanderborght and Yamasaki (2004), the new minimal formula even produced a much more parsimonious and elegant formula than the previous one (with CSAs). However, resolution of CSAs can become a technical and theoretical maze if their number is great—i.e., more than six or seven. The risk of having a large number of CSAs increases when diversity is more limited— i.e., when the number of empty zones (see Venn diagrams, Chapter 3) greatly exceeds the number of zones with observed cases. Hence, an overly heavy presence of CSAs may point to some more fundamental problem in the selection of conditions, and the user might need to go back to theoretical and empirical considerations, so as to amend the model.

Finally, it should be noted that the problem of CSAs is much less severe if researchers avoid relying on the most parsimonious solutions produced by QCA and instead use theoretical and substantive knowledge to specify intermediate solutions. Remember that, when deriving intermediate solutions, theoretical and substantive knowledge guides the incorporation of logical remainders and permits only those that are plausible (i.e., those that are "easy" from the viewpoint of counterfactual analysis) to be used (see pp. 110–118, 136). While the derivation of intermediate solutions does not guarantee the elimination of CSAs, practical experience indicates that this practice rids virtually all minimal formulas of CSAs. Plus, procedures for the derivation of intermediate solutions (for both crisp-set and fuzzy-set analyses) are now implemented in FSQCA. Users are presented a dialogue box in which they input basic information about how conditions should be connected to the outcome. This information is then used to guide the selection of logical remainders for inclusion in the intermediate solution.

Box 6.2
"Good Practices" (11): Technical Arbitrations and Practical Steps Throughout the QCA Procedures

This selective review of csQCA applications allows us to identify a series of additional, more transversal technical good practices (also applicable to mvQCA and fsQCA):

- For each technical arbitration (case selection, threshold setting, inclusion of logical remainders, etc.), always *justify* your choice and make choices transparent.

- Likewise, it might be useful to conduct a *sensitivity analysis* by rerunning the analysis with different technical arbitrations.

- Don't be afraid to alter some of your initial arbitrations throughout the process of your research. QCA techniques are *best used in an iterative manner.*

- In many situations, there is not a single "one size fits all" strategy to be applied. Problem-solving strategies are often best used in combination.

- Logical remainders (and the resulting simplifying assumptions) are not to be used mechanically—the theoretical implications of including them have to be seriously considered (see also p. 152).

- If contradictory simplifying assumptions are produced through the respective minimizations of the [1] and [0] outcome configurations, they have to be identified and addressed.

mvQCA

We hereby discuss one specific real-life application, Cronqvist and Berg-Schlosser's 2006 analysis of HIV prevalence trends in sub-Saharan Africa, because it illustrates a basic mvQCA and its added-value and limitations not only vis-à-vis csQCA but also vis-à-vis multiple regression.

To explain decreases in the prevalence of HIV between 1997 and 2003, the authors first examined a set of potential explanatory factors through bivariate analyses and multivariate analyses using multiple regression, applied to data on all 42 sub-Saharan African countries. They found that, when controlling for the literacy rate, the share of agriculture in the country's GDP, and the gender equity index (GDI), there was a positive correlation (0.51) between the predominance of Protestant churches and the decrease of the HIV prevalence rate. They conjectured that this might reflect some legacy of specific colonial patterns, especially situations in which "migrant labor . . . males had to live away from their families in the rural areas" (p. 151).

Next, csQCA and mvQCA procedures were applied to the 19 countries (cases) with a high (above 6%) HIV prevalence rate in 1997 in order to measure the impact of policies applied between 1997 and 2003. The conditions were restricted to contextual factors specific to this period (the religion factor was thus excluded): the literacy rate, the gender equality index, the share of agriculture in national GDP, and the mortality rate due to AIDS (proxy for the level of awareness of the danger of HIV/AIDS). Using csQCA, the truth table displayed two contradictory configurations (8 cases) out of a total of 9 configurations (embracing 19 cases altogether). When the mortality condition was trichotomized, the updated mvQCA truth table presented only one contradictory configuration (4 cases), in which, after reexamination of the cases in the contradictory row, the one case of Central African Republic appeared to require additional explanation. The truth table, after the removal of that case, then contained 18 cases and no contradictory configurations. The mvQCA minimized formulas ([1] outcome with inclusion of logical remainders and [0] outcome with inclusion of logical remainders) were, technically speaking, less parsimonious than the ones obtained with csQCA, but, substantially speaking, the explanatory paths pointed to overall similar patterns: a high AIDS-related mortality rate or a high share of agriculture in the national GDP were linked in most of the cases with a falling rate of HIV. Based on these findings, Cronqvist and Berg-Schlosser enumerated a number of policy recommendations and argued for a differentiated application of policies depending on the specific context of each country.

This application demonstrates that, through mvQCA, more can be learned from the same data using csQCA than by using multiple regression analyses and that an adapted threshold-setting procedure (with mvQCA) is a useful strategy for solving contradictory configurations. It also shows how different techniques can be used in a complementary way (see also pp. 169–170).

FUZZY SETS

In this section, we discuss five published fuzzy sets applications. Note that they are not applications of the fuzzy "truth table" algorithm (fsQCA) described in Chapter 5 but instead use the fuzzy "inclusion" algorithm described by Ragin (2000). Each application was chosen to illustrate a specific methodological point.

Hagan and Hansford-Bowles (2005): A Robust Application

During the Vietnam War, some 50,000 draft-age Americans emigrated to Canada as an act of political protest. Once in Canada, a large part of them became active in anti–Vietnam War movements. In this article, the authors addressed the issue of personal characteristics that led American Vietnam War resisters first to enter into activism and then to sustain their activism. They defined two outcomes: the intensity of personal involvement in anti-war activism and the level of current involvement in activism. For the first outcome, four conditions were selected: an "alternation experience" as a measure of individual efforts to help newly arrived Americans in Toronto; a measure of parental radicalism; the political stance of the individual; and the past participation in U.S. civil rights and peace movements; for the second outcome, six conditions were selected: the level of contacts sustained with other activists; the alternation experience measure (as above); the level of participation in anti-war activism after arriving in Canada; the level of current leftism; the level of parental radicalism (as above); and the past participation in U.S. civil rights and peace movements (as above). The main hypotheses tested by the authors concerned the explanatory power of the alternation experience for entering into activism and the gender-split patterns of explanations for staying into activism. The models were tested against interviews on a sample of 100 American resisters who settled in Toronto during the Vietnam War.

As a result of their fuzzy-set analyses, the authors found that the alternation experience was indeed a necessary condition for explaining the emergence of a collective anti-war activism in this group. Moreover, their findings pointed to the sustained contacts with activists as a necessary condition for women's continued activism and to a strong leftist political leaning as the necessary condition for men's continued activism. In conclusion, the authors argued for a distinction between mechanisms of emergent activism and mechanisms of sustained activism and suggested that these mechanisms might be different for men and women. This application is robust and shows all the practical steps of a fuzzy-set analysis, as well as the empirical usefulness of the configurational logic (which taps the diversity of paths toward an outcome) and the value of the thinking in terms of "necessity" and "sufficiency."

Katz, Vom Hau, and Mahoney (2005): Fuzzy Sets Versus Regression

In this article, the authors contrast the results obtained by fuzzy-set analyses and regression analyses to explain the reversal of socioeconomic development in 15 Spanish American countries during the 1750–1900 period. The two outcomes (economic and social development) are modeled with five conditions (concentration of indigenous populations; the labor intensity of agriculture; the degree of dependence on tropical agriculture and mineral exports; the strength of liberals in the colonial elites; and the strength of conservatives in the colonial elites).

The fuzzy-set analysis suggested that a strong liberal faction is probabilistically necessary for economic development, whereas a dense indigenous population is usually necessary for social underdevelopment. They also found two combinations of conditions that were sufficient for social underdevelopment, but these combinations were also subsets of the necessary condition "dense indigenous populations." On the other hand, the OLS regression analysis yielded less robust and highly unstable results, as conclusions drawn from bivariate analyses were sometimes reversed or lost their statistical significance when many variables were thrown into a multivariate regression.

In their methodological conclusions, the authors pointed to the fundamental differences between fuzzy-set and regression methods in their approaches to causality, and hence to the natural gap in their formulation of hypotheses. Moreover, they argued that in the world of small-N analyses, fuzzy-set techniques are less fragile than regression techniques when faced with issues of, for example, multicollinearity and degrees of freedom, partly because the necessary and sufficient approach to causality that they employ using fuzzy sets is mostly bivariate.

Jackson (2005): The Importance of Case Knowledge

In this article, Jackson tried to uncover necessary and sufficient conditions that would explain the presence of employee representatives in corporate boards in 22 OECD countries. He confronted four sets of potential conditions: corporate governance factors (ownership, rights of shareholders, etc.), type of legal system (civil law or common law), strength of labor unions, and finally the national political system (electoral system, consensus vs. majoritarian types of democracies). Since the total number of conditions (12) would weaken the robustness of the analysis, he first tested each set of conditions separately and then built several models with a limited number of conditions. The results ranged from the most parsimonious formula where the absence of common law proves to be a necessary condition for employee representation in corporate boards, to a theoretically more complex result with two broad paths reflecting sufficient combinations of conditions. These two paths displayed common factors (coordinated collective bargaining, consensual political systems, and concentrated corporate ownership) combined with either a strong political left accounting for the Scandinavian cases or a weaker political left and weaker investors' rights for the Germanic group.

Each model tested was confronted with the original case materials in order to bring about a dialogue between the obtained formulas and the author's case knowledge. This underlines the importance of qualitative knowledge for evaluating the validity and utility of logically derived formulas. Indeed, looking at the evidence, the most parsimonious formula was received with some skepticism by the author. He also reported that in the other formulas, France appears to be an exception and does not fit either model well.

Kogut, MacDuffie, and Ragin (2004): Informed Inclusion of "Simplifying Assumptions"

This research in firm management tried to uncover configurations of organizational characteristics and firm properties that led to high performance in both quality and productivity in 43 automobile production sites. Based on an earlier study by one of the authors, Kogut et al. selected three conditions reflecting sets of management practices and three other context or firm characteristics conditions. They first performed a separate sufficiency and necessity analysis (see also p. 47) for quality and productivity outcomes, before analyzing the pathways leading to high performance. The latter was obtained by intersecting the quality and productivity scores. In other words, the high performance outcome variable was measured as the combination of a high quality and a high productivity level of these plants, by taking the minimum scores of productivity and quality. The results showed the same three necessary conditions as in the separate analyses of quality and productivity: a low number of vehicles built during a standard day, the high level of automation, and the young age of the automobile model in construction. The automation level appeared especially important for explaining high performance, as it did for the other two outcomes. The authors accounted for the unexpected necessity of the first condition by proposing that "it is possible that in times of transition, smaller factories provide better experimental conditions" (p. 42).

What is most interesting from the point of view of fuzzy-set methodology is the strategy of informed inclusion of simplifying assumptions (see also p. 135). Kogut et al. began by recognizing the challenge of limited diversity (see also p. 27). The use of simplifying assumptions became critical in achieving some sort of general theoretical statements about the effects of a (combination of) condition(s) on the high performance of a firm. However, they warned that all simplifying assumptions should not be included in the analysis in a mechanistic, unthinking manner, and that they should first be assessed in light of their theoretical and empirical possibility or validity. They identified several simplifying assumptions that, they argued, should not, theoretically, lead to the outcome (high performance). These are combinations of conditions in which at least two out of the three management practice conditions displayed a low score. Kogut et al. excluded these simplifying assumptions because of their strong theoretical knowledge indicating that the lack of these practices is unlikely to be linked to high performance.

The authors also emphasized the advantage of configurational analyses over classical statistical analyses or qualitative methods with respect to the handling of simplifying assumptions (counterfactuals): "The researcher can explicitly identify the simplifying assumptions used in the minimization and decide, based on theory or field knowledge, if they should be eliminated or retained" (p. 26). More generally, this article illustrated the "good practice" of taking appropriate precautions when interpreting the most parsimonious solutions QCA is capable of generating and also the importance of using theoretical and substantive knowledge to guide the incorporation of logical remainders as simplifying assumptions and thereby crafting "intermediate" solutions that restrict implausible simplifying assumptions.

Gran (2003): Fuzzy Sets as a Typology-Building Tool

Gran compared institutions that provide services to abused children in order to demonstrate that they cannot be categorized with the simple dichotomy of public versus private. He hoped that moving beyond this dichotomy "may reveal overlooked political institutions and actors that have influenced systems of social service provision" (p. 85). Four ideal types of sectors—fully public institutions, fully social institutions, fully individual institutions, and fully private institutions—were constructed, based on four criteria: sources of finances, the universality of eligibility for program benefits, the type of stimulus for providing services to abused children, and the "who and how" of the management of the program. Within the 74 social service providers analyzed between 1999 and 2000 across the United States, he identified a subset of 15 providers as Faith-Based Organizations (FBOs).

By comparing the four ideal types of sectors and the social service providers, Gran brought forward two main conclusions: First, none of the social service providers purely belonged to one of the ideal-types of sectors. Rather, "the market and individual sectors appear to play small roles across all cases, . . . although the social sector has an important role in every case" (p. 97). Hence, it would be misleading to describe social service providers according to a dichotomous, public/private, scheme. Instead, the "social-service provision for abused children is fuzzy," and the "sectors often collaborate to provide social service to abused children" (p. 99).

Second, Gran concluded that FBOs were similar to other social service providers. In other words, there were no substantial differences between the 15 FBOs and the remaining 59 other social service providers in terms of their relationship to the four ideal typical sectors.

Faith-based providers do not strictly belong to any sector, . . . [but] perhaps more than other providers, faith-based organizations currently avoid reliance on the state sector as a [financial] source. The state sector, however, has a role in the management of every faith-based provider. (p. 100)

Building upon these conclusions, Gran also discussed the implication of the Bush Charitable Choice Policy, which advocates direct government funding of religious organizations for the purpose of carrying out government programs.

What is particularly interesting in this fsQCA application is the use of ideal types or the typology function (see also Aus, 2007; Kvist, 2000, 2006, Vis, 2006). He used fuzzy sets to "evaluate the degree to which a case conforms to an ideal type" (p. 94), and more substantially, to compare "a case of child-abuse service to a pure market, pure public, pure individual, and pure social case" (p. 95). The aim was thus the classification of cases according to the distance between their attributes and the attributes of some conceptual ideal types. In contrast with other fsQCA applications, it did not seek the explanation of some phenomenon but rather an analytical description of a multi-dimensional phenomenon. The use of the typological capabilities of fsQCA, or of csQCA, was rarely exploited, although it had the merit of giving meaningful boundaries to classifications. Often, classification techniques such as Multi-Dimensional Scaling (MDS) do not attribute meanings to the "corners" of its multidimensional spaces. By contrast, the scaling of fuzzy set scores on each factor is justified theoretically, so that any set of values for a case not only depicts the observed empirical measures of the case along the selected factors but also has a theoretical relationship to the ideal–typical corner of the vector space.

CONCLUSION

The applications overviewed in this chapter show the diverse ways in which QCA techniques can be exploited. They also show that those techniques can be used in inventive ways and that there are many ways to flexibly use them, also in combination, as the user meets challenges or difficulties. Many of these applications are recent and illustrate that innovations and refinements are quite numerous in this field—and indeed many more innovations and refinements are expected in the next few years (see Chapter 8). Finally, this chapter should make it even clearer to the reader that QCA techniques are designed to be used in an iterative and reflexive way (with an eye on theories and an eye on the empirical cases) and never following a "push-button" logic (see p. 14).

Key Points

With regard to all QCA techniques:

- In QCA, cases are not "given" but rather are constructed, carefully defined, and selected.
- There are several possible strategies to select conditions for QCA.
- Strategies to dichotomize (and trichotomize, etc.) conditions range from quantitative ones (e.g., clustering techniques) to qualitative, historical, and case-oriented ones.
- There are many possible strategies (and combinations of those strategies) to solve contradictory configurations; the solving of contradictory configurations is a challenging but most instructive task.
- Contradictory configurations and contradictory simplifying assumptions are not always "problems": They also can be heuristic tools to improve the model and the analysis.
- Case-based knowledge and the "dialogue" between the QCA procedures and the empirical cases is useful not only in csQCA but also in mvQCA, fsQCA, and fuzzy-set analysis, more generally.
- QCA techniques are designed to be used in an iterative and reflexive way (with an eye on theories and an eye on the empirical cases).

Key Complementary Readings

The selected published applications discussed in this chapter.

NOTES

1. Amenta and Poulsen (1994) list the first five approaches; we add the sixth one.

2. For example in the case of a secondary QCA based on an existing analysis using Inferential Statistical Methods (ISMs). When comparing these QCA to ISMs, Amenta and Poulsen argue that this "strategy underscores an advantage of QCA: that ISMs generally dismiss causal heterogeneity and can rule out factors that might matter for conjunctural explanations of social phenomena" (1994, p. 29).

3. For a perfect illustration, see Fischer, Kaiser, and Rohlfing (2006), who performed pre-tests using statistical techniques in order to discriminate among worthy and unworthy conditions.

4. However, the coding justification can be found in detail for each country in Bleiklie, Goggin, and Rothmayr (2003).

7

Addressing the Critiques of QCA

Gisèle De Meur
Benoît Rihoux
Sakura Yamasaki

Goals of This Chapter

After reading this chapter, you should be able to:

- Draw a distinction between relevant and less relevant critiques voiced vis-à-vis QCA techniques

- Have a clearer view of the respective strengths and limitations of csQCA, mvQCA, and fsQCA

- Distinguish critiques that are specific to QCA techniques from critiques that should be expanded to all formal empirical methodologies (including statistical ones)

- Reflect further on the strengths and limitations of any formal empirical methodology (not only QCA, but also other tools, including statistical)

As csQCA was launched earlier and has so far been used more extensively than the other QCA techniques, it has been the focus of more critiques than mvQCA and fsQCA.[1] In this chapter, we shall thus mostly concentrate on these critiques, some of which are specific to csQCA. Some critiques, however, can be expanded to the other QCA techniques. Most critiques of QCA concentrate on csQCA as a *technique* and less on QCA as an *approach* (as presented in Chapter 1). Building on a first attempt to review the critiques (De Meur, Rihoux, & Yamasaki, 2002), we draw a distinction between two very different sorts of critiques. On the one hand, there are those that we consider to be relevant, in the sense that they identify real limitations of csQCA.

On the other hand, there are those that are more disputable, or even simply not valid, for one of the two following reasons. First, some scholars voice critiques that would have been relevant in another framework but that are simply not relevant in the QCA paradigm whose assumptions, rules, and goals are, in essence, different. The most frequent problem of the sort occurs when one is embedded in a quantitative (read: mainstream statistical) paradigm that imposes (rightly so, *within that paradigm*) a whole series of formal constraints. For instance, following the statistical paradigm, "outliers" that run against the main explanatory scheme must be pushed aside, which is not the case with QCA (see pp. 7, 20). Further, following the statistical paradigm, the various explanatory variables must be considered as statistically independent, which is not the case with QCA either. And so on. Second, some critiques do not pertain solely to QCA but to the comparative approach more generally, or even to any empirical approach—for example, the critique with regard to loss of information through dichotomization, which overestimates the precision of the initial source of information and fails to recognize that some variation may be considered irrelevant, given specific theoretical and substantive interests. Thus, our ambition in this chapter shall be to clearly differentiate these two maincategories of critiques and also to use those critiques as a stepping stone to improve the QCA tools themselves as well as ways to present them, so as to better prevent misunderstandings.

This chapter is voluntarily restricted to critiques addressed specifically toward QCA techniques, so we will not cover the more general methodological critiques linked to small- and intermediate-N methods and research designs (for recent discussions, see e.g., Becker, 1998; Caramani, 2008; Gerring, 2006; Goertz, 2006b; King, Keohane, & Verba, 1994; Lieberson, 1991, 1994; Mahoney, 2000; Savolainen, 1994).

THE DICHOTOMIZATION OF DATA

One of the main characteristics of csQCA is that it can only treat dichotomized[2] variables. This constitutes an important limitation of the technique. If the researcher has fine-grained quantitative data at his or her disposal (e.g., interval-level data such as economic indicators or ordinal-level data such as a well-defined categorization of multiple professional groups with different income levels), the dichotomization can result in a loss of a great deal of information (Goldthorpe, 1997). Further, the choice of cutoff value for dichotomization may appear arbitrary or at least too manipulable.

This critique, though relevant to some extent, must be qualified. Many social phenomena—in particular (but not only) at the macro level—are of a qualitative nature; very often, then, the researcher will be able to determine if the phenomenon "happens" or "does not happen." Indeed, in many instances, decisive differences between cases of interest are differences in *nature* or *kind* rather than differences in *degree* (Ragin, 2002). In terms of operationalization of variables, this requires a decision, of course, but this may be done on the basis of theoretical considerations and familiarity with the cases, in this iterative "dialogue between ideas and evidence," which is a key advocacy of Configurational Comparative Methods more generally (see p. 14).

Dichotomization is one form of *simplification*—of reduction of complexity. Even if it comes with a loss of information, the simplification is very much legitimate. Indeed, all scientific research in the social sciences and beyond—whether "qualitative" or "quantitative," experimental or not—necessarily implies a step toward simplification in relation to the infinite complexity of the world (King et al., 1994, p. 42). Simplification is what allows us to make progress in our understanding of complexity. In fact, QCA "preserves the complexity of the situations underlying phenomena of interest while simplifying them as much as possible" (Becker, 1998, p. 186).

To say that a phenomenon is "complex" means several things at once. It can mean, on the one hand, that the phenomenon displays many dimensions, as well as a great deal of variation across each of these dimensions. On the other hand, it may also mean that interactions *among* different dimensions of the phenomenon are varied in number and in shape. In QCA, the latter understanding of "complexity" is fully taken into account. In fact, QCA places this complexity at the heart of the analysis. In short, dichotomization allows us, through simplification (the operationalization of the conditions), to conduct a rigorous comparison of a limited number of cases that present combinations of internally complex characteristics.

Another more technically specific problem associated with the dichotomization of the data is the threshold value. That is, where should the researcher place the threshold in order to dichotomize the data, to attribute the values [1] and [0]? Of course, many data can be dichotomized without much difficulty, as is the case for the sex of an individual, the presence or absence of illegal drugs in the blood, an increase or a decrease of a parameter in a given situation, a situation of crisis or stability in a stock market, and so on or in the example developed at large in this volume (a breakdown or survival of a democratic regime). Nonetheless, some data are more difficult to dichotomize. For example, some qualifications—old/not old, rich/poor, rural area/urban area, and so on—may require the researcher to make a more or less subjective choice in order to define the threshold value.

According to Bollen, Entwisle, and Alderson (1993), the researcher runs a serious risk in this decision process: "Ragin sets forth a strategy for analysis that could accentuate measurement problems when he proposes that variables be dichotomized" (p. 343). Goldthorpe (1997) shared this view and expressed his concern in strong language:

> where essentially continuous variables are involved, . . . these must be reduced (with, of course, much loss of information) to more or less arbitrary dichotomies; and all subsequent results will then be strongly dependent on the way in which particular cases are allocated. (p. 7)

Thus, according to Goldthorpe, setting the dichotomization threshold has an important impact on results, and any measurement or coding error has drastic consequences on robustness.

In response to these critics, we first note that various techniques make informed dichotomizations possible and actually also any form of threshold-setting, as well as for mvQCA and fsQCA (see p. 130, as well as Chapters 3 to 5). Recently, a number of authors have further countered this critique by performing systematic sensitivity analyses and testing the robustness of the results by varying dichotomization threshold values (see, e.g., Ishida, Yonetani, & Kosaka, 2006; Skanning, 2006; and Stokke, 2004, 2007, on both crisp and fuzzy sets).

Consider an interval-level variable that could take any value between 0 and 100, and for which there is no specific theoretical or empirical argument for locating the dichotomization threshold at a specific value. If most of the cases are distributed below the value of 60 *or* above the value of 80, without any cases situated between these two values, we could easily place the threshold value on 65, 70, or 75. If, however, the standard deviation is small—that is, if the data are grouped around similar values along the continuum from 0 to 100—dichotomization indeed becomes a challenge in csQCA.

The rules of common sense as well as solid theoretical and empirical knowledge often guide the researcher in making a decision regarding threshold values. Rihoux (2001), for example, managed to distinguish "major" from "minor" organizational adaptations by referring to the organizational theory literature. This is an example of theoretical justification. An example of using empirical knowledge is defining a "threshold of poverty" in Western democracies by the access to a shelter with basic commodities. This empirical definition is not numerical but is derived through relevant contextual knowledge. For instance, in countries with mild winters (say, south of Spain), a person without a fixed roof might not be considered below that threshold of poverty, but a person in such a situation in a country with very cold winters (say, Finland) would be considered well below the threshold. In this example, not having a fixed roof has different implications for the individuals, depending on the context.

Further, we want to emphasize again that, in many cases, dichotomization does not create any difficulty because phenomena under consideration present some clear-cut difference in the empirical world (man/woman, war/peace, guilty/not-guilty, success/failure, growth/decline, etc.). In many other instances, there are well-agreed-upon thresholds in the international social scientific literature or in indexes used by international organizations (e.g., UN, OECD).

Other techniques are also available. For example, a multi-categorical nominal variable can be transformed into several binary conditions. In the same way, an ordinal (or interval) variable can be transformed into a multi-categorical nominal variable, which may then in turn be transformed into several binary conditions (Ragin, 1987, pp. 86–87; 1994). This technique does raise two serious problems. On the one hand, there is no means by which to trace back the effect of the original variables. On the other, this type of procedure results in a multiplication of the total number of conditions, a problem when analyzing a limited number of cases (see p. 71). Note, however, that this problem can quite easily been circumvented by using mvQCA (see Chapter 4). Another technique, based on clustering, has also been applied convincingly (see p. 130, as well as Chapter 4 with mvQCA).

To sum up: Dichotomization—indeed any form of threshold-setting in data (e.g., also trichotomization)—forces the user to make choices that are often difficult. However, this is as much an advantage as a limitation of csQCA. Indeed, it allows the researcher to move beyond a gradualist perspective, which is sometimes considered an important pitfall of the comparative method. Sartori (1991) defined gradualism as the abusive application of the maxim according to which differences in kind would be better perceived as differences of degree, and that continuous treatments would invariably be more pertinent than dichotomized treatments.

Dichotomization, in particular, forces the researcher to make a clear choice of threshold. This introduces transparency into the research, which in turn reinforces the legitimacy of the analysis. It also allows for replication of the analysis by other scholars. In addition, dichotomization forces the investigator to get to the essentials. Because the threshold is a precise point, it is a strong indicator of the validity of the variable. Finally, remember that csQCA is best used in an iterative way. Along the way, the researcher may choose to modify or fine tune the threshold value of various variables, when this is justified on the basis of theoretical and/or empirical considerations, and in particular in the process of addressing contradictory configurations (see p. 48). Note, finally, that even when a phenomenon is measured in a fine-grained way, what matters from a QCA perspective is focusing on *relevant difference*. For instance, the physical size of an individual can be measured in a very fine-grained way (centimeters, millimeters), but to what extent is this extreme precision in measurement useful if our research question is whether or not the individual is too tall to pass through a door? In this example, the research would rather call for a focus on difference in kind, and the use of interval scaled values would be of less interest.

Thus, many of the critiques of dichotomization must be qualified, and in fact, the rigor associated with the dichotomization process may be considered a positive feature of the approach. Obviously, if these arguments are not convincing or if there is a theoretical interest in fine-grained data, there is still the option of using mvQCA or fsQCA.

THE USE OF NON-OBSERVED
CASES (LOGICAL REMAINDERS)

Recall that, in the process of performing Boolean minimization, we are able to make use of logical remainders—that is, cases that are not empirically observed, from which the software is then able to draw some simplifying assumptions (see Chapters 3 to 5).

This practice has attracted several critiques. Markoff (1990), for example, considered the use of non-observed configurations to be dangerous: "Ragin is speculating about different ways of imagining what would happen under configurations of variables that do not actually exist." Moreover, Markoff worried that this method can lead the researcher to an "unfortunate situation in which we are engaged in an imaginative act that often will be guided by producing a formula that is neat in appearance but essentially unverifiable" (p. 179). The underlying problem, according to Markoff, is that some of these logical cases are never observed in the real world. Romme (1995) shared these concerns: He argued that one should establish a distinction between logical cases that *could* exist in reality (which are not a problem to him) and those that *could not* possibly exist in reality. This latter type of cases, should not, according to him, be taken into consideration (p. 325).

There are several ways to address this critique. The first way—which we shall develop with some detail—is to make a strong argument that this critique is not relevant. The second way is to accept the critique and put forward some concrete strategies to make a distinction between what would be "plausible" versus "non-plausible" logical remainders, in order to include only the "plausible" ones in the minimization procedure.

Let us first start with a defense of the *unrestricted* use of logical remainders, even though, in most situations, we do not advocate this practice. From the outset, remember that the use of logical remainders only corresponds to a well-circumscribed step in the minimization procedure. Logical cases are not taken into account during the elaboration of the truth table. The researcher does not, as it were, give life to fictitious cases that would be treated as real-life cases but resorts to them very briefly during the analysis to achieve greater parsimony. Also remember that these logical remainders that receive an outcome value and subsequently become simplifying assumptions are, structurally, *never in contradiction* with the observed cases. In other words, the inclusion of the logical remainders does not change anything about the properties of the empirical (observed) cases (for a detailed argument and a constructed example, see De Meur et al., 2002, pp. 123–126). Logical remainders free up space, allowing us to obtain a more parsimonious solution. They constitute an "artifice," whose unique objective is to obtain a more parsimonious reduced expression. The software will select only those logical cases that will contribute to the production of a more parsimonious reduced expression.

Second and more fundamentally, if the researcher chooses to limit the analysis to the observed cases, he/she will not be able to draw on information beyond that which is observed in these cases. When the number of cases is small and the number of conditions great, this strategy tends to result in individualizing explanations. In these situations, only the use of logical remainders allows us to take a step toward theoretical elaboration. This requires a degree of generalization, even if moderate in scope: "Direct consideration of combinations of causal conditions that do not exist in the data . . . forces the investigator to confront the theoretical assumptions that permit more general causal statements" (Ragin, 1987, p. 112).

Indeed, to be qualified as "scientific," research must go beyond the mere description of observed phenomena. It must contain a complementary step: *inference*, not in the narrow, statistical sense, but in its more general meaning—moving beyond observed data, toward what is not directly observed. Such inference may be descriptive, when empirical observations are used to advance our knowledge of other non-observed phenomena. It can also be causal and advance our understanding of causal effects, beyond observed phenomena. Thus, "the key distinguishing mark of scientific research is the goal of making inferences that go beyond the particular observations collected" (King et al., 1994, p. 8). Whatever the scientific discipline, and whatever the method (statistical, experimental, etc.), any generalization necessitates going beyond the observed cases and therefore—necessarily—the use of some form of non-observed cases. This is often done unconsciously or at least without being made explicit in many different types of research (for a more detailed argument, see De Meur et al., 2002, pp. 127–129).

Thus the use of logical remainders by QCA is in fact a positive feature rather than a problem. Their use make it possible for researchers to find a creative solution to one of the greatest obstacles to systematic social inquiry—the problem of the limited diversity of human phenomena (Ragin, 1987, pp. 104–113; see p. 27). It is precisely this limited diversity that, among other things, enables one to conduct a quasi-experimental research design in many social science disciplines. By going beyond the observation of phenomena that are present in a limited variety, we can thus support theoretical inquiries beyond observed cases.

Third, and even more fundamentally, any method in the social sciences with an analytical claim necessitates the use of some form of simplifying assumptions—that is, assumptions related to cases not observed by the investigator. This is also true for the experimental sciences: biology, physics, and others. For example, the classic laws of physics rely on many "non-observed cases." Consider, for example, the fundamental equation of Newtonian mechanics: $F = m \cdot a$ (the force exerted on an object is equal to the product of its mass and acceleration). It is absolutely impossible to formulate this principle without going beyond the observed cases. Because the variables in this law are continuous, the number of required observations would be infinite and also inaccessible to laboratory experimentation. To state the general expression, then, it is necessary to make a leap beyond the finite universe of observations.

This is equally true in social sciences. In his reexamination of Rokkan's classic study of the development of cleavages in Western Europe, Ragin (1987) demonstrated that Rokkan (implicitly) included simplifying assumptions in his theory—that is, combinations of conditions he had not observed in the real world (pp. 132–133; see also De Meur & Rihoux, 2002, pp. 70–78). In other words, to reach his conclusions, Rokkan had to make assumptions related to combinations of conditions combined with various cleavages that he did not observe empirically. In most social scientific comparative research, the investigator actually observes an even smaller proportion of the total logically possible configurations of conditions than was the case for Rokkan—hence the importance of logical remainders as a key resource for the investigator.

In other methodologies, such as mainstream quantitative methods, where the goal is to make generalizations about relations between causes (the independent variables) and consequences (the dependent variables), simplifying assumptions are also called upon—though most often in an implicit manner (Ragin, 1987, p. 32). Yet, such simplifying assumptions do go beyond the universe of observed cases. Let us consider, for example, a multiple regression analysis, which examines several independent variables. In this type of analysis, the vector space formed by the independent variables contains de facto many zones or sectors that are almost or completely devoid of observed cases. When the researcher produces a predictive equation on the basis of independent variables, it is then possible to predict values (for the dependent variable). Such a prediction, however, is made on the basis of a huge number of non-observed values of conditions (i.e., in the empty zones of the vector space). Further, since multiple regression rests upon (among other things) an aggregation and linearity postulate, it *intrinsically* makes assumptions related to configurations of non-observed conditions (Ragin, 2000).

Finally, remember that the QCA minimization algorithms do not produce "explanations" of a given outcome—they simply offer a reduced expression that *describes* a set of (observed) cases in a logically shorthand manner. Thus, for that purpose—shorthand description—all "logical remainders" are potentially useful, whether they are empirically plausible or not. If we were to discover, in future research, a case that runs against a given "simplifying assumption" (especially an empirically less plausible one) used in a current research project, this will be most useful from a Popperian perspective: Refutation through observation enables scientific progress.

On the other hand, if some logical remainders are indeed considered problematic by the user, then there are strategies for coping with them. The first to make a more informed use of logical remainders (see "easy" versus "difficult" logical remainders, pp. 135, 110–118); the second is to address them as they arise in the process of dealing with contradictory simplifying assumptions (see p. 136). As noted previously, the FSQCA software now has built-in procedures allowing the investigator to automatically restrict the incorporation of logical remainders, using theoretical and substantive knowledge to guide their use (i.e., the derivation of "intermediate" solutions). Further, this practice often neutralizes the problem of contradictory simplifying assumptions.

To sum up: Also with regard to logical remainders, the distinctiveness of QCA is that it makes explicit what usually stays hidden in other methodologies (Ragin, 1987, pp. 111–112). Once again, in QCA, the researcher is "forced" to make choices explicit, a virtue in any scientific method. Such choices are transparent in QCA as the researcher has to decide whether to include or exclude logical remainders, and if to include them, which ones to include. In choosing not to include them, the user—voluntarily—chooses to keep a maximum level of complexity. The user can always decide to include them later to obtain a more parsimonious reduced expression. In the end, he or she can, with complete transparency, make a choice toward greater complexity or toward greater parsimony (Ragin & Sonnett, 2004).

CASE SENSITIVITY

This critique actually has two different sides to it. The first side, which refers more precisely to the method's sensitivity to *each* individual case, can be addressed in four ways. First of all, it is indeed true that QCA commonly gives equal weight to all combinations of conditions leading to the outcome, whether they are observed for 20 cases or for just 1. (fsQCA allows the setting of a frequency threshold for combinations.) From a case-oriented perspective, however, this not a weakness but rather a strength of QCA. While statistical techniques focus on mainstream explanations supported by the majority of cases and treat cases distant from the main path as "deviants" or "outliers," QCA leads researchers to "decide that the deviant case they discovered is not an exception to their theory, but a hitherto unsuspected phenomenon that deserves and will get its own category" (Becker, 1998, p. 193; see also Ragin, 2003).

Second, social phenomena are not uniform in their occurrence. Let us consider an example from the natural sciences. We know that earthquakes of magnitude 3 and higher on the Richter scale are not observed regularly in France but are frequent occurrences in countries such as Japan. The researcher may obtain a configuration covering many cases in Japan and another one covering only one French case. Is the latter less important than the former in explaining the factors leading to earthquakes of magnitude 3 and higher? Not at all. It is simply that such phenomena are not often observed in France. This does not imply that the "French" explanation is less significant than the "Japanese" one. It remains equally legitimate.

In the same way, in their QCA of American court decisions on issues related to AIDS victims, Musheno, Gregware, and Drass (1991) highlighted the importance of taking into account all cases, and in particular those that are not often observed:

> Because the cases we examine are among the first to confront the courts regarding AIDS, we must be sensitive to the possibility that stable routines for handling these cases have not yet emerged. Therefore, while it is certainly important to look for patterns among the combinations of attributes associated with different outcomes, we must also try to explain *all* cases, even those that deviate from the patterns. (p. 753)

This case sensitivity allows the investigator to discover, via QCA, all possible explanations, whether frequent or not. The researcher is thus compelled to look at all the cases and all paths of explanation. This practice in turn leads toward an important theoretical point: "Employing all potential causes makes it less likely that QCA results will be misleading" (Amenta & Poulsen, 1994, p. 26).

Coming to a third argument, Musheno et al. also referred to the scientific added-value of considering rarely observed cases:

> These unique cases may in fact represent important instances in which the social order is refracted rather than simply reflected. Statistical analysis, with an emphasis

on central tendency, is more likely to treat such deviation as error (and may actually be adversely affected depending upon the degree to which cases are different). [QCA], on the other hand, is comfortable with multiple explanations for outcomes and simply treats deviations in this manner. (p. 753)

Fourth and last, this obligation to take all cases into account removes the temptation for the researcher to present only those cases (or that part of the analysis) that would be "convenient." In QCA, all causal combinations present in the reduced expression are the result of this extra-case-sensitive analysis, and it is therefore impossible to put forward only a sample of the cases to explain the result. This is also why a "good practice" of QCA is to display the full and complete minimal formulas (see p. 65), without hiding the less convenient bits.

To summarize, the case-sensitivity of QCA with regard to individual cases is particularly well suited to the requirements of a small-N or intermediate-N analysis. Indeed, when the researcher considers a limited number of cases, his or her goal is not to identify a "central" or "average" tendency. On the contrary, the researcher strives to trace different paths leading to the same outcome and to understand the "deviations" that lead to different outcomes in apparently similar cases, each one of which has been selected with a purpose, in a self-conscious process of case selection (see p. 23).

The second side of the critique is that results generated with QCA are sensitive to cases in the sense that by excluding or including one case or another, rather different paths toward the outcome (i.e., different groupings of cases) can be generated. For instance, with case A in the analysis, a term in the minimal formula might group cases C, D, and E together on the one hand and F, G, and H together on the other. But without case A, case H might be singled out as following its own path. Hence, depending on case selection, different minimal formula terms might be produced for the same cases.

This critique is correct—indeed excluding or including some cases will have an influence on the "paths" identified toward the outcome for the other, "permanent" cases (i.e., those cases that remain in all the analyses). To curtail this problem, two good practices can be recommended. On the one hand, the more homogeneous the cases (in terms of background conditions not included in the model), and the more diverse they are with regard to their combinations of values on the conditions, the less severe this problem is likely to be (see selection of cases and conditions, Chapter 2). On the other hand, the use of "logical remainders" (see p. 152) is likely to make the minimal formula more stable, as an additional observed case could well be in line with a "simplifying assumption" already included to obtain the initial minimal formula (without that additional observed case).

THE DIFFICULTY IN SELECTING CONDITIONS

This critique originates primarily from Goldthorpe (1997) along with Amenta and Poulsen (1994). In any empirical scientific project, it is often difficult to choose the relevant "independent" variables. It is also true that this difficulty is even more apparent with QCA. Small-N and intermediate-N studies require a limited number of conditions, and thus these must be selected with utmost care (see p. 25). Based on this, Amenta and Poulsen argued that

> a large number of [conditions] makes QCA unwieldy and decreases the likelihood that any given combination will have an empirical referent or will be theoretically interpretable. . . . QCA's determinism means that omitting potentially causal variables or errors in measurement can provide misleading results. (pp. 23–24)

These authors made a critique that is in fact applicable to *any* empirical analysis involving a relatively large number of variables. Their critique is revealing—it "discovered" a reality that is shared by many empirical methodologies. QCA just brings it to light. This critique does not identify the real difficulty of the matter—to be able to take into account a relatively small number of conditions, without which the researcher would "individualize" the explanation of each case (see Box 2.3). Moreover, we argue that the difficulty in selecting conditions can be viewed as an advantage rather than a limitation of QCA—in that the researcher must be *rigorous* and *transparent* in his or her choice of variables and/or theories taken into consideration.

Concerning rigor, Ragin (1987) strongly insisted that the major part of the work, the most demanding part for the investigator, is the elaboration and selection of the conditions:

> the construction of a truth table involves considerable effort . . . . To construct a useful truth table, it is necessary to gain familiarity with the relevant theories, the relevant research literature, and, most important of all, the relevant cases. (pp. 120–121)

Thus, QCA acts as a guide rail for the researcher, forcing him or her to walk away from "push-button" logic and to instead apply a rigorous logic to the selection of variables—this is also exactly the motivation behind the development of MSDO/MDSO (see p. 28). Indeed, as soon as the investigator's selections directly influence the analysis in a visible way, it is then up to the researcher to use his or her skills and make further decisions to exclude random ingredients.

Concerning transparency, let us spell out again what has been said about the threshold value for dichotomization (see p. 151). In the process of selecting conditions, the researcher is exposed to a peril—that of making clear and explicit choices that have the potential to provoke critics, since

> by requiring all possible theoretical combinations, the initial truth table exposes and makes explicit one's own (implied) theoretical presumptions and postulates. . . . As such, examining the truth table is an ideal mechanism for evaluating selection bias . . . . (Boswell & Brown, 1999, p. 158)

Moreover, the software allows us to test the validity of the selected conditions. If the minimal formula is not convincing (if, for example, it is too complex) or if the truth table contains contradictory configurations, the researcher will have to reconsider the choice of conditions. Accordingly, if the software rejects one or more conditions, it should not be seen as a negative feature of the software but rather as a useful interpretive tool for the analysis. Of course, because of its encompassing approach to explanation (see p. 8), a valid QCA relies heavily on a good selection of conditions.

Since a QCA always produces a result (i.e., the minimal formula), it has been criticized as not being able to distinguish a real model from a random model (Lieberson, 2004) and as making too strong assumptions about omitted variables (Seawright, 2005). This critique is largely misplaced[3] because, in the QCA paradigm (and contrary to the mainstream statistical paradigm), there is no explicit connection with randomness, whether in the model, in the real world, or in the conception of causality. Neither are any assumptions made regarding conditions (variables) outside of the model—one chief reason being that, once again, the goal of QCA algorithms (the computer-run part of QCA) is not to provide an "explanation" of a given outcome (see p. 155).

To sum up, the critique related to the difficulty of selecting conditions is not specific to QCA: It is applicable to any empirical approach that attempts to explain a phenomenon through its characteristics. What is specific about QCA is that these difficulties are made more visible, in particular through the presence of contradictory configurations—but this is actually a positive feature of QCA, as those contradictions can actually be used as a heuristic device to further improve the model.

THE BLACK BOX PROBLEM

Simply said, this problem refers to the "mystery" of the complex processes underlying the analyzed phenomena. QCA has been criticized because it does not describe the process or the "how" of causal combinations that explain the outcome. According to Goldthorpe (1997), "logical methods . . . do not, in themselves, provide an account of the actual processes involved" (p. 14).

This problem does not constitute a real critique because QCA simply does not aim to explain the mechanisms at work behind the variables. QCA by design does not describe a process; it describes the conditions that are present or absent when an outcome of interest is observed or not observed. The more in-depth analysis of underlying processes, of causality, of the more concrete interplay among variables must be worked out by the researcher, by moving beyond the minimal formulas produced by the software. Thus the identification and comprehension of underlying processes can only come out of a dialogue between the investigator's knowledge of the cases and the conditions highlighted by QCA (see p. 65). Moreover, causality cannot be expressed solely through the conditions; the researcher must add an in-depth knowledge of the analyzed phenomenon to determine causality. This point can be illustrated by the following example.

Box 7.1
The Importance of Case-Based
Knowledge to Open Up the "Black Box" of Causal Processes

A professor shows students a series of geometrical figures of various sizes that are colored in different ways. One might notice that the small figures are either completely colored or colored only at the borders, while all of the large figures are only colored at the borders. We observe a pattern: When the figures are large, they are colored at the borders. Based on our observation, we would have a difficult time determining causality. There is, however, a reason. The professor, being mindful of the university's low budget for supplies, was careful not to waste the marker's ink on large figures.

Note that causality in this example is not visible from the conditions themselves; we must add a more detailed knowledge of the phenomenon. For example, we might want to know that it was the professor who actually colored the figures, the habits of the professor, the context in which the professor works, and so on. This sort of information can be supplied only by the researcher. In fact, this necessary dialogue between researcher and data constitutes an important feature of the technique: "What QCA embodies which is especially valuable in the context of small-N macro-comparisons is visibility of, intimacy with, and dialogue with the cases" (Shalev, 1998, p. 14; see also p. 6). In short, there is no "black box" inherent to QCA. Rather, there is a black box *in the world*, in the phenomena observed around us, but it is neither engendered nor explained by QCA, which simply provides some leverage along the way.

In fact, Goldthorpe himself acknowledged that this limitation applies more generally to quantitative methods, for they are equally incapable of explaining causality in observed phenomena. In addition, purely qualitative techniques, which often attempt to explain observed phenomena based on case studies, are criticized for being subjective and lacking rigor: The researcher will often try to explain a phenomenon based on a particular perspective or under a certain set of conditions that he or she considers important. Thus, QCA constitutes a *via media* between these two approaches—one that is limited by its great distance from the "real world" and its lack of understanding of underlying mechanisms and the other by its lack of rigor and too much subjectivity in the explanation of the causal links between observed phenomena. There would, of course, be much more to say, from an ontological, epistemological, and more practical perspective on this key topic of causality, but this discussion goes way beyond the purpose of this volume (some suggested readings: Abbott, 1995, 2001; George & Bennett, 2005; Gerring, 2005; Mahoney, 2003, 2004; Pierson, 2003; Rueschemeyer & Stephens, 1997; Stephens, 1998).

THE TEMPORALITY PROBLEM

This final critique is probably the most significant of all. On the surface, it may appear similar to the "black box" problem above, but these are clearly two distinct problems. The issue at stake is the consideration (or rather the absence of consideration) of temporality within QCA. In a nutshell, QCA does not explicitly integrate the time dimension and therefore does not allow for analysis of temporal processes. In more technical terms, QCA cannot order—or, rather, chronologically articulate—the conditions in the minimal formula. According to Boswell and Brown (1999), the price to be paid to systematically compare cases through QCA is "a static comparison that is not fully compensated by the use of temporally contingent determinants" (p. 181; see also Griffin, 1992).

Several techniques and procedures, however, allow us to make progress toward a resolution of this limitation. The first and most obvious one consists in re-interrogating the different terms in the minimal formula. This leads the researcher to return to the cases in a more qualitative manner and allows him or her to take into consideration—among other things—the temporal dimension.

For example, in an analysis of the presence of major organizational adaptations (the outcome) in West European Green parties, Rihoux (2001) obtained a minimal formula consisting of several terms. In some of these terms, one particular condition was regularly observed in combination with other conditions—the presence of a faction change in favor of "modernizers." By reexamining the cases in a qualitative way, he observed that in many of these parties, this faction change happened at the end of the "temporal chain" in the sequence of events leading to an organizational adaptation. This enabled him to conclude that this condition acted as a catalyst. Another good example of such a dynamic interpretation is the study by Cress and Snow (2000).

A second technique consists in building "dynamic" conditions, by integrating a temporal dimension into conditions themselves. Examples could be as follows: "revolution preceded by an economic crisis" or "electoral failure at two consecutive elections."

A third technique is to introduce the temporal dimension in the definition of the cases themselves. This is what Rihoux did, for example, in the above-mentioned study. He segmented each case (Green political parties) according to temporal events. This allowed him to obtain about 40 cases, or rather units of observations, some of which "preceded" others in a chronological sequence. This in turn allowed for a more dynamic interpretation of the outcome of interest. Such a technique must be implemented in a theoretically and empirically informed manner, to avoid potentially significant methodological problems. For instance, each "subunit" (a temporally defined case) must be rich enough to be well-differentiated from other subunits (King et al., 1994, p. 221). In the Rihoux study, indeed, the different cases (units of observation) within the same nation were linked—and thus were less independent or autonomous than cases across nations. More precisely, the cases segmented in time (for example, a party in a nation A at different periods of time: A1, A2, A3) are less independent among themselves than among other cases (for example, the party A1 compared to party B1 in nation B). This also implies that each added case (segmented in time) provides less new information than a more independent case would (King et al.,1994, p. 222).

Fourth and not least, the researcher can combine QCA with other techniques that are intended to include the temporal dimension of independent variables (conditions) vis-à-vis the outcome. Several potential concrete paths open up, especially around sequence analysis broadly defined (Krook, 2006). A first set of existing or developing techniques concentrates on structures of whole sequences, such as optimal matching (Abbott, 1995), comparative narrative analysis (Abell, 1987, 2004), or Gibbs sampling (Abbott & Barman, 1997). A second set of techniques breaks down the components of individual sequences, such as event-structure analysis (ESA) (Griffin, 1992; 1993; Heise, 1989), narrative analysis, or process tracing (George & Bennett, 2005; Rueschemeyer & Stephens, 1997). There are also other formal techniques, such as game-theoretic interaction models, which self-contain dynamic processes.

Already quite a few attempts have been made so far. In an analysis of the outcomes of local environmental policies in the United States, Stevenson and Greenberg (2000) applied both QCA and ESA. Quite similarly, in a research on closure processes of nonprofit organizations, Duckles, Hager, and Galaskiewicz (2005) first elaborated an expected sequence of events leading to the outcome of interest—i.e., organizational closure. Then they used thick case information (narratives, interviews) to reconstruct the actual sequence of events in the empirical cases. With the help of ESA, they were then able to construct 31 event structures, some of which were operationalized in sequential sub-models for successive QCA minimization procedures. Eventually they elaborated a complete model that enabled them to identify some key precipitating factors in the chain of events, at least for some clusters of cases. In another vein, Brown and Boswell (1995) combined QCA with game modeling in their study of ethnic conflicts in split labor market conditions. They used a game-theoretic model (which is dynamic by definition) to construct dynamic hypotheses, which were then tested using QCA.

An attempt of another kind, by Caren and Panofsky (2005), consisted of integrating temporality directly into QCA. Using a hypothetically constructed example, they argued that it is possible to develop an extension of QCA (TQCA—temporal QCA) to capture causal sequences. First, they included sequence considerations as a specific case attribute, hence increasing dramatically the number of logically possible configurations. Second, they placed theoretical restrictions to limit the number of possible configurations. Third, they performed a specific form of Boolean minimization; this allowed them to obtain richer minimal formulas, which also include sequences and trajectories. This is an interesting attempt, although it dramatically increases the problem of limited diversity (Ragin & Strand, 2008), and it should still be tested using empirical data.

In conclusion, the question of temporal articulation remains a major and complex issue, the detailed discussion of which goes beyond the scope of this volume. It is a difficult question extending far beyond QCA. For social scientific empirical research, the question of the temporal dimension represents a real methodological Pandora's Box (see Abbott, 2001; Bartolini, 1993). Everything depends, in the end, on what is meant by "including the temporal dimension" in QCA. If it is about taking into consideration *sequences* of events[4] along an objective timeline, then the solutions which have been presented here may be satisfactory. On the contrary, if it is about integrating into QCA a "richer" dimension of temporality—the "narrative" dimension, the subjective perceptions of time by the actors, the "social" production of time, feedback mechanisms, and so on—then much more work should still be done.

CONCLUSION: THERE IS NO "MIRACLE METHOD"

Among the seven main critiques voiced vis-à-vis QCA, the most potent one regards the non-inclusion of time and process in the QCA procedure itself. As for the six other critiques, some of them can be addressed technically (e.g., the use of mvQCA or fsQCA if dichotomization is viewed as too "rough") or nuanced in that they are not QCA-specific and hence should be extended to many other empirical approaches and techniques. Some of the critiques are disputable—or even misplaced—because they are issued using criteria from other paradigms (typically the statistical paradigm) that are not applicable to QCA. We hope that this chapter helps to clarify some of these misunderstandings—it is indeed a key ambition of this textbook to develop a "pedagogy" of QCA and try to bring scholars from other paradigms to at least understand (if not adhere to) the paradigm underpinning QCA.

Of course, neither csQCA nor the other QCA techniques are miracle techniques—ones that will resolve all dilemmas related to the comparative analysis in small- and intermediate-N research designs. Rather, they are best understood as complementary to other methods, as techniques that can help the researcher to overcome obstacles. In any case, those techniques "should not be used mechanically; they are conceived as aids to interpretive analysis" (Ragin, 1987, p. 120).

Key Points

- General point: Some critiques vis-à-vis QCA techniques are not valid because they are based on assumptions, rules, and goals that are not those of QCA as a paradigm.

- Dichotomization (and any form of threshold-setting) always induces some "loss" of information, but it also allows some progress in the understanding of complexity.

- Some technical difficulties of dichotomization can be met with csQCA and also by opting instead for mvQCA or fsQCA.

- The use of non-observed cases ("logical remainders") can be justified even when they are less plausible, if the goal is simply to derive a logical shorthand description of cases. It is important, however, to consider the plausibility of "simplifying assumptions" in most applications of QCA.

- Case-sensitivity is both an asset and a problem in QCA. Following "good practices" of case selection, model building, and minimization enables one to moderate the problematic side of this issue.

- The difficulty of selecting conditions is not specific to QCA and can be addressed through a rigorous research design.

- QCA, technically speaking, does not unravel "causal mechanisms" (the "black box") at work in the real world—this is the investigator's task, based on his or her understanding of cases.

- It is indeed a key limitation of QCA that it does not explicitly integrate the time and process dimensions. Various attempts are being made to address this limitation.

Key Complementary Readings

De Meur, Rihoux, & Yamasaki (2002), Ragin (2008), Ragin & Rihoux (2004b).

NOTES

1. See, however, a first critique of mvQCA by Vink and van Vliet (2007) and discussions of fuzzy sets by Verkuilen (2001), Hollander (2002), Cat (2006), Fiss (2007), and Smithson and Verkuilen (2006). See Ragin (2008) for a reply to some of the critiques on fuzzy sets.

2. With the possibility of adding a third "don't care" [-] value. However, remember that this does not constitute an intermediate value between [0] and [1] (see Box 3.1).

3. Marx (2006) nevertheless takes this critique onboard and suggests some technical responses with regard to the ratio between the number of cases and the number of conditions.

4. In this respect, a particularly relevant possibility would be to "cross" the logics of QCA with the Actor-Process-Event Scheme (APES) tool developed by Serdült, Vögeli, Hirschi, and Widmer (2005; Serdült & Hirschi, 2004).

8

Conclusions—The Way(s) Ahead

Benoît Rihoux
Charles C. Ragin
Sakura Yamasaki
Damien Bol

Goals of This Chapter

After reading this chapter, you should be able to:

- Have a clear view of the key "good practices" throughout the textbook
- Understand the key remaining challenges facing QCA techniques, as well as expected developments in the near future
- Possibly, in your own work, try to bring an original contribution to these developments
- Reflect on the possibility of combining (or confronting) QCA techniques with other methods in your own research

MAINSTREAMING "GOOD PRACTICES" IN APPLICATIONS OF QCA

Remember that a key goal of this textbook is to present the most important "good practices" for QCA techniques. During the last few years, more and more practitioners have become aware of these good practices, thus enabling an increasingly homogeneous quality of applications. Within the next few years, the further mainstreaming of good practices will be of crucial importance for the further progress of Configurational Comparative Methods in general and of QCA techniques in particular.

An important overarching good practice is that QCA techniques are best applied with transparency. In concrete terms, this means that at least some information must be provided with respect to each one of the practical steps and decisions made in the course of the analysis. Remember that transparency is what allows replicability, more pertinent critiques (hopefully), and more cumulative knowledge.

Box 8.1
"Good Practices" (12): Transparency

For all QCA techniques, the buzzword is *transparency*. Even in short publication format (e.g., conference papers and journal articles), the following elements should be provided in some form:

- The raw data table

- The operationalization (dichotomization, trichotomization, or fuzzy-set calibration) of all variables (conditions and outcome)

- The computer software used (TOSMANA or FSQCA, or other available program). The minimization should not be performed by hand

- The truth table

- The analysis of necessary conditions

- The treatment of contradictory configurations (if any)

- The main iterations leading to the final (contradiction-free) model

- The way logical remainders are being used (if applicable)

- The full minimal formulas, not only as narratives, but also in formal notation. If there are many possible minimal formulas, all should be mentioned— or at least, the choice of a specific minimal formula should be well-documented and justified

- The minimal formulas before and after you factor them by hand (if applicable; see Box 3.7)

- The consistency and coverage measures

- The interpretation of the minimal formulas (which "paths" are more important and why?, etc.)

Of course, in short publication format, it might be difficult to find enough room to lay out all these elements. Experience indicates that it can nevertheless be done, in a synthetic way (some good examples: Chan, 2003; Hagan & Hansford-Bowles, 2005; Kilburn, 2004; Osa & Corduneanu-Huci, 2003; Redding & Viterna, 1999; Vanderborght & Yamasaki, 2004). It is also always possible to make available (e.g., on a Web page) some elements that would be too cumbersome for a short publication (e.g., a raw data table that would be too large, qualitative threshold justification for some conditions, a long list of minimal formulas).

CONNECTING THE DIFFERENT QCA TECHNIQUES

Beyond their specifics, the different QCA techniques share a common perspective: contributing to the development of "meaningful 'medium-range' social science," situated "between the extremes of over-generalizing and 'universalizing' macro-quantitative approaches, on the one hand, and purely individualizing case-oriented approaches, on the other" (Cronqvist & Berg-Schlosser, 2006, p. 164; see also p. 6). Because they share this perspective, QCA techniques should be viewed as complementary. Depending on the researcher's needs, and on the nature of the data, it is possible to concentrate on a single technique, or possibly try different combinations.

As explained above (p. 28), MSDO/MDSO is useful mostly at the preliminary stages of research, in the process of case and condition selection. As for the three other techniques (csQCA, mvQCA, and fsQCA), there are different perspectives on how they articulate. Herrmann and Cronqvist (2008), for example, argue that the three respective techniques are best used in different research situations, following two dimensions: the sheer number of cases (the size of the data set) and the necessity to preserve the richness of the data information in the raw data set.

Another perspective is to consider that the crisp-set approach works best when there is a careful articulation with in-depth case knowledge, especially given the important impact that dichotomization has on findings. The fuzzy-set approach, by contrast, is probably more useful when the evidence is more quantitative in nature and lends itself to fine-grained calibration. Whether or not these perspectives on differences are accepted, there are important overlaps among these techniques. For instance, all three techniques can be used for large, intermediate, and small Ns. Indeed, it has been demonstrated that csQCA can be used fruitfully in larger-N settings and that fsQCA is also compatible with a small-N research design (see p. 174). Whatever choice is made, one should not be too rigid when approaching these techniques. Testing the different QCA techniques can indeed be part of the iterative research process.

In general, if the data are mostly dichotomous by nature, or if dichotomizing does not pose too serious difficulties, it is best to try csQCA first and then shift to mvQCA if contradictions are numerous and there is no way to resolve them via in-depth analysis of cases. By contrast, if the raw data vary systematically and meaningfully by degree, it is probably better not to dichotomize or trichotomize them and to use fsQCA instead. Also, as explained in Chapter 5, fsQCA has a stricter definition of sufficiency, and the assessment of each causal combination is based on data for all cases included in a study. Thus, the results of an application of fsQCA are likely to be more narrowly circumscribed—by the evidence—than the results of either csQCA or mvQCA.

CONNECTING QCA TECHNIQUES AND OTHER
QUALITATIVE AND QUANTITATIVE TECHNIQUES

Remember that Configurational Comparative Methods, and QCA techniques in particular, display some features (and strengths) of both "case-oriented" and "variable-oriented" approaches. In short, these techniques are case-oriented, holistic techniques, but at the same time they are also analytic in nature as it is necessary to break down cases into variables—conditions and an outcome (see pp. xviii, 6, 13). Because of the dual nature of QCA techniques, they can be fruitfully connected to many other techniques, be they "qualitative" or "quantitative."

By definition, most QCA applications are de facto developed in sequence with more qualitative, thick case-oriented methods. Especially in the smaller-N analyses, applications often stem from qualitative case studies. Thus, there is already a lot of upstream qualitative work involved in the process of achieving an in-depth understanding of cases. One of the recent illustrations is Grimm's (2006) analysis of entrepreneurship policy and regional economic growth in the USA and Germany. She uses QCA in an exploratory way, to enrich her qualitative knowledge of specific cases, by helping her to identify specific contextual factors that influence some cases but not others. Indeed, QCA minimal formulas can be interpreted in useful ways by qualitatively oriented researchers, for these results may shed light on key elements of their "thick" case narratives. In other words, QCA techniques can be used to gain leverage in the process of unraveling thick case narratives—both for individual cases (within-case perspective) and for comparisons across cases (cross-case perspective) (Curchod, Dumez, & Jeunemaître, 2004). True, as explained above, QCA does not in itself open up the "black box" of complex phenomena and processes (see p. 159). However, it rather acts like a flashlight that points at some crucial spots in the black boxes of the cases under investigation.

As for the connection with mainstream statistical methods, in numerous recent contributions, especially in medium-N and larger-N settings, researchers have used both statistical techniques and QCA techniques to analyze the same initial data and to confront the conclusions of both techniques. Quite often, the empirical conclusion is that QCA techniques help researchers learn more from their data. For instance, by reanalyzing with fsQCA the bell curve data on social inequalities in the United States, Ragin (2006a) demonstrates that there is much more to be found when one takes into account the configurational nature of social phenomena, which cannot be grasped with standard statistical procedures. Another example is Luoma's (2006) study of social sustainability in local Finnish communities, in which QCA enriches the conclusions reached by prior regression analyses. The same goes for Cronqvist and Berg-Schlosser's

(2006) aforementioned mvQCA analysis of explanatory factors of AIDS prevalence in sub-Saharan Africa (see p. 138).

Other examples include the confrontation between fuzzy-set analysis and regression analyses by Katz, Vom Hau, and Mahoney (2005) (see p. 140). csQCA has in fact already been confronted with quite a few different statistical techniques: discriminant analysis (Berg-Schlosser & De Meur, 1997), factor analysis (Berg-Schlosser & Cronqvist, 2005), descriptive statistics on individual conditions (Sager, 2004), various types of multiple regression (e.g., Amenta & Poulsen, 1996; Ebbinghaus & Visser, 1998; Kittel, Obinger, & Wagschal, 2000; Nelson, 2004), logistic regression (Amoroso & Ragin, 1999; Ragin & Bradshaw, 1991), and logit regression (Dumont & Bäck, 2006; Heikkila, 2003; Peters, 1998). Other attempts to "cross" QCA techniques with other (non-statistical) formalized techniques have been made, such as social network analysis (Stevenson & Greenberg, 2000; Yamasaki & Spreitzer, 2006) and game theory (Brown & Boswell, 1995).

At this stage, the most contested topic is probably the respective pros and cons of QCA techniques versus statistical techniques. This debate can become somewhat confrontational. Probably a useful way to put things is that the intention of QCA techniques is certainly not to supplant regression and related analyses, especially since the underlying logic and goals of the respective methods display stark differences (see Chapter 7). As mentioned above (see p. 9), one of the key differences is that regression-based methods focus primarily on the problem of estimating the net, independent effect of each variable included in an analysis on the outcome. By contrast, it would be a serious mistake to apply QCA techniques to this task, as the latter focus on combinations of conditions. From the perspective of QCA, the idea of isolating the net, independent effect of each condition variable makes no sense (Ragin & Rihoux, 2004b; Ragin, 2006a). Fundamentally, QCA techniques attempt to explain specific outcomes in particular cases (hopefully also producing "modest" generalizations; see p. 11); statistical analysis, by contrast, tries to generalize about averages across all cases in a population, without attention to any specific case. Without taking into account this ontological difference, it is all too easy to formulate misplaced critiques with regard to QCA (see Chapter 7), and it is difficult to meaningfully confront the two approaches. Probably a useful way to combine QCA techniques and other formal (typically statistical) techniques is to consider them sequentially. This is a rejoinder to growing debates on how to combine, or possibly even "mix," methods in real-life empirical research (see, e.g., Creswell, 2003; Creswell & Plano Clark, 2007; Tashakkori & Teddlie, 2003). Note that one should always remain cautious when confronting different types of methods: To what extent is it meaningful to compare results obtained using different methods with different ontological assumptions? Researchers who wish to seriously compare results from different methods should first become knowledgeable of the literature on methodological triangulation (see references in: Flick, 2004; Lobe, 2006; Massey, 1999).

To sum up: There is still much work to be done on this topic—the added value of comparing different methods—and more specifically on the confrontation between QCA techniques and other techniques. In any event, it is important to take into account the type of (causal) relationships we expect to find in a given universe of investigation, as Skaaning (2006) argues:

> [If] the area under investigation is best described by a general linear, additive logic, then conventional statistics . . . is probably the most appropriate methodological tool, and if it is characterized by complex causality and sufficient and/or necessary explanations, the QCA methods have a strong standing because of their ability to handle set-theoretical propositions. . . . [In] general it depends on the character of the phenomena under consideration whether it is more rewarding to see [statistics and QCA] as complementary or competitive alternatives. As we cannot determine the character of social phenomena a priori, we have to apply methods based on different assumptions and subsequently evaluate the plausibility of their respective results based on theoretical and substantial insight. (p. 184)

On the more qualitative, case-oriented side as well, there is a lot to be gained from a rich dialogue between QCA techniques and more interactive qualitative methods (see Rihoux & Lobe, 2009).

PURSUING INNOVATIONS

As we write these lines, many avenues are being opened up for further innovation in the use and development of QCA techniques as well as for MSDO/MDSO. On the one hand, software development (see the "software" page at www.compasss.org) is continually underway. At this stage, the two major programs, FSQCA and TOSMANA, offer complementary tools, in user-friendly environments. Some additional tools have been developed. For instance, in addition to implementing the procedures described in Ragin (2000), FSQCA now has new routines for truth table analysis of fuzzy-set data (fsQCA, as described in Chapter 5). It now also includes calculations of "consistency" and "coverage" measures for both crisp- and fuzzy-set analyses, as described in Ragin (2006b, 2008; see also pp. 47, 67). Additionally, coverage can be partitioned to show the relative empirical weight of the combinations of conditions shown in a truth table solution. The task of calibrating interval and ratio scales as fuzzy sets is now automated, based on thresholds for full membership, full nonmembership, and the crossover value, input by the user. Finally, a new procedure has been implemented that allows the derivation of three solutions for each analysis: the complex solution, the parsimonious solution, and the intermediate (theory and knowledge informed) solution, as described in pp. 110–118 and in Ragin (2008). As for TOSMANA, in addition to the standard csQCA procedure, this software fully implements mvQCA as described in Chapter 4. A number of tools have also been developed to make the csQCA and mvQCA procedures more accessible and to enable a more dynamic use of the software. A "visualizer" tool allows one to display Boolean data as Venn diagrams, with different visualizing options. Further tools have also been developed to help the user in the threshold-setting exercise (e.g., the "thresholdssetter" tool, see p. 79, as well as some clustering algorithms; see p. 84) and to easily compute contradictory simplifying assumptions. All these are documented in the TOSMANA manual (Cronqvist, 2007b).

Thanks to increasing computing capacity, both programs now enable the treatment of a larger number of conditions. Nevertheless, such capacities should be used sparingly in order to avoid "individualizing" cases completely in the ongoing dialogue between theory and evidence. Indeed, just because a computing operation is *technically feasible doesn't mean that it is useful or even desirable*. Once again: The QCA programs should never be used in a "push-button" manner but rather in a reflexive way. Needless to say, the same should apply to any formal tool—statistical tools as well—in social science research.

Some further software innovations will surely follow in the next few years. Some other efforts are being undertaken on other platforms, especially R, by Dusa (2007) as well as STATA (Longest & Vaisey, 2008). Here are some issues on the agenda, which will hopefully materialize at some stage in the software development, through FSQCA, TOSMANA, or other platforms: a more explicit inclusion of the time dimension in the procedures, some further improvements in the user-friendliness of the platforms, new ways to visualize the configurations as well as the minimal formulas (Schneider & Grofman, 2006, 2007), better linking between the minimal formulas and the cases, some interconnections with other software (e.g., importing/exporting data), and so on. The developers of those programs are open to comments and suggestions from users.

On the other hand, the range of QCA applications, and the way QCA techniques are being exploited, is broadening in at least four directions. First, a new trend that is only just now beginning concerns the *level* at which cases are defined. So far, in almost all QCA applications, cases and outcomes are situated at the macro- or meso-levels, such as policy fields, collective actors, organizations, and country or regional characteristics. Only a few users have applied QCA to micro-level data, though there is arguably a potential to do so, especially in fields such as educational research and psychology—and surely other disciplines as well (sociology, political science, criminology, etc.), where it makes sense to engage in a small- or intermediate-N research design with individuals as cases. Apart from some already mentioned large-N micro-level analyses (e.g., Ragin, 2006b, using the bell curve data; see p. 170), original applications of this type have been recently completed or are currently in progress—e.g., the work of Lobe (2006) on students taking part in an experiment or that of Scherrer (2006) on the political socialization of individuals. Especially in more participatory research designs—i.e., when the researcher is able to engage in regular interaction with the individuals (the "cases") that are the object of the study—it is possible to argue that he or she gets an even better understanding of each individual case than would be the case for meso- or macro-level phenomena. Indeed, the researcher is literally able to interact directly with each and every case, which is much more difficult when cases are meso- or macro-level entities (Lobe, 2006; Lobe & Rihoux, forthcoming).

Second, with regard to the *number* of cases, there is already a lot of variation in the applications. Up to the present, quite a few applications have very small N's, as few as three (Häge, 2005), five (e.g., Kitchener, Beynon, & Harrington, 2002), six (e.g., Vanderborght & Yamasaki, 2004), or seven cases (e.g., Brueggemann & Boswell, 1998; Hellström, 2001). In the intermediate-N range, most applications are to be found in the broad range from 10 to 50 cases. However, several applications address between 50 and 80 cases (e.g., Williams & Farrell, 1990; Rudel & Roper, 1996; Nomiya, 2001). Still further, some applications are to be found in the large-N domain, up to a more than 100 (Drass & Spencer, 1987; Ishida, Yonetani, & Kosaka, 2006) or even more than 1,000 cases (Ragin & Bradshaw, 1991; Amoroso & Ragin, 1999; Miethe & Drass, 1999). There is surely further room for innovation when one "stretches" the potential of techniques such as QCA on very small-N or, conversely, large-N situations. Of course, the key question to be asked in such situations is: what "added value" does QCA bring, as compared with other techniques? For instance, if one only has four cases, what is the added value of a QCA as compared to four "thick" case studies compared in a more (non-formal) qualitative way?

Third, in terms of disciplinary and topical profiles, more than two-thirds of existing applications are still found in political science (comparative politics, welfare state studies, policy analysis, etc.) and sociology (historical sociology, organizational sociology, etc.). However, there is a growing number of applications in other disciplines such as political economy, management studies, and criminology, and a few applications can be found in history, geography, psychology, and education. For sure, many other fields of study could exploit QCA techniques—even in the natural and biological sciences. For instance, in medical research, for some topics (e.g., rare diseases, infections in very specific subgroups of a population), it is impossible to engage in large-N designs where biostatistical tools can be applied or to fulfill strict conditions of an experimental procedure. QCA techniques could offer some solutions in these research areas.

Fourth and finally, there is still a largely untapped potential in the use of QCA, specifically in terms of exploratory (hypothesis-testing) applications. If QCA is used in this way, we strongly recommend that researchers present their hypotheses in algebraic form (e.g., as Boolean statements). This simple step raises several important questions as to how hypotheses are structured and also as to how the results will be interpreted. For example, in csQCA, there is a difference between positing that a given phenomenon is associated with or caused by the presence of condition A or the presence of condition B or the presence of condition C and positing that the same phenomenon is associated with or caused by the simultaneous presence of condition A and condition B and condition C. In Boolean terms, these two hypotheses appear, respectively, as:

$$H1 = A + B + C$$

$$H2 = A * B * C$$

Needless to say, their implications are very different. Remember that the methodological assumptions behind QCA are those of conjuncturality (see p. 8) and that, as Amenta and Poulsen (1994; and pp. 125, 128) have already pointed out, QCA hypotheses should also posit conjunctural, contextual, or conditional hypotheses. Until now, QCA hypotheses have mainly rested on the expected *individual* effect of a condition on the outcome, and even if an overall joint effect was expected (see "multiple conjunctural causation," p. 8), the precise joint effects between specific conditions have seldom been exposed (for some exceptions, see Amenta, Caren, & Olasky, 2005 [see p. 128]; Bochsler, 2006; Peillon, 1996; Watanabe, 2003; Yamasaki, 2003, 2007).

ENGAGING IN COLLECTIVE RESEARCH EFFORTS AND INFORMED METHODOLOGICAL DEBATES

Until the last few years, there were several factors hampering the growth and diversification of QCA techniques and their applications (De Meur & Rihoux, 2002, pp. 143–144). One factor was the lack of training opportunities and the lack of guidance for students and researchers not (yet) specialized in these techniques. This limitation has now broadly been lifted, as the training opportunities increase (standard courses and seminars, summer courses, etc.) and as many resources are now available online through the COMPASSS resource site (www.compasss.org) and related Web sites. The pool of published applications is also quite broad and diversified at this stage, which constitutes another key resource for users. Further, as an increasing number of scholars have actually used the techniques to some extent, they are more able to provide guidance to beginners.

A second obstacle had to do with limitations in the first versions of the QCA software. In the late 1980s and 1990s, though they were technically operational, QCA-DOS 2.0 and 3.0 were not user-friendly, operating under a DOS environment and rather slow as the number of conditions increased. This limitation has now been largely lifted, through the development of the more user-friendly, Windows-type FSQCA and TOSMANA software (see p. 172).

A third obstacle was the lack of a full-size, English-language textbook designed to reach a broad audience across various disciplines. This is exactly the ambition of this volume, so hopefully this hampering factor will also be lifted.

So what other obstacles remain? Let us rather phrase them in terms of challenges, two of which are probably particularly crucial. The first challenge is to further improve case knowledge in systematic comparative, small- or intermediate-N research designs. Remember that case knowledge—empirical "intimacy" with each case—is a key pillar for QCA techniques (p. 24). However, also remember that, as the number of cases grow, it becomes increasingly difficult to develop a sufficient level of knowledge of all individual cases. This task is especially difficult if it is the *individual* effort of a solitary researcher. Probably some key advancements will be achieved by bringing together *pools* of researchers—typically case specialists—in concerted efforts. Provided that flows of communication and the design of the case studies is well thought out, such concerted research efforts could provide excellent material for even richer QCA applications. For example, if a researcher wants to apply QCA to a phenomenon of interest across the 25 European Union member states, the ideal template would be to rely on a network of country experts to help with data collection and the operationalization of the variables with due consideration of context-specific features and, last but not least, to develop meaningful interpretations of the results, taking these findings back to the individual cases. The inter-war project (revisited in Chapters 3 to 5) is a good illustration of such a research effort.

The second challenge is to pursue the debates on the strengths and limitations of QCA techniques, obviously also as compared with those of other techniques (qualitative or quantitative). However, only very seldom do such discussions produce sufficient progress, probably because, on the one hand, when it comes to methodological debates (not only with regard to QCA, also much more broadly), they are much more often destructive than constructive. They look more like "paradigms wars," where the goal is to destroy or disqualify the enemy—namely, the advocate of some other methodological perspective. On the other hand, until recently at least, relatively few scholars were adequately informed regarding the underpinnings of QCA as an *approach*, let alone on the more technical aspects of QCA techniques. One can only hope that, with the further development, broadening, and sophistication of QCA applications, potential detractors will become better informed regarding these techniques, so they can also make more useful critiques. Hopefully, this textbook will be of some help in this process.

Key Points

- Transparency: Because QCA techniques require an active input from the user at several stages of the procedure, the key choices have to be well-documented in any publication or report.

- QCA techniques can be connected with other techniques in several different ways, including both "qualitative" and "quantitative" techniques. A lot of progress can be expected in this field.

- When confronting or connecting QCA techniques with statistical techniques, one should not forget their ontological differences (different purposes, assumptions, and conceptions of causality); the same holds for any endeavor of methodological "triangulation."

- User-friendly programs are available and offer many useful tools; these programs are still under development and being improved on a regular basis.

- QCA applications are opening up to various disciplines, to different levels of analysis (micro, meso, macro), and to a broad range of research designs (from very small-N to large-N).

- A still underexploited and yet powerful feature of QCA is its "hypothesis-testing" function.

- *Collective* research projects (bringing case experts together) are a suitable environment for fruitful applications of QCA techniques.

- Debates on the strengths and limitations of QCA techniques need to be pursued in an informed way, so as to pursue the improvement of these techniques.

Key Complementary Readings

Ragin (2008), Rihoux (2006, 2008a, 2008b), Schneider & Wagemann (2007, forthcoming).

Appendix: Further Resources for Configurational Comparative Methods

WHERE TO FIND FURTHER INFORMATION

There are two key locations where you will find further information and a large amount of resources on Configurational Comparative Methods. The first one, specifically as a companion to this textbook, is the *textbook resource page* (URL: www.compasss.org/Textbook.htm), in which we have compiled more detailed information on many aspects and practical points presented in the textbook. It is designed to be a help for users, at all levels (from beginners to more advanced), working on their own applications.

The second one is the *COMPASSS international resource site* (URL: www.compasss.org), which also contains many useful resources. In particular, as you start working with CCM and QCA techniques, you will probably be mostly interested in the "didactics," "working papers," and "international bibliographical database" sections. There are also many links to other sites—for example, the FSQCA and TOSMANA pages, where you can freely download the programs.

Glossary

In this glossary, we have gathered key technical terms used in QCA and its techniques, along with concise definitions. Some equivalent terms, used by some authors in the literature, as well as by the FSQCA or TOSMANA programs, are also mentioned.

Binary variable (equivalents: **Boolean variable, dichotomous variable**): variable that takes only two values: [0] or [1].

Boolean distance: the number of Boolean (i.e., dichotomized, with [0] or [1] values) *conditions* by which two cases differ from one another.

Boolean minimization: see *Minimization*.

Complex solution: *minimal formula* derived without the aid of any *logical remainders*.

Condition (equivalents: **condition variable, causal[1] condition**): an explanatory variable that may affect the *outcome*. Note: It is not an "independent variable" in the statistical sense.

Configuration: a combination of *conditions* relevant to a given *outcome*. It may correspond to one, more than one, or no empirical case(s). It corresponds to one row of a *truth table*.

> *[-] outcome configuration:* a configuration whose outcome value is always [-], indicating it could be [1] or [0]; also known as a "don't care" configuration.

> *[0] outcome configuration:* a configuration whose outcome value is always [0].

> *[1] outcome configuration:* a configuration whose outcome value is always [1].

Consistency: the degree to which empirical evidence supports the claim that a set-theoretic relation exists. A subset relation may signal a necessary or a sufficient condition, depending on which is the subset, the cause (*sufficiency*), or the outcome (*necessity*).

Contradictory configuration: a *configuration* whose *outcome* value is [1] for some cases and [0] for other cases. It therefore covers a set of empirical cases, which, although they share the same set of *condition* values, display different outcome values.

Contradictory simplifying assumption: when the same *logical remainder* is used both in the *minimization* of the *[1] outcome configurations* and in the *minimization* of the *[0] outcome configurations,* thereby making two contradictory assumptions regarding the outcome value of that logical remainder.

Coverage: an assessment of the way the respective *terms* of the *minimal formulas* "cover" observed cases (three types of coverage: raw coverage, unique coverage, and solution coverage).

Fuzzy set membership score: the degree to which a given case belongs to a *set,* which can be any value between two qualitatively defined states: full membership (1) and full nonmembership (0) in the set.

Implicant: see *Prime implicant.*

Intermediate solution: *minimal formula* derived with the aid of only those *logical remainders* that are consistent with the researcher's theoretical and substantive knowledge.

Interval level (of measurement): quantitative data that are ordered on a constant scale, with equivalent differences between values; an interval scale with a meaningful zero point is known as a *ratio scale.*

Logical remainder (equivalents: **logical case, logical remainder case, remainder, counterfactual, non-observed case**): a *configuration* (combination of conditions) that lacks empirical instances. Logical remainders may be included in the Boolean *minimization.*

Membership score: see *Fuzzy set membership score.*

Minimal formula (equivalents: **reduced expression, minimal equation, solution**): formula obtained through Boolean or set-theoretic *minimization.* It typically consists of a reduced set of *prime implicants* (*terms*), connected by the Boolean "OR" [+] operator, also known as a "sums of products" expression.

Minimization (equivalents: **Boolean minimization, Boolean synthesis, Boolean reduction**): the process of reducing, through Boolean or set-theoretic algorithms, complex expressions into a *minimal formula.*

Necessary condition: see *Necessity.*

Necessity: a *condition* is *necessary* for an *outcome* if it is always present when the outcome occurs, and if it is never absent when the outcome occurs (thus the outcome cannot occur in the absence of the condition). The outcome is a *subset* of the cause.

Nominal level (of measurement): the data are classified, but not ordered (e.g., religion, gender [male/female]).

Ordinal level (of measurement): the data are ordered, but the differences between the values or ranks are not equal (e.g., social class, rank order of preference for political parties).

Outcome (equivalent: **outcome variable**): the variable to be explained by the *conditions*; usually the outcome is the main focus of a study.

Parsimonious solution: *minimal formula* derived with the aid of *logical remainders,* without any evaluation of their plausibility.

Prime implicant: reduced expressions derived in the course of Boolean *minimization.* Typically, a subset of the prime implicants that are derived constitute a *minimal formula,* the endpoint of Boolean minimization. A prime implicant is usually a set of *conditions* joined by the Boolean "AND" [*] operator. Each prime implicant in a minimal formula covers a series of *configurations* from the *truth table* with a given *outcome.*

Property space: the analytic frame that is defined by a given set of *conditions;* with fuzzy set, it is a multidimensional vector space defined by the fuzzy-set conditions. The corners of this multidimensional vector space correspond to *truth table* rows.

Remainder: see *Logical remainder.*

Set: any collection of distinct objects (called *members*) considered as a whole. A set can be described by certain properties or characteristics.

Simplifying assumption: assumption made on the *outcome* value of a *logical remainder,* so it can be included in the *minimization* procedure, in order to obtain a simpler *minimal formula.*

Solution: see *Complex solution; Intermediate solution; Parsimonious solution.*

Subset relation: with crisp sets, a subset relation exists whenever all the members of one *set* are contained within another set; with fuzzy sets a subset relation exists whenever *membership scores* in one set are consistently less than or equal to membership scores in another set.

Sufficiency: a *condition* (or combination of conditions) is *sufficient* for an *outcome* if the outcome always occurs when the condition (or combination) is present (however, the outcome can occur for other reasons as well). In short, the cause is a *subset* of the outcome. Most *terms* in *minimal formulas* (e.g., the term AB in the minimal formula AB + CD → Y) constitute subsets of the outcome and therefore can be interpreted as sufficient (but not *necessary*) for the outcome.

Sufficient condition: see *Sufficiency*.

Term: an element within a Boolean sum. In Boolean or set-theoretic expressions, it is usually a combination of *conditions* joined by the Boolean "AND" [*] operator *(set* intersection).

Truth table (equivalent: **table of configurations**): synthetic display of all *configurations* (combinations of conditions) based on a given data set.

Venn diagram: a graph showing all the possible mathematical or logical relationships between *sets*.

NOTE

1. It is, however, recommended to be cautious in the use of the "causality" terminology, unless you have a clear view of the causal mechanisms at work in your field of study.

References

Note: This reference list can be complemented by further resources in the "international bibliographical database" on the COMPASSS Web site (see the Appendix). You are welcome to indicate missing references (in any format or language) in the database to the COMPASSS team.

Aarebrot, F. H., & Bakka, P. H. (2003). Die vergleichende Methode in der Politikwissenschaft. In D. Berg-Schlosser & F. Müller-Rommel (Eds.), *Vergleichende Politikwissenschaft: Ein einführendes Studienhandbuch* (4th ed.) (pp. 57–76). Wiesbaden, Germany: VS-Verlag.

Abbott, A. (1995). Sequence analysis: New methods for old ideas. *Annual Review of Sociology, 21,* 93–113.

Abbott, A. (2001). *Time matters. On theory and method.* Chicago: University of Chicago Press.

Abbott, A., & Barman, E. (1997). Sequence comparison via alignment and Gibbs sampling: A formal analysis of the emergence of the modern sociological article. *Sociological Methodology, 27*(1), 47–87.

Abell, P. (1987). *The syntax of social life: The theory and method of comparative narratives.* Oxford: Clarendon.

Abell, P. (2004). Narrative explanation: An alternative to variable-centered explanation? *Annual Review of Sociology, 30,* 287–310.

Achen, C. H. (2005). Two cheers for Charles Ragin. *Studies in Comparative International Development (SCID), 40*(1), 27–32.

Alber, J. (1982). *Vom Armenhaus zum Wohlfahrtsstaat. Analysen zur Entwicklung der Sozialversicherung in Westeuropa.* Frankfurt am Main: Campus Verlag.

Amenta, E., Caren, N., & Olasky, S. J. (2005). Age for leisure? Political mediation and the impact of the pension movement on US old-age policy. *American Sociological Review, 70,* 516–538.

Amenta, E., & Poulsen, J. D. (1994). Where to begin: A survey of five approaches to selecting independent variables for Qualitative Comparative Analysis. *Sociological Methods and Research, 23*(1), 22–53.

Amenta, E., & Poulsen, J. D. (1996). Social politics in context: The institutional politics theory and social spending at the end of the New Deal. *Social Forces, 75*(1), 33–60.

Amoroso, L. M., & Ragin, C. C. (1999). Two approaches to understanding control of voluntary and involuntary job shifts among Germans and foreigners from 1991 to 1996. *Quarterly Journal of Economic Research, 2,* 222–229.

Andersen, S. C. (2005). How to improve the outcome of state welfare services. Governance in a systems-theoretical perspective. *Public Administration, 83*(4), 891–907.

Aus, J. P. (2007). Conjunctural causation in comparative case-oriented research. *Quality and Quantity,* DOI: 10.1007/s11135-007-9104-4.

186 CONFIGURATIONAL COMPARATIVE METHODS

Bailey, K. D. (1994). *Typologies and taxonomies: An introduction to classification techniques.* Beverly Hills, CA: Sage.

Bartolini, S. (1993). On time and comparative research. *Journal of Theoretical Politics, 5*(2), 131–167.

Becker, H. S. (1998). *Tricks of the trade: How to think about your research while you're doing it.* Chicago: University of Chicago Press.

Befani, B., Ledermann, S., & Sager, F. (2006). Realistic evaluation and QCA: Conceptual parallels and an empirical application. *Evaluation, 13*(2), 171–192.

Berg-Schlosser, D. (1998). Conditions of authoritarianism, fascism and democracy in inter-war Europe. A cross-sectional and longitudinal analysis. *International Journal of Comparative Sociology, 39*(4), 335–377.

Berg-Schlosser, D. (2004). Evaluation critique des indicateurs de la démocratisation et de la bonne gouvernance. In C. Thiriot, M. Marty, & E. Nadal (Eds.), *Penser la politique comparée. Un état des savoirs théoriques et méthodologiques* (pp. 249–278). Paris: Editions Karthala.

Berg-Schlosser, D., & Cronqvist, L. (2005). Macro-quantitative vs. macro-qualitative methods in the social science. An example from empirical democratic theory employing new software. *Historical Social Research, 4* (30), 154–175.

Berg-Schlosser, D., & De Meur, G. (1994). Conditions of democracy in interwar Europe: A Boolean test of major hypotheses. *Comparative Politics, 26*(3), 253–279.

Berg-Schlosser, D., & De Meur, G. (1997). Reduction of complexity for a small-N analysis: A stepwise multi-methodological approach. *Comparative Social Research, 16,* 133–162.

Berg-Schlosser, D., & Mitchell, J. (2000). *Conditions of democracy in Europe, 1919–39: Systematic case studies.* Basingstoke, UK, New York: Macmillan Press, St Martin's Press.

Berg-Schlosser, D., & Mitchell, J. (2003). *Authoritarianism and democracy in Europe, 1919–39. Comparative analyses.* Hampshire, UK: Palgrave Macmillan Limited.

Berg-Schlosser, D., & Quenter, S. (1996). Macro-quantitative versus macro-qualitative methods in political science. Advantages and disadvantages of comparative procedures using the welfare-state theory as an example. *Historical Social Research, 21*(1), 3–25.

Blalock, H. M. (1984). *Basic dilemmas in the social sciences.* Beverly Hills, CA: Sage.

Bleiklie, I., Goggin, M. L., & Rothmayr, C. (2003). *Comparative biomedical policy: Governing Assisted Reproductive Technologies.* London: Routledge.

Bochsler, D. (2006). *Electoral engineering and inclusion of ethnic groups: Ethnic minorities in parliaments of Central and Eastern European countries* (COMPASSS Working Paper, 38), 35p.

Bollen, K. A., Entwisle, B., & Alderson, A. S. (1993). Macrocomparative research methods. *Annual Review of Sociology, 19,* 321–351.

Boole, G. (1847). *The mathematical analysis of logic: Being an essay towards the calculus of deductive reasoning.* Oxford: Basil Blackwell.

Boole, G. (1958). *An investigation of the laws of thought on which are founded the mathematical theories of logic and probabilities.* New York: Dover Publication.

Boswell, T., & Brown, C. (1999). The scope of general theory. Methods for linking deductive and inductive comparative history. *Sociological Methods and Research, 28*(2), 154–185.

Brady, H. E., & Collier, D. (2004). *Rethinking social inquiry: Diverse tools, shared standards.* Lanham, MD: Rowman & Littlefield.

Brayton, R. K., & Khatri, S. P. (1999). Multi-valued logic synthesis. Paper presented at the 12th International Conference on VSLI Design—"VSLI for the Information Appliance."

Brown, C., & Boswell, T. (1995). Strikebreaking or solidarity in the Great Steel Strike of 1919: A split labor market, game-theoretic, and QCA analysis. *American Journal of Sociology, 100*(6), 1479–1519.

Brueggemann, J., & Boswell, T. (1998). Realizing solidarity: Sources of interracial unionism during the Great Depression. *Work and Occupations, 25*(4), 436–482.

Caramani, D. (2008). *Introduction to comparative method with Boolean algebra.* Thousand Oaks, CA: Sage.

Caren, N., & Panofsky, A. (2005). TQCA. A technique for adding temporality to Qualitative Comparative Analysis. *Sociological Methods & Research, 34*(2), 147–172.

Cat, J. (2006). Fuzzy empiricism and fuzzy-set causality: What is all the fuzz about. *Philosophy of Science, 73,* 26–41.

Chan, S. (2003). Explaining war termination: A Boolean analysis of causes. *Journal of Peace Research, 40*(1), 49–66.

Clément, C. (2003). *State collapse: A common causal pattern? A comparative analysis of Lebanon, Somalia, and the former-Yugoslavia.* Louvain-la-Neuve: Université catholique de Louvain.

Clément, C. (2004). Un modèle commun d'effondrement de l'Etat? Une AQQC du Liban, de la Somalie et de l'ex-Yougoslavie. *Revue Internationale de Politique Comparée, 11*(1), 35–50.

Clément, C. (2005a). *Failing states, failing data: The case for QCA (Qualitative Comparative Analysis).* Annual Meeting of the American Political Science Association, Qualitative Methods Panel.

Clément, C. (2005b). *The nuts and bolts of state collapse: Common causes and different patterns?* (COMPASSS Working Paper, 32), 34p.

Cohen, M. R., & Nagel, E. (1934). *An introduction to logic and scientific method.* New York: Harcourt Brace.

Coleman, J. S. (1990). *Foundations of social theory.* Cambridge, MA: Belknap Press.

Collier, D., Mahoney, J., & Seawright, J. (2004). Claiming too much: warnings about selection bias. In H. E. Brady, & D. Collier (Eds.), *Rethinking social inquiry: diverse tools, shared standards* (pp. 85–102). Maryland: Rowman & Littlefield.

Collier, R. B. (1999). *Paths toward democracy: The working class and elites in Western Europe and South America.* New York: Cambridge University Press.

Cook, T. D., & Campbell, D. T. (1979). *Quasi-experimentation: Design and analysis issues for field settings.* Boston: Houghton Mifflin.

Cress, D. M., & Snow, D. A. (2000). The outcome of homeless mobilization: The influence of organization, disruption, political mediation, and framing. *American Journal of Sociology, 105*(4), 1063–1104.

Creswell, J. W. (2003). *Research design qualitative, quantitative and mixed methods approaches* (2nd ed.). London: Sage.

Creswell, J. W., & Plano Clark, V. L. (2007). *Designing and conducting mixed methods research.* London: Sage.

Cronqvist, L. (2004). *Presentation of TOSMANA: Adding multi-value variables and visual aids to QCA* (COMPASSS Working Paper, 20).

Cronqvist, L. (2005). *Introduction to multi-value Qualitative Comparative Analysis (MVQCA)* (COMPASSS Didactics Paper, 4).

Cronqvist, L. (2006). *Using multi-valued outcomes with MVQCA.* TOSMANA technical Note, 2.

Cronqvist, L. (2007a). TOSMANA. Tools for small-N analysis. Version 1.3. http://www.tosmana.org.

Cronqvist, L. (2007b). TOSMANA user manual. Version 1.3.

Cronqvist, L. (2007c). *Konfigurationelle Analyse mit Multi-Value QCA als Methode der vergleichenden Politikwissenschaft.* Unpublished doctoral dissertation, University of Marburg.

Cronqvist, L., & Berg-Schlosser, D. (2006). Determining the conditions of HIV/AIDS prevalence in sub-Saharan Africa. Employing new tools of macro-qualitative analysis. In B. Rihoux & H. Grimm (Eds.), *Innovative comparative methods for policy analysis* (pp. 145–166). New York: Springer.

Curchod, C., Dumez, H., & Jeunemaître, A. (2004). Une étude de l'organisation du transport aérien en Europe: Les vertus de l'AQQC pour l'exploration de la complexité. *Revue Internationale de Politique Comparée, 11*(1), 85–100.

Cuvier, G. (1812). *Recherche sur les ossements fossiles des quadrupèdes.* Paris: Flammarion.

Dahl, R. A. (1971). *Polyarchy, participation and opposition.* New Haven: Yale University Press.

Dahl, R. A. (1989). *Democracy and its critics.* New Haven: Yale University Press.

De Meur, G. (1996). La comparaison des systèmes politiques: Recherche des similarités et des différences. *Revue Internationale de Politique Comparée, 3*(2), 405–437.

De Meur, G., & Berg-Schlosser, D. (1994). Comparing political systems: Establishing similarities and dissimilarities. *European Journal of Political Research, 26*(2), 193–219.

De Meur, G., & Berg-Schlosser, D. (1996). Conditions of authoritarianism, fascism and democracy in inter-war Europe: Systematic matching and contrasting of cases for "small N" analysis. *Comparative Political Studies, 29*(4), 423–468.

De Meur, G., Bursens, P., & Gottcheiner, A. (2006). MSDO/MDSO revisited for public policy analysis. In B. Rihoux, & H. Grimm (Eds.), *Innovative comparative methods for policy analysis* (pp. 67–94). New York: Springer.

De Meur, G., & Rihoux, B. (2002). *L'analyse quali-quantitative comparée (AQQC-QCA): Approche, techniques et applications en sciences humaines.* Louvain-la-Neuve, Belgium: Academia-Bruylant.

De Meur, G., Rihoux, B., & Yamasaki, S. (2002). Revue critique . . . des critiques de l'AQQC. In G. De Meur & B. Rihoux (Eds.), *L'analyse quali-quantitative comparée (AQQC-QCA): Approche, techniques et applications en sciences humaines* (pp. 119–144). Louvain-la-Neuve: Academia-Bruylant.

Diagne, S. B. (1989). *Boole. L'oiseau de nuit en plein jour.* Paris: Belin.

Diamond, L. (1992). Economic development and democracy reconsidered. *American Behavioral Scientist, 35*(3), 450–499.

Drass, K. A., & Spencer, J. W. (1987). Accounting for pre-sentencing recommendations: Typologies and probation officers' theory of office. *Social Problems, 34,* 277–293.

Duckles, B. M., Hager, M. A., & Galaskiewicz, J. (2005). How nonprofits close. Using narratives to study organizational processes. *Qualitative Organizational Research,* 169–203.

Dumont, P., & Bäck, H. (2006). Why so few and why so late? Green parties and the question of governmental participation. *European Journal of Political Research, 45*(S), 35–68.

Dusa, A. (2007). User manual for the QCA(GUI) package in R. *Journal of Business Research, 60*(5), 576–586.

Easton, D. (1965). *A systems analysis of political life.* New York: Wiley and Sons.

Ebbinghaus, B. (2005). When less is more: Selection problems in large-N and small-N cross-national comparisons. *International Sociology, 20*(2).

Ebbinghaus, B., & Visser, J. (1998). When institutions matter: Union growth and decline in Western Europe, 1950–95. *MZES Arbeitspapiere/Working Papers* (I/30), 1–37.

Eisinger, P. K. (1973). The conditions of protest behavior in American cities. *American Political Science Review,* (67), 11–28.

Esping-Andersen, G. (1990). *The three worlds of welfare capitalism.* Princeton, NJ: Princeton University Press.

Esser, H. (1993). *Soziologie. Allgemeine Grundlagen.* Frankfurt am Main: Campus Verlag.

Fischer, J., Kaiser, A., & Rohlfing, I. (2006). The push and pull of ministerial resignations in Germany, 1969–2005. *West European Politics, 4*(29), 709–735.

Fiss, P. C. (2007). A set-theoretic approach to organizational configurations. *Academy of Management Review 32*(4), 1180–1198.

Flick, U. (2004). Triangulation in qualitative research. In U. Flick, E. von Kardorff, & I. Steinke (Eds.), *A companion to qualitative research* (pp. 178–190). London: Sage.

Geddes, B. (2003). *Paradigms and sand castles. Theory building and research design in comparative politics.* Ann Arbor: University of Michigan Press.

George, A. L., & Bennett, A. (2005). *Case studies and theory development in the social sciences.* Cambridge, MA: MIT Press.

Gerlich, P., & Campbell, D. (2000). Austria: From compromise to authoritarianism. In D. Berg-Schlosser & J. Mitchell (Eds.), *Conditions of democracy in Europe, 1919–39. Systematic case-studies* (pp. 40–58). London: Macmillan.

Gerring, J. (2005). Causation: A unified framework for the social sciences. *Journal of Theoretical Politics, 17*(2), 163–198.

Gerring, J. (2006). *Case study research: Principles and practices.* Cambridge, UK: Cambridge University Press.

Glaser, B. G., & Strauss, A. L. (1967). *Discovery of grounded theory: Strategy for qualitative researcher.* London: Wiedenfeld and Nicholson.

Goertz, G. (2006a). Assessing the trivialness, relevance, and relative importance of necessary and sufficient conditions in social science. *Studies in Comparative International Development, 41*(2), 88–109.

Goertz, G. (2006b). *Social science concepts: A user's guide.* Princeton, NJ: Princeton University Press.

Goldthorpe, J. H. (1997). Current issues in comparative macrosociology: A debate on methodological issues. *Comparative Social Research, 16,* 1–26.

Gran, B. (2003). Charitable choice policy and abused children: The benefits and harms of going beyond the public–private dichotomy. *International Journal of Sociology and Social Policy, 23*(11), 80–125.

Grassi, D. (2004). La survie des régimes démocratiques: Une AQQC des démocraties de la "troisième vague" en Amérique du Sud. *Revue Internationale de Politique Comparée, 11*(1), 17–33.

Griffin, L. J. (1992). Temporality, events, and explanation in historical sociology: An introduction. *Sociological Methods and Research, 20,* 403–427.

Griffin, L. J. (1993). Narrative, event-structure analysis and causal interpretation in historical sociology. *American Journal of Sociology, 98*(5), 1094–1133.

Griffin, L. J., Botsko, C., Wahl, A.-M., & Isaac, L. W. (1991). Theoretical generality, case particularity: Qualitative Comparative Analysis of union growth and decline. *International Journal of Comparative Sociology, 32,* 110–136.

Grimm, H. (2006). Entrepreneurship policy and regional economic growth. Exploring the link and theoretical implications. In B. Rihoux & H. Grimm (Eds.), *Innovative comparative methods for policy analysis* (pp. 123–144). New York: Springer.

Hagan, J., & Hansford-Bowles, S. (2005). From resistance to activism: The emergence and persistence of activism among American Vietnam war resisters in Canada. *Social Movements Studies, 4*(3), 231–259.

Häge, F. M. (2005). *Constructivism, fuzzy sets and (very) small-N: Revisiting the conditions for communicative action* (COMPASSS Working Paper, 33), 32p.

Hall, P. A. (2003). Aligning ontology and methodology in comparative politics. In J. Mahoney & D. Rueschemeyer (Eds.), *Comparative historical research* (pp. 373–405). Cambridge, UK: Cambridge University Press.

Heikkila, T. (2003). Institutional boundaries and common-pool resource management: A comparative analysis of water management programs in California. *Journal of Policy Analysis and Management, 23*(1), 97–117.

Heise, D. R. (1989). Modelling event structures. *Journal of Mathematical Sociology, 14,* 139–169.

Hellström, E. (2001). *Conflict cultures. Qualitative comparative analysis of environmental conflicts in forestry* (Silva Fennica Monographs No. 2). Helsinki: The Finnish Society of Forest Science/The Finnish Forest Research Institute.

Herrmann, A., & Cronqvist, L. (2008). When dichotomisation becomes a problem for the analysis of middle-sized datasets. *International Journal of Social Science Research Methodology.*

Hodson, R., & Roscigno, V. J. (2004). Organizational success and worker dignity: Complementary or contradictory? *American Journal of Sociology, 110*(3), 672–708.

Hollander, J. F. (2002). A quick look at Ragin's "Fuzzy set social science." *Comparative & Historical Sociology, 14*(1), 7–9.

Hume, D. (1758). *An enquiry concerning human understanding.* Chicago: Open Court Publishing Co.

Ishida, A., Yonetani, M., & Kosaka, K. (2006). Determinants of linguistic human rights movements: An analysis of multiple causation of LHRs movements using a Boolean approach. *Social Forces, 84*(4), 1937–1955.

Jackson, G. (2005). Employee representation in the board compared: A fuzzy sets analysis of corporate governance, unionism and political institutions. *Industrielle Beziehungen, 3*(12), 28.

Katz, A., Vom Hau, M., & Mahoney, J. (2005). Explaining the great reversal in Spanish America: Fuzzy set analysis versus regression analysis. *Sociological Methods and Research, 33*(4), 539–573.

Kilburn, H. W. (2004). Explaining U.S. urban regimes. A qualitative comparative analysis. *Urban Affairs Review, 39*(5), 633–651.

King, G., Keohane, R. O., & Verba, S. (1994). *Designing social inquiry: Scientific inference in qualitative research.* Princeton, NJ: Princeton University Press.

Kitchener, M., Beynon, M., & Harrington, C. (2002). Qualitative Comparative Analysis and public services research: Lessons from an early application. *Public Management Review, 4*(4), 485–504.

Kitschelt, H. (1986). Political opportunity structures and political protest: Anti-nuclear movements in four democracies. *British Journal of Political Science, 16*(1), 57–85.

Kittel, B., Obinger, H., & Wagschal, U. (2000). Wohlfahrtsstaaten im internationalen vergleich. Politisch-institutionelle Faktoren der Entstehung und Entwicklungsdynamik. H. Obinger & U. Wagschal (Eds.), *Der "gezügelte" Wohlfahrtsstaat: Sozialpolitik in Australien, Japan, Schweiz, Kanada, Neuseeland und den Vereinigten Staaten* (pp. 329–364). Frankfurt am Main: Campus Verlag.

Klir, G. J., Clair, U. St., & Yuan, B. (1997). *Fuzzy sets theory. Foundations and applications.* Englewood Cliffs, NJ: Prentice Hall PTR.

Kogut, B., MacDuffie, J. P., & Ragin, C. C. (2004). Prototypes and strategy: Assigning causal credit using fuzzy sets. *European Management Review, 1,* 114–131.

Kosko, B. (1993). *Fuzzy thinking: The new science of fuzzy logic.* New York: Hyperion.

Krook, M. L. (2006). *Temporality and causal configurations: Combining sequence analysis and fuzzy set/Qualitative Comparative Analysis.* Paper presented at the annual meeting of the APSA, Philadelphia.

Kvist, J. (2000). Idealtyper og fuzzy mèngdelère i komparative studier—Nordisk familiepolitik i 1990erne som eksempel. *Dansk Sociologi, 11*(3), 71–94.

Kvist, J. (2006). Diversity, ideal types and fuzzy sets in comparative welfare state research. In B. Rihoux & H. Grimm (Eds.), *Innovative comparative methods for policy analysis* (pp. 167–184). New York: Springer.

Lieberson, S. (1991). Small N's and big conclusions: An examination of the reasoning in comparative studies based on a small number of cases. *Social Forces, 70*(2), 307–320.

Lieberson, S. (1994). More on the uneasy case for using Mill-type methods in small N comparative studies. *Social Forces, 72*(4), 1225–1237.

Lieberson, S. (2004). Comments on the use and utility of QCA. *Qualitative Methods: Newsletter of the American Political Science Association Organized Section on Qualitative Methods, 2*(2), 13–14.

Lijphart, A. (1971). Comparative politics and the comparative method. *American Political Science Review, 65*(3), 682–693.

Lijphart, A. (1975). The comparable-cases strategy in comparative research. *Comparative Political Studies, 8*(2), 158–177.

Linnaeus, C. (1753). *Species plantarum.* Stockholm: Impensis Laurentii Salvii.

Lipset, S. M. (1960). *Political man.* London: Mercury Books.

Lipset, S. M. (1994). The social requisites of democracy revisited: 1993 presidential address. *American Sociological Review, 59*(1), 1–22.

Lobe, B. (2006). *Mixing qualitative and quantitative methods in the environment of new information-communication technologies.* Unpublished doctoral dissertation, University of Ljubljana, Faculty of Social Sciences.

Lobe, B., & Rihoux, B. (forthcoming). The added value of micro-level QCA: Getting more out of rich case knowledge.

Longest, K. C., & Vaisey, S. (2008). Fuzzy: A program for performing qualitative comparative analyses (QCA) in Stata. *The Stata Journal, 8*(1), 79–104

Luoma, P. (2006). Social sustainability of community structures: A systematic comparative analysis within the Oulu region in Northern Finland. In B. Rihoux & H. Grimm (Eds.), *Innovative comparative methods for policy analysis* (pp. 237–262). New York: Springer.

Mahoney, J. (2000). Strategies of causal inference in small-N analysis. *Sociological Methods and Research, 28*(4), 387–424.

Mahoney, J. (2003). Strategies of causal assessment in comparative historical analysis. In J. Mahoney & D. Rueschemeyer (Eds.), *Comparative historical research* (pp. 337–372). Cambridge, UK: Cambridge University Press.

Mahoney, J. (2004). Revisiting general theory in historical sociology. *Social Forces, 83*(2), 459–489.

Mahoney, J., & Goertz, G. (2004). The possibility principle: Choosing negative cases in comparative research. *American Political Science Review, 98*(4), 653–669.

Mahoney, J., & Rueschemeyer, D. (2003). *Comparative historical research.* Cambridge, UK: Cambridge University Press.

Markoff, J. (1990). A comparative method: reflections on Charles Ragin's innovations in comparative analysis. *Historical Methods, 23*(4), 177–181.

Marradi, A. (1985). Natura, forme e scopi della comparazione: Un bilancio. In D. Fisichella (Ed.), *Metodo scientifico e ricerca politica.* Roma: La Nuova Italia Scientifica.

Marx, A. (2006). *Towards a more robust model specification in QCA results from a methodological experiment* (COMPASSS Working Paper, 43), 25p.

Massey, A. (1999). Methodological triangulation, or how to get lost without being found out. In A. Massey & G. Walford (Eds.), *Studies in educational ethnography* (Vol. 2) (pp. 193–197). Stamford, CT: JAI Press.

McCluskey, E. J. (1966). *Introduction to the theory of switching circuits.* New York: McGraw-Hill.

Merton, R. K. (1968). *Social theory and social structure* (Enlarged ed.). New York: The Free Press.

Miethe, T. D., & Drass, K. A. (1999). Exploring the social context of instrumental and expressive homicides: An application of Qualitative Comparative Analysis. *Journal of Quantitative Criminology, 15*(1), 1–21.

Mill, J. S. (1967 [1843]). *A system of logic: Ratiocinative and inductive.* Toronto: University of Toronto Press.

Mjøset, L. (2001). Theory: Conceptions in the social sciences. In N. J. Smelser & P. B. Baltes (Eds.), *The international encyclopedia of the social and behavioral sciences* (pp. 15641–15647). Amsterdam: Elsevier.

Mjøset, L. (2003). Versuch über die Grundlagen der vergleichenden historischen Sozialwissenschaft. In H. Kaelble & J. Schriewer (Eds.), *Vergleich und Transfer: Komparatistik in den Sozial-, Geschichts- und Kulturwissenschaften* (pp. 167–220). Frankfurt am Main: Campus Verlag.

Musheno, M. C., Gregware, P. R., & Drass, K. A. (1991). Court management of AIDS disputes: A sociolegal analysis. *Law and Social Inquiry, 16*(4), 737–776.

Nelson, K. (2004). The last resort. *Determinants of the generosity of means-tested minimum income protection in welfare democracies* (COMPASSS Working Paper, 21), 44p.

Nomiya, D. (2001). Minsyuu no hanran to shakai hendou: Rekishiteki deita heno ouyou [Peasants' rebellion and social change: Application [of QCA] to historical data]. In N. Kanomata, D. Nomiya, & K. Hasegawa (Eds.), *Shituteki hikaku bunseki [Qualitative comparative analysis]* (pp. 79–94). Kyoto: Mineruva Syobo.

Nomiya, D. (2004). Atteindre la connaissance configurationnelle: Remarques sur l'utilisation précautionneuse de l'AQQC. *Revue Internationale de Politique Comparée, 11*(1), 131–133.

Osa, M., & Corduneanu-Huci, C. (2003). Running uphill: Political opportunity in non-democracies. *Comparative Sociology, 2*(4), 605–629.

Peillon, M. (1996). A qualitative comparative analysis of welfare legitimacy. *Journal of European Social Policy, 6*(3), 175–190.

Pennings, P., Keman, H., & Kleinnijenhuis, J. (1999). *Doing research in political science. an introduction to comparative methods and statistics.* London: Sage.

Peters, B. G. (1998). *Comparative politics, theory and methods.* Basingstoke, UK: Palgrave.

Petersen, T. (1993). Recent advances in longitudinal methodology. *Annual Review of Sociology, 19,* 425–454.

Pierson, P. (2003). Big, slow-moving, and . . . invisible: Macrosocial processes in the study of comparative politics. J. Mahoney & D. Rueschemeyer (Eds.), *Comparative historical research* (pp. 177–207). Cambridge, UK: Cambridge University Press.

Pierson, P. (2004). *Politics in time: History, institutions, and social analysis.* Princeton, NJ: Princeton University Press.

Popper, K. R. (1959). *The logic of scientific discovery.* London: Hutchinson.

Popper, K. R. (1963). *Conjectures and refutations: The growth of scientific knowledge.* London: Routledge & Kegan Paul.

Przeworski, A., & Teune, H. (1970). *The logic of comparative social inquiry.* New York: Wiley-Interscience.

Quine, W. V. (1952). The problem of simplifying truth functions. *American Mathematical Monthly, 59,* 521–531.

Ragin, C. C. (1987). *The comparative method. Moving beyond qualitative and quantitative strategies.* Berkeley, Los Angeles, and London: University of California Press.

Ragin, C. C. (1994). *Constructing social research. The unity and diversity of method.* Newbury Park, CA: Pine Forge Press.

Ragin, C. C. (1995). Using Qualitative Comparative Analysis to study configurations. In U. Kelle (Ed.), *Computer-aided qualitative data analysis* (pp. 177–189). London: Sage.

Ragin, C. C. (2000). *Fuzzy-set social science.* Chicago: University of Chicago Press.

Ragin, C. C. (2002). Préface. In G. De Meur & B. Rihoux (Eds.), *L'analyse quali-quantitative comparée (AQQC-QCA): Approche, techniques et applications en sciences humaines* (pp. 11–14). Louvain-la-Neuve: Academia-Bruylant.

Ragin, C. C. (2003). *Making comparative analysis counts* (COMPASSS Working Paper, 10), 24p.

Ragin, C. C. (2004). Turning the tables: How case-oriented research challenges variable-oriented research. In H. E. Brady & D. Collier (Eds.), *Rethinking social inquiry: Diverse tools, shared standards* (pp. 123–138). Lanham, MD: Rowman & Littlefield.

Ragin, C. C. (2006a). The limitations of net-effects thinking. In B. Rihoux & H. Grimm (Eds.), *Innovative comparative methods for policy analysis* (pp. 13–41). New York: Springer.

Ragin, C. C. (2006b). Set relations in social research: Evaluating their consistency and coverage. *Political Analysis, 14*(3), 291–310.

Ragin, C. C. (2007). Calibration versus measurement. In D. Collier, H. Brady, & J. Box-Steffensmeier (Eds.), *Methodology volume of Oxford handbooks of political science.* New York: Oxford University Press.

Ragin, C. C. (2008). *Redesigning social inquiry:* Fuzzy sets and beyond. Chicago: University of Chicago Press.

Ragin, C. C., & Becker, H. S. (1992). *What is a case? Exploring the foundations of social inquiry.* Cambridge, UK: Cambridge University Press.

Ragin, C. C., Berg-Schlosser, D., & De Meur, G. (1996). Political methodology: Qualitative methods. In R. E. Goodin, & H.-D. Klingemann (Eds.), *A new handbook of political science* (pp. 749–768). Oxford: Oxford University Press.

Ragin, C. C., & Bradshaw, Y. W. (1991). Statistical analysis of employment discrimination: A review and a critique. *Research in Social Stratification and Mobility, 10,* 199–228.

Ragin, C. C., & Rihoux, B. (2004a). Qualitative Comparative Analysis (QCA): State of the art and prospects. *Qualitative Methods: Newsletter of the American Political Science Association Organized Section on Qualitative Methods, 2*(2), 3–13.

Ragin, C. C., & Rihoux, B. (2004b). Replies to commentators: Reassurances and rebuttals. *Qualitative Methods: Newsletter of the American Political Science Association Organized Section on Qualitative Methods, 2*(2), 21–24.

Ragin, C. C., & Sonnett, J. (2004). Between complexity and parsimony: Limited diversity, counterfactual cases, and comparative analysis. In S. Kropp & M. Minkenberg (Eds.), *Vergleichen in der Politikwissenschaft.* Wiesbaden, Germany: VS Verlag für Sozialwissenschaften.

Ragin, C. C., & Strand, S. I. (2008). Using Qualitative Comparative Analysis to study causal order: Comment on Caren and Panofsky (2005). *Sociological Methods & Research, 36*(4), 431–441.

Redding, K., & Viterna, J. S. (1999). Political demands, political opportunities: Explaining the differential success of left-libertarian parties. *Social Forces, 78*(2), 491–510.

Rihoux, B. (2001). *Les partis politiques: Organisations en changement. Le test des écologistes* (Coll. Logiques Politiques). Paris: L'Harmattan.

Rihoux, B. (2003). Bridging the gap between the qualitative and quantitative worlds? A retrospective and prospective view on Qualitative Comparative Analysis. *Field Methods, 15*(4), 351–365.

Rihoux, B. (2006). Qualitative Comparative Analysis (QCA) and related systematic comparative methods: Recent advances and remaining challenges for social science research. *International Sociology, 21*(5), 679–706.

Rihoux, B. (20092008, forthcoming). Case-oriented configurational research using QCA (Qualitative Comparative Analysis). In J. Box-Steffensmeier, H. Brady, & D. Collier (Eds.), *Oxford handbook of political science: Methodology.* Oxford: Oxford University Press.

Rihoux, B. (2008b, forthcoming). Qualitative Comparative Analysis (QCA) and related techniques: Recent advances and challenges. In S. Pickel, G. Pickel, H.-J. Lauth, & D. Jahn (Eds.), *Neuere Entwicklungen und Anwendungen auf dem Gebiet der Methoden der vergleichenden Politikwissenschaft—Band II.* Wiesbaden, Germany: Westdeutscher Verlag.

Rihoux, B., & Lobe, B. (2009). The case for QCA: Adding leverage for thick cross-case comparison. In D. Byrne & C. C. Ragin (Eds.), *Handbook of case based methods.* Thousand Oaks, CA, and London: Sage.

Romme, A. G. L. (1995). Boolean comparative analysis of qualitative data: A methodological note. *Quality and Quantity, 29*(4), 317–329.

Roscigno, V. J., & Hodson, R. (2004). The organizational and social foundations of worker resistance. *American Sociological Review, 69,* 14–39.

Rudel, T. K., & Roper, J. (1996). Regional patterns and historical trends in tropical deforestation, 1976–1990: A qualitative comparative analysis. *Ambio, 25*(3), 160–166.

Rueschemeyer, D., & Stephens, J. D. (1997). Comparing historical sequences—a powerful tool for causal analysis. A reply to John Goldthorpe's "current issues in comparative macrosociology." *Comparative Social Research, 16,* 55–72.

Sager, F. (2004). Metropolitan institutions and policy coordination: The integration of land use and transport policies in Swiss urban areas. *Governance: An International Journal of Policy, Administration, and Institutions, 18*(2), 227–256.

Sartori, G. (1970). Concept misformation in comparative politics. *American Political Science Review, 64*(4), 1033–1053.

Sartori, G. (1991). Comparing and miscomparing. *Journal of Theoretical Politics, 3*(3), 243–257.

Savolainen, J. (1994). The rationality of drawing big conclusions based on small samples: In defence of Mill's methods. *Social Forces, 72*(4), 1217–1224.

Scherrer, V. (2006). *Citoyens sous tensions. Analyse qualitative des rapports à la politique et des configurations d'appartenances à partir d'entretiens projectifs sur les proches.* Unpublished doctoral dissertation, Institut d'Etudes Politiques de Paris, Paris.

Schneider, C. Q., & Grofman, B. (2006). *It might look like a regression equation . . . but it is not! An intuitive approach to the presentation of QCA and FSQCA results* (COMPASSS Working Paper, 39), 61p.

Schneider, C. Q., & Grofman, B. (2007). *Graphical representations of fuzzy set results: How not to get your audience confused*. Paper presented at the 4th ECPR General Conference, Pisa, Italy. Panel on "Comparative Research Design and Configurational Methods."

Schneider, C. Q., & Wagemann, C. (2006). Reducing complexity in Qualitative Comparative Analysis (QCA): Remote and proximate factors and the consolidation of democracy. *European Journal of Political Research, 45*(5), 751–786.

Schneider, C. Q., & Wagemann, C. (2007). *Qualitative Comparative Analysis (QCA) und fuzzy sets. Ein lehrbuch für anwender und jene, die es werden wollen.* Opladen and Farmington Hills: Verlag Barbara Budrich.

Schneider, C. Q., & Wagemann, C. (2008). Standards guter Praxis in Qualitative Comparative Analysis (QCA) und fuzzy-sets. In S. Pickel, G. Pickel, H.-J. Lauth, & D. Jahn (Eds.), *Neue vergleichende sozialwissenschaftliche Methoden.* Wiesbaden, Germany: VS-Verlag.

Schneider, C. Q., & Wagemann, C. (forthcoming). *Qualitative Comparative Analysis (QCA) and fuzzy sets. A user's guide.*

Scouvart, M. (2006). *Une analyse quali-quantitative comparée des causes de la déforestation en Amazonie brésilienne.* Unpublished doctoral dissertation, Université catholique de Louvain, Louvain-La-Neuve, Belgium.

Scouvart, M., Adams, R. T., Caldas, M., Dale, V., Mertens, B., Nédélec, V., et al. (2007). Causes of deforestation in the Brazilian Amazon: A Qualitative Comparative Analysis. *Journal of Land Use Science, 2*(4), 257–282.

Seawright, J. (2005). Qualitative Comparative Analysis vis-à-vis regression. *Studies in Comparative International Development (SCID), 40*(1), 3–26.

Serdült, U., & Hirshi, C. (2004). From process to structure: Developing a reliable and valid tool for policy network comparison. *Swiss Political Science Review, 10*(2), 137–155.

Serdült, U., Vögeli, C., Hirschi, C., & Widmer, T. (2005). APES—Actor-Process-Event Scheme. http://www.apes-tool.ch.

Shalev, M. (1998). *Limits of and alternatives to multiple regression in macro-comparative research.* Paper presented at the Second Conference on the Welfare State at the Crossroads.

Skaaning, S.-E. (2006). *Democracy besides elections: An inquiry into (dis)respect for civil liberty in Latin American and post-communist countries after the third wave.* Unpublished doctoral dissertation, University of Aarhus, Aarhus.

Skocpol, T. (1984). *Vision and method in historical sociology.* Cambridge, UK: Cambridge University Press.

Smithson, M., & Verkuilen, J. (2006). *Fuzzy set theory. Applications in the social sciences.* London: Sage.

Stephens, J. D. (1998). Historical analysis and causal assessment in comparative research. *APSA-CP. Newsletter of the APSA Organized Section in Comparative Politics, 9*(1), 22–25.

Stevenson, W. B., & Greenberg, D. (2000). Agency and social networks: Strategies of action in a social structure of position, opposition, and opportunity. *Administrative Science Quarterly, 45*, 651–678.

Stokke, O. S. (2004). Boolean analysis, mechanisms, and the study of regime effectiveness. In A. Underdal & O. R. Young (Eds.), *Regime consequences. Methodological challenges and research strategies.* Dordrecht, Netherlands: Kluwer.

Stokke, O. S. (2007). Qualitative Comparative Analysis, shaming and international regime effectiveness. *Journal of Business Research, 60*(5), 501–511.

Swanson, G. (1971). Frameworks for comparative research: structural anthropology and the theory of action. In I. Vallier (Ed.), *Comparative methods in sociology. Essays on trends and applications* (pp. 141–202). Berkeley: University of California Press.

Tarrow, S. (1994). *Power in movement. Social movements, collective action and politics.* Cambridge, UK: Cambridge University Press.

Tashakkori, A., & Teddlie, C. (2003). *Handbook of mixed methods in the social and behavioral research.* Thousand Oaks, CA: Sage.

Tiemann, G. (2003). Das "most different system design" als Instrument zum Umgang mit multipler Kausalität. In S. Pickel, G. Pickel, H.-J. Lauth, & D. Jahn (Eds.), *Vergleichende politikwissenschaftliche Methoden. Neue Entwicklungen und Diskussionen* (pp. 265–287). Wiesbaden, Germany: Westdeutscher Verlag.

Tilly, C. (1984). *Big structures, large processes, huge comparisons.* New York: Russell Sage Foundation.

Vanderborght, Y., & Yamasaki, S. (2004). Des cas logiques . . . contradictoires? Un piège de l'AQQC déjoué à travers l'étude de la faisabilité politique de l'Allocation Universelle. *Revue Internationale de Politique Comparée, 11*(1), 51–66.

Vanhanen, T. (1984). *The emergence of democracy: A comparative study of 119 states, 1850–1979. Commentationes Scientarum Socialium n0.24.* Helsinki: Finnish Society of Sciences and Letters.

Varone, F., Rothmayr, C., & Montpetit, E. (2006). Regulating biomedicine in Europe and North America. A Qualitative-Comparative Analysis, *European Journal of Political Research, 45*(2), 317–343.

Verkuilen, J. (2001). [Book review] Charles Ragin, fuzzy set social science. *APSA-CP: Newsletter of the APSA Organized Section in Comparative Politics.*

Verkuilen, J. (2005). Assigning membership in a fuzzy set analysis. *Sociological Methods and Research, 33*(4), 462–496.

Vink, M., & Van Vliet, O. (2007). *Not quite crisp, not yet fuzzy? . . . Assessing the potential and pitfalls of multi-value QCA* (COMPASSS Working Paper, 52), 29p.

Vis, B. (2006). *States of welfare or states of workfare? A fuzzy-set ideal type analysis of major welfare state restructuring in sixteen advanced capitalist democracies, 1985–2002* (COMPASSS Working Paper, 42), 40p.

Wagemann, C., & Schneider, C. Q. (2007). *Standards of good practice in Qualitative Comparative Analysis (QCA) and fuzzy-sets* (COMPASSS Working Paper, 51), 35p.

Watanabe, T. (2003). *Where theory and reality meet: Using the full potential of QCA by exploiting the intersection function of the QCA software. International comparison analysis about the occurrence of social movement* (COMPASSS Working Paper, 13), 14p.

Williams, L. M., & Farrell, R. A. (1990). Legal response to child sexual abuse in daycares. *Criminal Justice and Behavior, 17*(3), 284–302.

Yamasaki, S. (2003). *Testing hypotheses with QCA: Application to the nuclear phase-out policy in 9 OECD countries.* Second ECPR General Conference. Section: "Methodological Advances in Comparative Research: Concepts, Techniques, Applications"; Panel: "QCA (Qualitative Comparative Analysis) in Comparative Research: Applications."

Yamasaki, S. (2007). *Policy change in nuclear energy. A comparative analysis of West European countries.* Unpublished doctoral dissertation, Université catholique de Louvain, Louvain-la-Neuve, Belgium.

Yamasaki, S., & Spreitzer, A. (2006). Beyond methodological tenets. The worlds of QCA and SNA and their benefits to policy analysis. In B. Rihoux & H. Grimm (Eds.), *Innovative comparative methods for policy analysis* (pp. 95–120). New York: Springer.

Zadeh, L. A. (1965). Fuzzy-sets. *Information and Control, 8,* 338–353.

Zelditch, M., Jr. (1971). Intelligible comparisons. In I. Vallier (Ed.), *Comparative methods in sociology. Essays on trends and applications* (pp. 267–307). Berkeley: University of California Press.

Index

Abbott, A., 161
Abell, P., 10
Actor-Process-Event Scheme (APES), 165(n4)
Alber, J., 8
Alderson, A. S., 149
Amenta, E., 26, 125–129, 132, 145(n1, 2), 156, 158, 171, 175
Analytic induction, 20
Anchors, qualitative, 90(box), 92
Andersen, S. C., 17
Assumptions, 153, 164, 171, 172, 177
   of conventional statistics, 8–9, 135, 148, 155
   of QCA, xx(box), 9, 18(n18), 67(n3), 135, 148, 159, 175
   of positivism, 2
   simplifying. *See* Logical remainders

Becker, H. S., xxv, 148–149, 156
Bennett, A., 161–162
Berg-Schlosser, D., 8–9, 40–41, 67(n4), 77, 138–139, 169–170
Binary variables, 27, 33, 34(box), 36, 66(box), 85(n1)
Bleiklie, I., 145(n4)
Bochsler, D., 175
Bollen, K. A., 149
Boole, G., 34
Boolean algebra 16, 34, 58, 66(box)
   addition. *See* Boolean algebra, logical OR
   concentration, 20, 140, 147, 169
   factoring, 8, 22, 28, 58, 64, 65, 139, 142, 144, 168, 171, 175, 176
   logical AND, 34(box), 96, 99(box)
   logical OR, 34(box), 96–97, 99(box)
   multiplication. *See* Boolean algebra, logical AND
   negation, 94, 99(box)

Boolean distance, 29–30, 130, 144
Boolean minimization. *See* Truth tables, minimization of
Boolean variables. *See* Binary variables
Boswell, T., 159, 161, 163
Bourdieu, P., 7, 17
Brady, H. E., 4
Brayton, R. K., 85(n2)
Breakpoints, qualitative. *See* Anchors, qualitative
Brown, C., 159, 161, 163

Calibration, 78, 88, 89, 90, 92, 93, 118(box), 121(n2)
Campbell, D., 83
Caramani, D., xxiv, 17, 34, 148
Caren, N., 128–129, 163, 175
Case-oriented research, 6, 17(box), 20, 23, 89
Cases:
   as configurations, xix, xxiv(box), 6, 13, 44–47, 82, 89
   knowledge of. *See* Knowledge, substantive
   selection of, 7, 20, 21–24, 32(n3), 124–125, 138(box), 157, 164(box), 169
Cat, J., 165(n1)
Causality, *See* Multiple conjunctural causation
Chan, S., 132, 168(box)
Clément, C., 129, 136
Clustering, 42(box), 67(n6), 79, 84, 130, 145(box), 151, 173
   of cases, 15, 29–30, 31(box), 58, 77
   of conditions, 29–30, 31(box)
Cohen, M. R., 3
Coleman, J. S., 7
Collier, D., 4, 8
Comparative analysis, 4

About the Editors

The editors and contributors of this textbook are all active in the COMPASSS research group (www.compasss.org).

Benoît Rihoux is professor of political science at the Centre de Politique Comparée of the Université catholique de Louvain (Belgium). His substantive research interests include political parties, new social movements, organizational studies, political change, environmental politics, and policy processes. He is coordinator of the COMPASSS research group and oversees the management of its linked Web pages, databases, and archives. He is also joint convener of international initiatives around methods more generally, such as the ECPR Standing Group on Political Methodology, the ECPR Summer School in Methods and Techniques, and the ECPR Research Methods book series (Palgrave; editor, with B. Kittel). In connection with the topic of this book, he has also recently published *Innovative Comparative Methods for Policy Analysis: Beyond the Quantitative–Qualitative Divide* (Springer/Kluwer, with H. Grimm, 2006).

Charles C. Ragin holds a joint appointment as professor of sociology and political science at the University of Arizona. In 2000–2001 he was a Fellow at the Center for Advanced Study in the Behavioral Sciences at Stanford University, and before that he was professor of sociology and political science at Northwestern University. His substantive research focuses on the welfare state in advanced industrial societies, comparative ethnic political mobilization, nationalism, and international inequality. His books include *The Comparative Method: Moving Beyond Qualitative and Quantitative Strategies* (University of California Press, 1987), *Issues and Alternatives in Comparative Social Research* (E. J. Brill, 1991), *What Is a Case? Exploring the Foundations of Social Research* (Cambridge University Press, with Howard S. Becker, 1992), *Constructing Social Research: The Unity and Diversity of Method* (Pine Forge Press, 1994), *Fuzzy-Set Social Science* (University of Chicago Press, 2000), and *Redesigning Social Inquiry: Fuzzy Sets and Beyond* (University of Chicago Press, 2008).

About the Contributors

Dirk Berg-Schlosser, PhD in political sciences, is professor at the Institute of Political Science at the University of Marburg (Germany). His major areas of research and teaching include comparative politics, African and Third World politics, political culture, democratization, and comparative methodology. He was chair of the European Consortium for Political Research (ECPR) from 2003 to 2006 and has since 2006 been vice president of the International Political Science Association (IPSA).

Damien Bol is a fellow researcher at the National Fund for Scientific Research (FNRS) and at the Centre de Politique Comparée of the Université catholique de Louvain (Belgium) and maintains the COMPASSS research group Web pages and linked databases. His research focuses on political and electoral institutions (especially change and choice), approaches and techniques in comparative politics (especially those dealing with "small populations" and with the time dimension), political representation, and strategic interactions between political players

Lasse Cronqvist, PhD in political sciences, is lecturer at the Institute of Political Science at the University of Trier (Germany). He teaches German and comparative politics as well as social science methods. His research focuses on comparative methodology and comparative policy studies. He has also authored software for Configurational Comparative Analysis (TOSMANA).

Gisèle De Meur is professor of mathematics at the Université Libre de Bruxelles (Belgium). She teaches mathematics for social scientists, methodology, introduction to computing, and epistemology and is director of the Laboratory for Mathematics and Social Sciences (MATsch) at the ULB. Her more recent research interests include study of "pseudoscience" discourse, geometric patterns in arts, mathematical models applied in anthropology, as well as political science, methodology (quali-quantitative comparative analysis), and gender studies.

Sakura Yamasaki, PhD in political sciences, was a Fellow Researcher at the National Fund for Scientific Research (FNRS) and at the Centre de Politique Comparée of the Université catholique de Louvain, Belgium. She has elaborated and maintained the COMPASSS research group Web pages and linked databases since their launching (2003–2007). Her areas of interest include comparative methodology (especially QCA), network analysis, nuclear energy policy, policy change and new social movement theories. She is now working in the energy trading sector.